Winding Quest

Man hath still either toys or care;
He hath no root, nor to one place is tied,
But ever restless and irregular
   About this earth doth run and ride.
He knows he hath a home, but scarce knows where;
      He says it is so far,
That he hath quite forgot how to go there.

   He knocks at all doors, strays and roams;
Nay, hath not so much wit as some stones have,
Which in the darkest nights point to their homes,
   By some hid sense their Maker gave;
Man is the shuttle, to whose winding quest
      And passage through these looms
God ordered motion, but ordained no rest.

Henry Vaughan

Winding Quest

The Heart of the Old Testament
in Plain English

by

Alan T. Dale

Oxford University Press

Oxford University Press, Ely House, London W.1

GLASGOW NEW YORK TORONTO MELBOURNE WELLINGTON
CAPE TOWN IBADAN NAIROBI DAR ES SALAAM LUSAKA ADDIS ABABA
DELHI BOMBAY CALCUTTA MADRAS KARACHI LAHORE DACCA
KUALA LUMPUR SINGAPORE HONG KONG TOKYO

Colour Illustrations by Geoffrey Crabbe

First published 1972
Reprinted with corrections 1974, 1975

Filmset by BAS Printers Limited, Wallop, Hampshire
and printed in Great Britain at the University Press, Oxford,
by Vivian Ridler, Printer to the University.
Colour plates printed in Great Britain
by Colour Reproductions, Billericay

Foreword

The story is told that once, Oscar Wilde heard someone utter a witty remark and said 'I wish I could have said that'; to which Whistler replied 'You will, Oscar, you will'. I suspect that many an Old Testament scholar will find himself in a similar position if he reads this book by Mr Dale. For the task of the scholar is twofold. He must first understand what the Old Testament speakers are saying. This requires a knowledge of the ancient language, of the thought-forms of the speakers and their background, of the way in which their words were recorded and transmitted over the centuries, of the strange history of those to whom the Word of the Lord was given and of the way in which their response to that Word enabled them to overcome disasters which ought to have destroyed them. But when he has done all that he can to understand, there remains a further task, and that is to share this with others.

There are books that do this, and do it well. They are like bridges across the Jordan from the desert into the Promised Land. But no one will get into the land by studying the bridges. Perhaps after all we need a Joshua to take us across the Jordan into this unknown land and to say to us: 'Look! Here you are. This is yours. Now enjoy it.'

Mr Dale would not claim to be a Joshua. But he has that gift which many a teacher will envy, which belongs especially to the poet and dramatist. Having this gift, he has also the mind of a scholar. He knows moreover that what he has seen in the Old Testament is as important for life today as it was for Israel of old. He has brought to the writing of this volume an enthusiasm and a reverence for life of which the Old Testament is full. But there is also what I can only describe as a love and sympathy for young people with whom he would share what he has received from the Old Testament.

Winding Quest is incomplete. It is meant to be. It will succeed if it stimulates the reader to go on to read the Old Testament as a whole, preferably in a form such as the New English Bible. I can only add that I am grateful for the many occasions on which Mr Dale and I have talked about this work, and for all that I have received from reading it.

A. S. Herbert *Selly Oak Colleges, Birmingham*

Preface

Here is protest: the protest of a small highland people against the 'beasts' of brutal military empires; the protest of individual men against a baffling and apparently meaningless universe.

Here is the protest of a small people—far enough away for us to look at what was happening with clear eyes and to see in their experience a parable of the total human situation; yet brought close to us by the magic of enduring speech, the speech of men who had their backs to the wall and their lives at stake, who had once been slaves and who, after several hundred years of political independence, saw their city lie in ruins, a mass of debris—and survived.

Here is the protest of individual men—

> What does a man get by endless toil,
> sweating under the hot sun?
> Families come and families go,
> only the earth goes on for ever . . .
> What has been will be,
> what's done must be done again,
> there's nothing new under the sun!

and—

> Our enemies have thrown us back
> plundering to their heart's desire—
> we are butchered like sheep,
> scattered over the world . . .
> a byword and a laughing-stock
> to everybody.

and—

> Why should a man be doomed
> to grope his way blindfold
> shut in by God's unceasing No?

and yet (one can say of God in spite of everything)—

> I shall lack nothing—
> he lets me lie down on green grass,
> leads me by quiet streams,
> makes me a new man.
> He guides me along right tracks
> because he is what he is;
> when I go through the pitch-black gorge,
> nothing frightens me . . .
> God's home is my home
> for ever!

Whatever else may be said of the Old Testament, nobody who has really read it would ever call it dull. It is crowded with colour—little, tidy, dogmatic minds may think too much colour. A man can speak his mind—paint even his king in earthy colours. Here is rebel—and 'establishment'. The Old Testament is a bewildering book largely because so many voices are speaking. They are asking 'Why?'—speaking for themselves, and speaking for obscure men and women all over the world and in every century. The very variety ensures that everybody somewhere will hear his own voice.

The Old Testament is a lively book; it is also an important one. It is a pioneering book, asking, for the first time in human history (before the Greeks to whom we owe so much) and in language that can still speak directly to men's imagination, ultimate questions about the meaningfulness—or meaninglessness—of human experience, questions which serious men and women have been asking ever since and which they—especially young people—are asking today.

There are no short answers to such questions—it sometimes seems that all we can do is to get the questions straight. Everybody, anyhow, has to ask his own questions and seek his own answers in his own way—learning from others but doing his own thinking, 'listening to all but giving his soul to none'. Here is a living introduction to this perennial enquiry.

The Old Testament is an important book for a further and more impressive reason: this is no academic debate. Men speak from a threatened country or from exile in a foreign land; they speak frankly and directly—even brutally—with a contempt for conventional cant. There are questioners and doubters among them, but their profoundest minds believe they have found both the secret of living as human beings in a dehumanizing situation and the clue to the making of a genuinely human world. They are searching for a new world and they speak to those in every generation who care. Here is a community of men and women—

> 'growing not as any collective urge
> would have them
> (in its own placable image) but into
> their own more wayward value—strong,
> untidy, original, self-possessed.'[1]

It is the *reading* of the Old Testament that matters—not just *reading about* it. I offer this version of the heart of it to all who care. I once thought it was a book of little significance today—until I started to read it again for myself. I had to learn how to come to terms with it the hard way, and I owe an immense debt to the Old Testament scholars who helped me; I made this version in the light of their discoveries and insights. This is how

[1]Alan Brownjohn, from *For my Son* (Penguin Modern Poets).

I read it and I offer it as first steps to the reading of the splendid modern translations of the full text.

But there is one thing to remember. I have spoken about the Old Testament as if it were a book in the ordinary sense of that word. It is not, of course. It is more like a library of books, written at different times by different authors. The collection and editing of these books was carried out by many editors over a period of many centuries; the final discussion about what books should be included did not take place until the year 90 of our era. The books themselves are very varied in style and contents. Here is prose—history, biographies, diaries, tracts for the times, short stories, legal documents; here, too, is poetry—ballads, love lyrics, dramatic poetry, hymns, prophetic poems.

The Old Testament, in a word, is like a shelf of books, and there is no more need to start at the traditional beginning than to read a shelf of library books by beginning with the one on the left. So we shall begin to read, not at the traditional beginning which you will find in the editions of the full text, but at an important and dramatic moment in the story of the Hebrew People[1] (*Brief Hour of Glory*). We then look back over their past history as they remembered it (*Memories of the Past*). In *The Death of Two Cities* we see how they became the victims of powerful military empires. We then turn to see how they mastered their tragic suffering (*Making Sense of the Story*) and what they learned from it (*Enduring Convictions*). These, then, will be our first steps into the Old Testament.

[1] See John Bowden, *What about the Old Testament?*

Contents

Note: 'GOD' translates 'Yahweh'; 'God' other divine names. 'South' translates 'Judah'; 'North' 'Israel' (see pp. 412–3).

Acknowledgements

The brief words on this page can be but a symbolic gesture of my indebtedness. Every page—indeed, every sentence—bears the marks of my borrowing. Every teacher is an incorrigible borrower; the shortness of the time and the nature of his work forces him to be so. And he is the more so when he is concerned, as I have been here, to help his students to read a great book in the light of the work of present-day scholars. I have made this version of the Old Testament in the light of the work of those Old Testament scholars to whom I myself have been most indebted. Those who know will recognise how shameless my borrowing has been everywhere—in the choice and arrangement of the material and in the interpretation of word and phrase.

I have kept before me the translations of the Old Testament which young people in school and the ordinary reader at home will be most likely to use or consult: the Revised Standard Version, the New English Bible (which only became available after I had begun this version) and the Jerusalem Bible. What I have done is intended to encourage the reader, younger or older, to tackle these full translations and to read them with understanding and imagination.

But my chief debt is to Prof. Arthur S. Herbert who has guided me with his generous help (I fear to recall how often I intruded into his busy life) throughout the making of this book. To travel through the Old Testament with him—surveying the whole landscape or stopping to examine one small spot—was to widen my horizons and deepen my sense of the importance and relevance of the experience of the Israelite people. He encouraged me to go on and made innumerable suggestions. These I have gladly accepted; any mistakes and misjudgments that remain are mine.

I am again indebted to Dr. Francis A. D. Burns, Head of the English Department of Newman College, Birmingham. He has read through *Winding Quest* and helped me with many comments and suggestions about vocabulary and idiom.

Much of this volume has been read aloud to groups of young people and adults in various parts of the country. I am greatly indebted to them for their comment and questions.

I must thank Mr Geoffrey Crabbe for his paintings. He has painted what excited his imagination as he explored this volume. It was illuminating to talk it over with him and to look at it through his eyes.

And I must thank the staff of the Clarendon Press whose untiring help has been so generously given to me at all the stages of the making of this book. I am indebted to them for many comments and suggestions—and not least for drawing my attention to Henry Vaughan's poem *Man* from which the title of this book, *Winding Quest,* has come.

Finally, I must thank my wife for her encouragement, insight and comment—and not least for carrying the burden of the typing and re-typing that the making of a book like this involves.

Alan T. Dale

The publishers would like to thank the following for permission to reproduce photographs:—
P. R. Ackroyd, p. 198; Aerofilms, pp. 137, 181 top; Ashmolean Museum, Oxford, p. 105 top; Bildarchiv Foto Marburg pp. 152, 181 bottom; British Museum, pp. 168, 176, 323; Camera Press, pp. 48, 113, 222, 235, 245, 280, 285, 304, 307, 380, 387, 395, 399, 403, 407; J. Allan Cash, pp. 37, 99, 115, 120 top, 316; Graphische Sammlung Albertina, Vienna, p. 346; Grollenberg *Atlas de la Bible* (Elsevier), p. 158; Raymond Irons, p. 218; Israel Department of Antiquities and Museums, p. 171; Israel Museum, Jerusalem, pp. 52, 53; Kathleen M. Kenyon, p. 77; A. F. Kersting, p. 104; Keystone Press, pp. 210, 270, 291, 297; Kupferstich-Kabinet, Staatliche Museen Zu Berlin, p. 67; Laporte Industries Limited, p. 354; Matson Photo Service, Alhambra, California, pp. 24, 29, 43, 61 top, 80, 85, 92, 95, 116, 134, 146, 150, 162, 253; Metropolitan Museum of Art, New York, pp. 105 bottom, 268 (copyright S.P.A.D.E.M.); Oriental Institute, Chicago, pp. 23 bottom, 120 bottom, 121, 149; Palestine Exploration Fund, p. 23 top; Roland Penrose Collection, London (copyright S.P.A.D.E.M.) p. 214; Pennsylvania University Museum, p. 34; Rijksmuseum, Amsterdam, pp. 334, 338; M. Shaeffer, p. 166; David Newell Smith (copyright *The Observer*) p. 312; The illustrations on pp. 359, 361, 366, and 369 are from William Blake's *Illustrations of the Book of Job*, (1825).

Prelude

How can they live in GOD's Way?

Farmer
  ploughing the field, proud of his goad,
  driving his oxen, lost to the world,
  talking, talking of cattle,
  following the furrow by day,
  fattening the heifers by night?

Blacksmith
  sitting by his anvil in a world of pig-iron,
  scorched by the forge, fighting the furnace heat,
  deafened by hammers' din, rapt in his pattern,
  firm to finish his work, fashioning it into the night?

Potter
  working at his wheel, turning it with his feet,
  lost in his task of making up his tally,
  slapping and puddling the clay,
  engrossed in his glazing,
  staying awake cleaning out his kiln?

These men trust their hands;
  their craftsmanship is their wisdom.
Without them cities would be empty—
  nobody living there,
  nobody coming and going.
You won't hear them in the City Council
  or see them sitting in the Assembly;
you won't find them among the judges—
  they can't make head or tail of the Law;
they don't talk like scholars—
  they can't quote the critics.

Yet
they hold the world in their hands;
  their worship is in their work.

Brief Hour of Glory

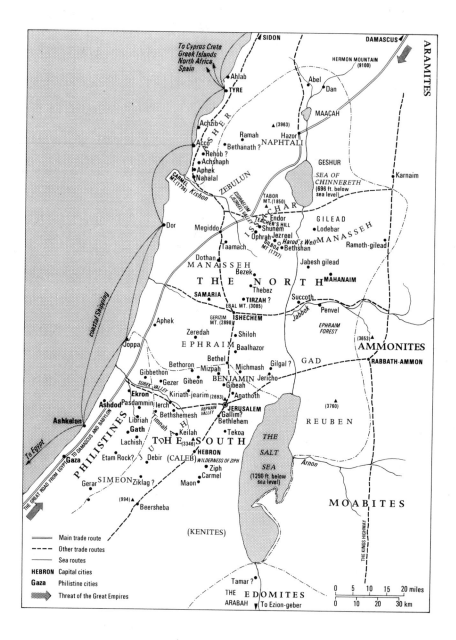

SIDON
DAMASCUS
ARAMITES

To Cyprus Crete
Greek Islands
North Africa
Spain

HERMON MOUNTAIN
(9100)

Ahlab
Abel
Dan

TYRE
MAACAH

Achzib
▲(3963)

Acco
Ramah
Hazor
Bethanath?
NAPHTALI

Rehob?
GESHUR
Achshaph
SEA OF
Aphek
Karnaim
Nahalal
CHINNERETH
ZEBULUN
(696 ft. below
sea level)

CARMEL
MT.(1736) Kishon

TABOR
MT.(1850)

Dor
Megiddo
Endor
GILEAD
TEACHER'S HILL
Shunem
Ophrah
Jezreel
Lodebar
Harod's Well
MANASSEH
Taanach
Bethshan
Ramoth-gilead
BILBOA
MT.(1737)

Dothan
Jabesh gilead

MANASSEH
Bezek
THE NORTH
MAHANAIM

SAMARIA
Thebez
Succoth

TIRZAH?
EBAL MT. (3085)

GERIZIM
MT.(2890) ISHECHEM
Jabbok
Penvel

Aphek
EPHRAIM
FOREST

Zeredah
Shiloh

Joppa
EPHRAIM Baalhazor
(3653)▲
AMMONITES

Bethel
Bethoron
Mizpah
Michmash
Gilgal?
GAD
RABBATH-AMMON
Gibbethon
Gezer Gibeon
BENJAMIN Jericho
Ekron
Kiriath-jearim (2693)
Gibeah
Anathoth

Ashdod Pasdammin Ierch
(3760)
REPHAIM
Bethshemesh
JERUSALEM
VALLEY
Libriah
Gallim?
REUBEN
Ashkelon
Gath
Timnah
Bethlehem

Keilah
Tekoa
THE
Lachish
(3346)
THE SOUTH
SALT
Gaza
HEBRON
SEA
Etam Rock?
Debir (CALEB) WILDERNESS OF ZIPH
(1290 ft. below
Gerar SIMEON Ziklag?
Ziph
sea level)
Maon
Carmel
Arnon

(994)▲
Beersheba
MOABITES

(KENITES)

Main trade route
Other trade routes
Sea routes
THE KINGS HIGHWAY
HEBRON Capital cities
Gaza Philistine cities
Threat of the Great Empires

0   5   10   15   20 miles
Tamar?
0   10   20   30 km
THE EDOMITES
ARABAH ▼To Ezion-geber

Introduction

About the year 1000 B.C.E.,[1] two hundred and fifty years after the escape from Egypt under the leadership of Moses, David became king of the South in Hebron City in the southern highlands. This was a turning point in the story of the Israelite people. Before this, they had been a tribal league whose story we will come back to later. Now they were to become a nation, the most powerful small nation in the Middle East. King David captured an old Canaanite fortress, Jerusalem, and made it his new capital. Here he established his court and government and ruled as a great king. And at his court, for the first time, records were made of the story of this remarkable rise to power and nationhood.

Up to this time, little had been written down. There had not been peace enough for writing; holding the highlands, fighting with the fortified cities or the camel-riding nomads from the eastern deserts, had drained the energy of the scattered tribes. The stories of these exciting days was handed on, from generation to generation, as tribal traditions, recited at the religious festivals at the central tribal shrine. Now there was peace and time to put the stories down in writing.

Most important of all, they were able to write down accounts of what was happening in their own time. They began to make official records —lists of army officers and their exploits, court documents, temple records. It was at Solomon's court that the first history books in the world were written, five hundred years before historical writing began in Greece. So, in the eighty years following David's coronation in Hebron, the Israelites moved out into the light. They had strong memories of the decisive two hundred years or so that followed their escape from Egypt, memories which governed their lives in this historic moment and which were to govern their lives over the succeeding centuries. But they were now standing on their own feet, building an empire which was to stretch from the far north to the Egyptian frontiers.

The world lay before them. The dreams and hopes and convictions of Moses could now be made a living reality. They could be GOD's people as God intended them to be. They had a capital city and an empire; their country was to be the centre of a new world. The glory of these days was to sustain them even in the darkest hours of disaster; it haunts the Jewish people still.

It will be best for us to get to grips with the story that lies behind the Old Testament at this historic moment in the fortunes of the Israelite people. Their tribal past, remembered in their traditions, lies behind them; the future is as yet all unknown. We can see what kind of people they were. We can see them, through the eyes of a contemporary, as real

[1] Before the Common Era.

people, facing the same kind of human situation all people have to face, and not, as they have been so often presented to us, as 'pious puppets in a fairy tale'. This—or something very much like it—actually happened. This is the real world; if religion is to mean anything at all, it has to make sense in this kind of world and help men to live in it and deal with it.

The sources that these first historians used were varied.

When the story begins the Philistines—the 'Sea Peoples', as the Egyptians called them—were already masters of the plain that lies between the highlands and the sea and they were about to launch their attack on the highlands. For information about these days, the writers had only the popular stories which circulated among the Israelite tribes; only a few of these—like *The Story of the Ark* with which we begin—had already been written down.

However, for the stories of the two great commanders, who became their first kings, they had written documents as well as popular tales. The kind of men Saul and David were and what they had tried to do was public knowledge. They were not far-off, misty figures; many of the men from whose lips the stories come had marched with them on their campaigns. Their stories give us, as it were, 'snapshots' of their commanders, vivid glimpses of incident and character. Here is no step-by-step account of all that happened, set in chronological order; many of the details of the various campaigns are now lost for ever—for example, the campaigns of David's Philistine War, when he subdued the five proud cities. But here is enough to see what kind of world it was, what sort of men they were and what they were trying to do. The stories are among the great stories of the world.

In addition, for the end of this part of the story, the writers had a vivid contemporary account, *The Court History*, written, it may be, by one of David's high officers. It is the account of the last days of David when he was no longer the able and vigorous king he had been (he is now painted as a disillusioned old man) and there was a harem quarrel about who should succeed him. A modern scholar writes:

This document . . . has the factual accuracy of contemporary chronicle. But, unlike the mere annalist, the writer reveals the relationship of character with event, and of one event with another, by the sheer skill of his narration. In the whole of the Old Testament, only the work of the Yahwist is comparable with the superbly simple prose of The Court History. As history, it is unequalled in ancient Hebrew literature. At this period, and for centuries afterwards, the neighbouring civilizations produced nothing comparable. The writer has seen history made in David's reign; and when, probably in the reign of Solomon, he wrote his narrative, he himself made literary history.[1]

[1] G. W. Anderson, *A Critical Introduction to the Old Testament*, p. 80. The 'Yahwist' is the name used for the author (or authors) of the 'first national history' (referred to as 'J') which we use for the Story of Moses (pp. 93–117) *What Kind of World do we live in ?* and *What Kind of Persons Should we be ?* (pp. 305–345).

The Philistine Attack

The Opening Battle

War at last broke out between the Philistines in their fortified cities on the plain and the Israelites in the highlands.

The Philistines began it—they called out their army and took up their position at Aphek on the road to the north. The Israelites took the field against them at a place called the Stone of Help.

Battle lines were drawn up, and in the general fighting that followed the Israelites were defeated—many of their soldiers lay dead on the battlefield.

Back at the Israelite camp, there was heated debate among the sheiks.

'Why has GOD routed us like this,' they asked, 'and let the Philistines defeat us? Let us take the Ark out from the temple at Shiloh. If we've got it with us, GOD will rescue us from our enemies however strong they are!'

They sent to Shiloh and fetched the Ark. Hophni and Phinehas, sons of the aged priest Eli, were its guardians. There was a tremendous shout as the Ark was carried into the camp. The Philistine soldiers heard it across the valley.

'What are they shouting about over there?' they were asking one another.

Scouts soon brought the news—the Ark had been brought from Shiloh. The Philistines were in a panic.

'A god has come down to the camp!' they shouted. 'We're lost!'

'Screw up your courage!' said their officers. 'Be the soldiers you are! You're not going to be the slaves of these bandits, are you? We've defeated them before. You're soldiers—get on with the fighting!'

They fought hard, and the Israelite soldiers broke and fled in disorder, nobody bothering about what happened to his comrade. The Ark was captured and its guardians, the sons of the old priest Eli, were killed.

A soldier escaped from the battlefield and ran all the way to Shiloh in the highlands, his clothes torn and earth on his head to mark his grief.

The old priest Eli was sitting on a seat near the town gate, looking down the road, wondering anxiously what had happened to the Ark. The soldier ran into the town and told the bad news. There was uproar in the streets and Eli heard the wailing.

'What's all this wailing about?' he asked the men standing near.

The soldier himself ran across and told him.

'I'm the soldier from the camp,' he said. 'I escaped this morning from the battlefield.'

'How did the fighting go, my son?' asked the old man.

'Our soldiers fled in panic,' he said. 'There have been heavy casualties —your two sons are dead and the Ark's been captured!'

At the word 'Ark', the old man fell back from his seat by the gate. He broke his neck and died—he was a very old and heavy man.

The Capture of the Ark

The Philistines carried the captured Ark to Ashdod, took it to the temple of their god Dagon and set it beside his image there.

Early next day, worshippers found the image of Dagon lying face down on the ground in front of the Ark. They put the image back in its place. Next morning the same thing happened. This time its head and its broken hands were lying on the floor beside the platform—nothing was left of Dagon but his trunk.

Worse followed: plague broke out in the city—people were suffering from boils.

'The Ark's not staying here,' they said. 'It's destroying both us and our god!'

A council of the Philistine chieftains was called.

'What are we going to do with it?' people of Ashdod asked them.

'Let it go to Gath,' they said.

That's where they took it; and then there was trouble there. The city was in a panic; young and old were struck with boils.

They sent the Ark on to Ekron, and there was uproar in that city.

'Have they brought the Ark round here to kill us?' they protested.

Another council of the chieftains was called.

The people of Ekron were in no doubt what should be done.

'Send the Ark back to where it belongs,' they said. 'We want no more deaths here.'

Panic had spread throughout the city. Many people were dead or plague-stricken, and there was uproar in the streets.

The Ark had now been seven months in Philistine territory. The priests and diviners were called together to advise the chieftains what to do with it and how to send it home.

'If you're going to send it home,' they said, 'don't send it home empty. You must send an offering to the God of the Israelites with it to acknowledge your guilt. Then you will be healed and you will find out why the God of the Israelites is against you.'

Above where the Philistines probably landed: the coast near Ashkelon, one of the oldest cities in the world It became one of the Philistine 'Five Cities'

Right relief of heads of Philistine soldiers. The Pharaoh who defeated the Philistines (the Sea Peoples) when they invaded Egypt set up these reliefs on the north wall of his palace and temple at Thebes to celebrate his victory. The headdress has a thick crest like a crown, probably made of horse-hair

Shiloh, north of Bethel. Eli was the priest in charge of the ark in the shrine there. It was the central shrine for a number of tribes. The town and shrine were burned by the Philistines. A later town, built on the ruins, was also destroyed (see p. 248)

'What sort of offering?' they asked.

'Five golden plague-boils,' they said, 'and five mice, one of each for each of the cities; the plague attacked you all and your chieftains. Give honour to the Israelite God; perhaps he will relax his grip on you and your gods and your land. Then get a new farm cart ready and two milking cows that have not yet been trained to pull carts. Hitch the cows to the cart, but keep their calves at home, away from them. Put the Ark on the cart and put your offering in a box beside it. Let cart and cows go and watch what happens. If the Ark goes back to Israelite territory—to Bethshemesh over there—you will know that the Israelite God is the cause of all your trouble. If it doesn't do that, then we can be sure that he had nothing to do with the plague—it was just an accident.'

The Philistine chieftains followed this advice. They took two milking cows, hitched them to a cart, and shut their calves up.

The cows made straight for Bethshemesh, keeping to the road and lowing as they went. They just went straight on. The Philistine chieftains followed them to the borders of Bethshemesh—and watched what happened.

It was wheat harvest in the valley and the townspeople were out reaping. They suddenly saw the Ark and ran excitedly to meet it. It came into farmer Joshua's field and stopped by the Great Stone there. So they broke up the wood of the cart, made a fire and sacrificed the cows as an offering to GOD.

The Philistine chieftains went back to Ekron.

Some time later, the citizens of Kiriath-jearim came and took the Ark to their own town and put it in Abinadab's house on the hill. They made his son, Eleazar, its guardian.

The Beloved Captain

Saul was a Northerner; the stories that now lie before us, we must remember, are Southern stories, and Southerners disliked Saul just because he was a Northerner. In their account of these times they 'write him down', and forget that it was the North that first realized the great danger they were all in and did something about it.

Saul is indeed 'the Beloved Captain'—he never had to face (as David did) any rebellion against his authority. We shall see later how loyal David was to him in spite of the trouble that arose between them. He was a deeply religious man and never turned his back on his country's enemies. But the task was too great for him—you can't fight trained soldiers with tribal levies.

'Where have you been?'

Kish, a rich farmer of the Benjamin clan, lived in the central highlands. Saul was his son, a handsome young man, head and shoulders taller than most of his fellows; there was not a handsomer young man in the country.

One day the farmer found that some of his donkeys had strayed away.

'Take one of the farm lads,' he said to Saul, 'and go and find them.'

The two of them searched everywhere in the highlands, but no donkeys were to be found. They came at last to a small Benjamin town.

'We'd better go home,' Saul said to the boy. 'It won't be the donkeys my father will be worried about—it'll be us.'

'Wait!' said the boy. 'There's a man of God in the town here. Everybody talks about him—what he says always comes true. Let's go into the town; perhaps he can tell us where the donkeys are.'

'Well,' said Saul, 'suppose we do—what are we going to pay him with? We've no present to give him; our bags are empty.'

'I've got a silver coin,' said the boy. 'We can give him that to tell us what to do.'

'All right,' said Saul. 'Let's try.'

They went toward the town.

The town was built on a hill, and girls were coming down the road to draw water from the well.

'Is the seer at home?' they asked the girls.

'Yes,' they said, 'he's ahead of you, over there. He's just got here;

we're going to have a sacrifice today on the hill. You'll easily find him when you get into the town—you may catch him before he goes to the hill for the meal there. Be quick—you may meet him now.'

Just as they got to the town gate, the seer (Samuel by name) was coming out of it on his way up to the hill.

Saul met him in the gateway.

'Can you tell me where the seer lives?' he asked.

'I am the seer,' said Samuel. 'Go ahead of me to the hill—you must share the meal with me there. Tomorrow I'll send you on your way, and tell you what you want to know. Forget about the donkeys—they've been found. Who are GOD's people waiting for? Isn't it you—and your family?'

'My tribe doesn't count,' said Saul, 'it's the least important in the land. My family doesn't count, either—we're nobody that matters. Why do you talk to me like this?'

Samuel just took Saul and the boy to the high hill, the holy place of the town, and into the guest-chamber. There were about thirty people there at the sacred meal. He set the two of them at the head of the table.

He turned to the cook.

'I told you to put a joint aside,' he said. 'Serve it now.'

The cook set the shoulder and fat tail in front of Saul.

'That was kept for you,' Samuel said to Saul. 'Eat it with the guests. It was kept for this important moment.'

So Saul shared the meal with Samuel.

They all went down the hill back to the town. Saul was given a bed on the flat roof of the house, and went to sleep.

At dawn, Samuel called up to him.

'Get up,' he said. 'I want to send you on your way.'

Saul got up, and he and Samuel went out into the street, and walked along until they came to the outskirts of the town.

'Tell the boy to go on ahead,' said Samuel.

The boy went on.

'Stand here,' Samuel said to Saul. 'I must tell you what GOD has said.'

He took some oil, poured it on Saul's head and kissed him (as if he were crowning a king).

'GOD anoints you as the leader of his people,' he said. 'You are to be their king and rescue them from their enemies who are attacking them on all sides. A sign will prove this to you. At Rachel's Tomb you'll meet two men who'll tell you that the donkeys have been found and that your father's worrying about you now. Then when you come to the Tabor Oak, three men, on their way to Bethel, will meet you. They will be carrying their gifts for the sacrifice there—one carrying three kids, another three bread loaves, the third a skin of wine. They will greet you and offer you two loaves—take them. After that you will come to God's Hill—there's a Philistine outpost there. A company of prophets will be marching down from the high hill there, playing on musical instruments, speaking excitedly words from GOD. GOD's spirit will seize you, and you will join them and speak as they do—you will become an inspired man. When all this has happened, you must do as you think best—GOD will be with you!'

Saul said goodbye to Samuel.

All happened as Samuel had said. When Saul's friends saw him acting like a prophet they were amazed.

'What's happened to Saul?' they asked. 'Has he joined the prophets?'

His uncle met them.

'Where've you been?' he asked.

'Looking for the donkeys,' said Saul. 'When we couldn't find them, we went to Samuel.'

'Oh!' said his uncle. 'And what did he talk to you about?'

'The donkeys,' said Saul. 'He told us they'd been found.'

Crowned King

A month later, Ammonite tribesmen, under their chieftain Nahash, attacked Jabesh town.

'We'll submit,' said the townsmen, 'if you will make a binding treaty with us.'

'I'll make a treaty with you all right—on one condition,' said the chieftain. 'I'll gouge all your right eyes out and make you a disgrace to all your fellow countrymen!'

'Give us a week's armistice, then,' said the townsmen. 'Let us send messengers to our countrymen. If nobody comes to our rescue, we'll surrender to you!'

The messengers came to Saul's town, Gibeah. They had just told their news—there was a great noise of wailing people—when Saul came home from the fields driving his oxen before him.

'What's the matter?' he asked.

They told him.

GOD's spirit seized him when he heard the news. In a blaze of anger he cut his oxen in pieces, and sent couriers with the pieces to his fellow countrymen everywhere, with a proclamation:

'Follow me! Anyone who doesn't will have his cattle cut up like this!'

The fear of GOD fell upon everyone, and they rallied as one man.

The roll call was held at Bezek, and Saul gave the Jabesh messengers their orders. 'Go home,' he said. 'Tell your fellow-townsmen that they will be rescued by noon tomorrow.'

There was great rejoicing in Jabesh town, and the townsmen sent word to the Ammonite chieftain.

'We will surrender tomorrow,' they said. 'You can do what you want with us.'

Saul marched all night with three companies. They stormed the Ammonite camp in the darkness before dawn. The fighting went on till noon—the Ammonite survivors fled in all directions, every man for himself.

The Israelite people gathered at Gilgal, and there Saul was crowned king in GOD's presence; there was a religious service with a sacrifice to GOD—and great celebrations.

Backs to the Wall

Saul (now fifty years old) set about dealing with the Philistines.

He organized an army and sent the rest of the tribal levies home. Two thirds of the men, under his own command, were encamped at Michmash and in the highlands of Bethel; one third, under his son Jonathan's command, were encamped at Gibeah in the Benjamin hills where they destroyed the Philistine outpost.

News reached the Philistine cities—'The highlanders have revolted.' They called out their troops, marched into the highlands and occupied Michmash. This threw the Israelites into a panic—they knew they were now in grave danger. They left their villages, and hid themselves any-where they could—in caves, holes, rocks, tombs or wells—or fled over Jordan River to the eastern mountains.

Saul held a roll call of his troops; they numbered about six hundred men. He and Jonathan now set up camp at Gibeah. The Philistines held Michmash and sent out three raiding parties to capture strategic points in the highlands—towards Ophrah (Gideon's home town), Beth-horon and the hill looking down the Valley of the Hyenas toward the desert.

The Michmash Pass

The main body of the Philistines at Michmash pushed out an outpost to the heights above the Michmash Pass.

One day Jonathan spoke to his young armour-bearer.

'Let's go and have a look at the Philistine outpost over there on the other side of the pass,' he said.

The gorge at Michmash Pass. Jonathan and his armour-bearer climbed one of these ▶ cliffs and destroyed the Philistine outpost on the cliff-top. The cliffs shown are probably 'Slippery Rock' and 'Thorny Rock'

Saul had taken his stand, with his six hundred soldiers, outside Gibeah where he had his headquarters under the pomegranate tree by the threshing-floor. Jonathan said nothing about his plans to his father; even the soldiers didn't know he had gone off.

Now on either side of the Michmash Pass there were two steep cliffs, one on each side, north and south. (Their local names were 'Slippery Rock' and 'Thorny Rock').

'Let's go over to these heathen Philistines,' said Jonathan. 'GOD will be on our side, perhaps—he doesn't depend on numbers.'

'Go ahead,' said his armour-bearer. 'I'm your man!'

'Now listen,' said Jonathan. 'We'll let them see us. If they shout at us "You stay where you are till we get at you!" we'll just stay put. But if they shout "Come on up and try your luck!" then up we go. That's a sure sign GOD's put them at our mercy.'

They both stepped out and let themselves be seen.

'Look,' shouted the Philistine sentries, 'the highlanders are coming out of their hide-outs!'

The sentries hailed the two men.

'Come on up!' they shouted. 'We'll show you a thing or two!'

'After me!' ordered Jonathan. 'GOD's put them at our mercy!'

He scrambled up on his hands and knees, the soldier after him. They caught the sentries by surprise (they had no idea there was a path up the cliff). Jonathan knocked them down and his armour-bearer killed them off—twenty men on the narrow ledge.

Panic spread throughout the Philistine camp—and beyond. There happened to be an earthquake just at that moment too; the Philistine army and the raiding columns were terrified and the panic became a rout.

The Israelite look-outs in Gibeah were watching the Philistine camp and saw the soldiers suddenly scattering in all directions.

'Who's missing?' asked Saul. 'Find out!'

Jonathan and his armour-bearer were missing at the roll-call.

'Bring the Ark here,' said Saul to Ahijah its guardian.

While Saul was talking like this to the priest, the uproar in the Philistine camp grew louder.

'Wait,' said Saul.

He and his men raced over to the fight. Everybody seemed to be fighting everybody else; it was complete chaos. Even the Israelites who had gone over to the Philistines and were serving with their army deserted and joined Saul and Jonathan. Men who had been hiding in the highlands came out and joined in the pursuit. So GOD rescued the Israelites that day.

But Saul made a big mistake.

He had put all his soldiers under oath—'Cursed be the man who eats anything until evening, until I have had my revenge on my enemies'.

The soldiers were exhausted; nobody had eaten anything all day, not even the honeycombs in the open fields which the bees had abandoned. The oath had frightened them.

Jonathan knew nothing about all this. Walking along, he pushed his staff into a honeycomb and put some of the honey into his mouth with his hand. It did him good.

A soldier told him about the oath.

'My father's made it very hard for the soldiers,' was all Jonathan said. 'See how much better I am with a little taste of honey. If the soldiers could have eaten when they wanted to today—there's plenty of loot—what a victory it would have been! We would have wiped them out!'

That day the Israelites fought the Philistines from Michmash to Aijalon, although they were weak with hunger.

'And now for a night attack!' ordered Saul. 'Loot until dawn and finish them all off!'

'As you command,' his men said.

'Let us ask GOD first,' said Ahijah the priest.

This is what Saul did.

'Shall I go after the Philistines?' he asked. 'Will you make us the victors?'

GOD gave no answer.

'Somebody's broken the oath,' said Saul. He ordered all the officers to meet and find out who the culprit was.

'By the GOD who rescues us,' he said, 'the culprit shall die—even though he is Jonathan, my son!'

The soldiers stood in silence.

'We'll soon find out,' said Saul. 'All of you shall be on one side— I and Jonathan on the other.'

'As you command,' said the soldiers.

Saul prayed to GOD.

'O GOD,' he said, 'why haven't you given me an answer today? Guide the lots, and if the guilt is mine or Jonathan's, give URIM; if it is the soldiers', give THUMMIM.'

Jonathan and Saul were chosen.

'Now cast the lots between me and Jonathan,' said Saul.

Jonathan was chosen.

'What have you done?' said Saul. 'Tell me!'

'I used my staff and tasted a bit of honey,' he said. 'I am ready to die.'

'And die you shall!' said Saul.

The soldiers protested.

'Jonathan die?' they shouted. 'Jonathan who rescued us today? Never! By GOD, not a hair of his head shall fall on the ground. He's been GOD's fellow-worker today!'

So the soldiers ransomed Jonathan and saved his life.

Saul called off the pursuit of the Philistines; by now they had retreated to their cities.

Night In the Valley

The last great battle was about to begin. The Philistines had massed their forces in the Jezreel valley with Shunem as headquarters. Saul and his men pitched camp on Gilboa Hill.

Saul surveyed the Philistine troops massed in the valley below. What he saw filled him with fear and foreboding.

He prayed to GOD, but GOD was silent. Whatever he tried—dreams, the stones,[1] prophets—he got no answer.

'I must get help from someone,' he said to his officers. 'Find me a woman who can conjure up the dead—I'll try her.'

'There's a woman in the valley below,' they told him, 'at Endor.'

He disguised himself as a private soldier and went, with two of his men, out into the night.

'You're a woman who can conjure up the dead,' he told the woman. 'Use your art to tell me my fortune—let me talk to the man whose name I'll give you.'

'You know Saul's orders,' said the woman. 'He's banished witches and wizards. You're trying to trap me, aren't you? You know I'll be put to death if I'm found out.'

Saul put her at her ease.

'As GOD lives,' he said, 'you're quite safe; our visit tonight won't get you into any trouble.'

'Who do you want to talk to?' she asked.

'Samuel,' he said.

When she heard the name of 'Samuel', she screamed and turned on Saul.

'Why have you played this trick on me?' she said. 'You are Saul himself!'

'Don't be frightened,' he said. 'Tell me what you are seeing.'

'A ghost,' she said, 'coming up out of the ground.'

---

[1] The flat stones called 'Urim' and 'Thummim'. See under 'Notes on Important Words and Names' (p. 410).

The Tabor Oak (p. 26) ▶

'What's it look like?' asked Saul.

'An old man,' she said, 'an old man wrapped in a cloak.'

Saul knew it was Samuel, and he bowed to the ground before him.

'Why have you disturbed me,' asked Samuel, 'bringing me back like this?'

'I'm at my wits' end,' said Saul. 'The Philistines are attacking me in force, and GOD has left me and won't listen to my prayers any more. So I've called you back—tell me what I'm to do.'

'If GOD won't have anything to do with you,' said Samuel, 'why ask me? This is GOD's will: tomorrow you and your sons will die in battle —the Israelites will be defeated.'

Saul fell full length on the floor; Samuel's words terrified him. He hadn't any strength left—for a whole day and a whole night he'd eaten nothing.

The woman knelt down beside him and saw his look of terror.

'I've done what you told me to do,' she said. 'I've done it at the risk of my life. Now listen to me, please. Let me get you something to eat. You need a bit of food if you're going to get back to the camp.'

'No,' he said, 'I couldn't touch anything.'

The three of them—his two men and the woman—went on arguing with him.

At last he gave way. He got up and sat on the bed in the room.

The woman killed a calf she had and made unleavened cakes from some flour. She made a meal for the three men.

They ate it and went back to the camp in the darkness.

Death on the Hill

The Philistines launched their attack. The Israelites broke before them and left their dead and dying on the slopes of Gilboa Hill.

The Philistines made for the king's standard and round it raged the fiercest fighting. Saul's sons were killed and, at last, the Philistine archers found their mark—Saul was badly wounded in the stomach.

'Draw you sword,' he said to his armour-bearer. 'Finish me off. I don't want these heathen beasts to come and make sport of me.'

His armour-bearer was too frightened to obey; so Saul got hold of his own sword and threw himself on it.

At the sight of his dead king, the armour-bearer threw himself on his own sword and died by his side. So Saul and his sons and his armour-bearer died together on the same day.

◄ David playing before King Saul (p. 40).

When the Israelites on the other side of the valley saw the rout of their own men, they abandoned their towns in panic.

Next day, the Philistine soldiers came back to the battlefield for booty. They found Saul's body and the bodies of his three sons where they had fallen on Gilboa Hill. They cut off Saul's head and stripped his body of his armour.

They sent heralds back to their own cities with the good news of victory. They announced it to the people in the streets and to the gods in their temples; they put Saul's armour in the temple of Astarte and hung his body on the wall of Bethshan.

News of all this reached the citizens of Jabesh-Gilead in the highlands east of Jordan River. A company of their bravest soldiers marched through the night across the river, to Bethshan, and took Saul's body—and those of his sons—down from the city wall. They carried them back home and buried their ashes under the tamarisk tree in their town. Everybody went into mourning for a week.

Walls of the temple at Bethshan. The Philistines, after defeating the Israelites on Gilboa Hill, hung Saul's armour in the temple and his body on the town walls

Salute to the Dead

David (whose story we have still to tell) was stationed at this time in Ziklag, a small town far away in the south. He had been out raiding and had only been home a day or two.

A young man, with his clothes torn and earth on his head, came running into the town. He threw himself on the ground in front of him in homage.

'Where have you come from?' asked David.

'I've escaped from the Israelite camp on Gilboa,' he said.

'What happened?' asked David. 'Tell me.'

'It was just a rout,' said the man. 'There are many killed and wounded on the battlefield. Saul and Jonathan are dead.'

'How do you know?' asked David.

'I just happened to be on Gilboa Hill. Saul was leaning on his spear. The Philistine chariots and cavalry were charging down on him. He turned round, saw me and called me over to him. "Here, sir!" I said. "Stand beside me," he said, "and put me out of my misery—I'm in terrible pain and I can't die". I did what he ordered me; he couldn't have lived much longer, I'm sure. I took the crown from his head and the armlet from his arm. Here they are. They are yours, my lord.'

'Where do you come from?' David asked.

'I'm the son of an Amalekite immigrant,' he said.

'What?' said David. 'Weren't you too overawed to kill GOD's anointed king?'

'Here!' David called to one of his young soldiers. 'Strike him down!' The soldier struck him dead.

'You signed your own death warrant,' said David. 'Your own words —"I killed the king"—are evidence against you.'

David and his men tore their clothes in their grief, lamenting and fasting for all who had died in the battle and for the whole tribal league. So they spent the day until darkness fell.

This is the 'Lament' which David composed about Saul and Jonathan:

      O Captain,
         dead in the highlands!
      Heroes fallen
         in the thick of the fight!

      Keep the news from Gath,
         no word of it in Ashkelon's streets—
      lest Philistine girls start singing,
         heathen girls make merry.

O Gilboa Hill! No dew be on you!
   No rain fall on you, you fields of death!
The hero's shield, the king's sword
   were stained there
      with dead men's blood,
      strong men's flesh.

Jonathan's bow faced the foe,
   Saul's sword wreaked havoc—
Saul and Jonathan,
   loved and lovely,
     together in life and death,
      swifter than eagles,
      stronger than lions!

Girls in the villages,
   cry your eyes out for Saul;
     he clothed you in scarlet and splendour,
     he braided your dresses with gold!

Alas for the heroes
   fallen in the fierce fighting!

O Jonathan, my heart breaks for you,
   my brother, my closest friend!
You loved me more dearly
   than any woman could!

Alas for the dead heroes!
   Alas for their broken swords!

Gilboa Hill, where Saul made his last stand against the Philistine armies

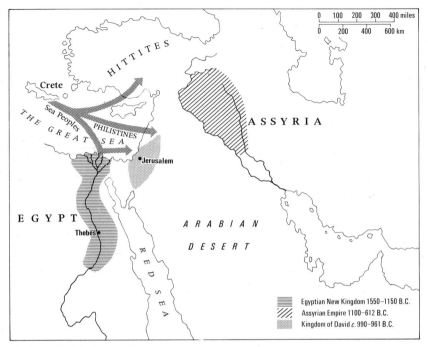

The Near East in 1000 B.C.E.

The Great King

The story of King David begins before Saul's death and we must now go back in time in order to tell it. King David is one of the outstanding kings in history, although his empire was a small affair beside the great empires of Egypt and Assyria. It was only because, as we have said, these powerful empires were having trouble at home and had no time for foreign adventures that David could dominate the small countries of the Middle East as he did.

His character and achievements made him the most famous Israelite king; later centuries were to remember him as the ideal king—a sort of King Arthur—beside whom all other kings were judged. When, after the Exile, small groups of Jews returned to rebuild their city but had no king of their own (they were part of the vast Persian Empire), they began to dream that one day God would again give them a king like David.

Saul had failed to drive the Philistines back to the plain and defeat them; David believed God had called him to carry out this task. He saw plainly that it could not be done with unreliable tribesmen whose interest very rarely went beyond their tribal boundaries and who were not capable of sustained warfare. He set himself to create a proper state, a nation, with a central government and a standing army. He enlisted and trained his famous 'Foreign Legion' from soldiers who had served under him in his days as a freebooter in the hills or as an officer under one of the Philistine chieftains. He was a great soldier and many Philistine soldiers were glad to serve under him. The Captain of his 'Foreign Legion' was a Philistine, and one of his most loyal officers, Captain Uriah, was a Hittite.

But David, like Saul, was a deeply religious man and cared greatly that the Israelite people should really be GOD's People. The tribal league had failed. David set himself to create a nation which could be GOD's People.

The new nation, including as it did Philistines and Canaanites as well as Hebrews, made a great change in Israelite religion. It brought them into close touch with neighbouring peoples; the new capital city itself ('David's Town', 'Zion') had been a Canaanite fortress with its temple and priests. The Israelites believed GOD had chosen it as his 'place' and David as his king. So for them the nation was founded on a new Covenant—a covenant made by GOD with David (representing the people). Many Israelites, especially in the North, had their doubts about all this, as we shall see.

David was a great man and a great king; a thousand years later one of his descendants—Jesus—was to deal with the problems he faced in a very different way and to call into being a new 'People of God' which would transcend national politics and be a world community.

Captain of the King's Bodyguard

Called to the Court

Saul suffered from sudden and unreasoning fits of terror.

'Some evil demon's tormenting you,' his courtiers told him. 'Let us find a clever harpist—you've only to give us the command; he can soothe you with his music when these fits of terror seize you.'

'Good,' said the king. 'Find me a clever musician and bring him to court.'

'I know a man who can play the harp,' said one of the pages. 'He's the son of Jesse, a farmer in Bethlehem.'

Saul asked Jesse to send his son David to court. Jesse sent him along —with a present of five loaves of bread, a skin of wine and a kid. Saul took a great fancy to him and made him his armour-bearer.

'I like David very much,' he sent word to his father. 'Let him become one of my officers.'

Whenever he had his fits of terror, David played his harp. He was soothed, the fits passed off and he felt himself again. He took David into his service, and wouldn't let him go home.

Jonathan, his son, and David became bosom friends and swore an oath of friendship with one another; in proof of his friendship, Jonathan gave his royal cloak to David, along with his weapons—his sword and his bow—and his belt.

David proved a first-class soldier. Saul promoted him to the rank of Commander-in-Chief. Everybody liked him—even the king's officers. He was a popular hero.

When he came back from a campaign village girls came out to meet him, dancing to music and singing songs. One of the popular songs of the day ran—

> 'Saul has killed his thousands—
> David his tens of thousands.'

Saul didn't like that!

'Tens of thousands to David,' he growled, 'but only thousands to me!' That's how his jealousy of David started; from now on he kept an eye on him.

The King's Daughter

Michal, Saul's daughter, fell in love with David. When Saul heard about it, he seemed very pleased; but he had his own reasons.

He told his courtiers to find out what David himself thought.

'Get him talking,' he said. 'You can start him off with something like this: "You're a lucky fellow—you're on the right side of the king, and we are all your friends. Is it such a wild dream to think of being the king's son-in-law?'' '

This was the way the conversation went when David was present.

'Nonsense,' he said. 'I'm nobody; you talk as if anybody could become the king's son-in-law!'

His words were reported to the king.

'Tell him I want no marriage present,' said Saul, 'but that there's one thing I would like: a little revenge on my enemies—the death of a hundred Philistine soldiers.'

The officers quickly told David. He thought it was an easy way of becoming the king's son-in-law. So he called out his men, raided the Philistines, and killed two hundred of them. He brought back to Saul evidence that he had killed them, and claimed his right to be his son-in-law.

So Saul gave David his daughter Michal in marriage. He knew in his heart that David was a good man and that Michal was really in love with him.

All this deepened his jealousy of David; and he began to plan his murder. One night he sent agents to keep watch outside David's house, with orders to murder him as he left home next morning.

Michal got wind of her father's plans and told David.

'Get out tonight,' she said. 'If you don't, you're as good as dead.'

She let him down through a window and he got away and made good his escape.

Michal then took the household gods and put them in his bed, with a goat's-hair pillow at its head and a cloak covering gods and pillow.

When David didn't come out of the house in the morning, Saul ordered his agents to break in and arrest him. Michal faced them and told them he was ill.

Saul wasn't being stopped by that. He ordered his agents to bring him, bed and all; he would see him killed himself.

The agents soon discovered the trick—there were household gods in the bed with the pillow at the head!

'Why have you played this trick on me?' Saul asked his daughter. 'You helped him to escape and get away—and you know he's my enemy!'

'He made me do it,' she said. 'He said he'd kill me if I didn't.'

Escape to Nob

David reached Nob where the priest was a man called Ahimelech. Ahimelech saw him coming and ran out to meet him.

'Why are you alone?' he asked. 'And where are your men?'

'I'm on a mission from the king,' said David, 'and on the king's orders, it must be kept secret. I am meeting my troops at a rendezvous. What have you got to eat? Give me four loaves of bread—or anything else you can lay your hands on.'

'There's only sacred bread here,' said the priest. 'There's no ordinary bread. Have your soldiers kept free from women?'

'Indeed they have,' said David. 'We maintain the sexual taboo whenever we go out on raids. Their equipment is dedicated to GOD.'

So the priest let him have the sacred bread. (This is special bread kept only for the worship of GOD; it is always replaced with fresh bread on the day it is taken away.)

'Haven't you got a spare sword or spear here?' asked David. 'The king's mission was so urgent that I left unarmed.'

'Goliath's Philistine sword is kept here,' said the priest. 'It's wrapped in a cloth over there behind the image. You can take it if you want to. We haven't anything else.'

'Fine! Let me have it,' said David. 'There isn't another sword like it!'

All this time, one of Saul's soldiers happened to be staying in the temple—Doeg, an Edomite, Saul's strongest cattleman. He was under a vow to GOD which he had to carry out in the shrine itself.

Outlaw

The Massacre at Gibeah

News about David and his men and where they were reached Saul at Gibeah. He was holding court at the time, sitting, spear in hand, under the tamarisk tree on the high hill. His officers were standing at attention round him.

'I've got something to say to you, men of Benjamin,' he said to them. 'Will this Bethlehem farmer David give you fields and vineyards—will he make you commanders of regiments and companies—that none of you breathed a word to me that my son Jonathan had actually set one of my officers up as my rival?'

'I've seen David,' called out Doeg the Edomite. 'I saw him at Nob. He came while I was staying in the temple there. The priest Ahimelech prayed to GOD for him, fed him and gave him Goliath's sword.'

Saul sent for Ahimelech and his assistant priests and commanded them to attend court.

'Now listen, Ahimelech,' said Saul.

'I am at your majesty's service,' said Ahimelech.

'What's this conspiracy against me about?' asked Saul. 'Why have

---

Gibeah ('hill'), Saul's home, a fortress on the main road running north-south through ▶
the hill country. It was, for a time, a Philistine outpost

you sided with David? I hear you've fed and armed him—and prayed to GOD for him. Why? He's now set himself up as my rival; he's out looking for me!'

'What else could I do?' asked Ahimelech. 'David's your son-in-law, the captain of your bodyguard, one of the most important men here in your court. If I couldn't trust him, who could I trust? Is praying to GOD for him an irreligious thing to do? I deny your charge against me. You have no reason to suspect me of conspiracy. I don't know what you're talking about.'

'I've already passed the death sentence on you,' said Saul, 'and on your fellow priests.'

The King turned to his guards.

'Kill them,' he ordered. 'They're hand-in-glove with David. They knew all about his escape, and they never reported it to me.'

The guards still stood at attention; they refused point-blank to have anything to do with such a murder.

The King turned to Doeg.

'You kill them,' he ordered.

Doeg stepped forward and killed them.

Eighty-five men died that day.

The Relief of Keilah Town

David heard that the Philistines were raiding Keilah Town; they had surrounded it and were looting the threshing floors. He immediately went to the town's rescue. He and his men routed the raiders and carried off their cattle.

Saul heard about all this.

'GOD's put him just where I want him,' he said. 'He's gone inside a walled town—he's walked into a trap!'

He called his army out; he would go down and catch him in the town.

Now Abiathar, the son of Ahimelech—the priest Saul had murdered—had escaped from Nob and joined David; and he had brought the ephod with him to Keilah.

When Saul's plans were reported to David, he called Abiathar to him.

'Bring the ephod here,' he ordered.

Then he prayed to GOD.

'O GOD,' he prayed, 'will Saul attack me here, as the reports say? Tell me, I am your servant.'

'He will,' said GOD.

'Will the citizens of this town hand me and my men over to him?'

'They will,' said GOD.

David acted straight away. He marched his six hundred men out of the town and they lived as guerrillas in the hills.

Saul heard of David's escape and called off his expedition.

Hachilah Hill

The people of Ziph took the news that David was hiding near them to Saul in Gibeah.

He called out his crack troops and marched to the wilderness of Ziph to hunt him out. He pitched camp on Hachilah Hill on the road facing 'The Desert'.

David was out in the rough moorlands when he heard that Saul was tracking him down. He sent scouts to find out where he was.

Then he moved quickly. He marched by night to the outskirts of Saul's camp. Saul and his commander-in-chief, Abner, were asleep—Saul lying in the trench, the soldiers in their tents round him as guard.

David called two men, the Hittite Ahimelech and Abishai.

'Which of you will go down with me to the camp—to Saul?' he asked.

'I will,' said Abishai.

So, through the darkness, the two men stole down to the camp. There was Saul lying asleep in the trench—his spear stuck in the ground at his head, Abner and the soldiers lying round him.

'GOD has put your enemy at your mercy,' whispered Abishai. 'I'll pin him to the earth with his own spear. One stroke's enough.'

'No murder,' said David. 'Saul is GOD's anointed king—murder of GOD's anointed king is a dreadful thing. In GOD's name, no murder!

'We'll leave him in GOD's hands, to die an ordinary death or meet a soldier's violent end,' he went on. 'But GOD forbid that I should lay my hand on his anointed king. Get the spear at his head, and the water-jug there—and let's get out!'

So they took the spear and the water-jug from near Saul's head and slipped away. Nobody saw or heard them, and nobody woke up. They were all sound asleep.

David crossed the valley and stood at a safe distance on a hilltop on the other side. He was so far off that he had to shout as loud as he could to be heard.

'Why don't you answer, Abner?' he shouted.

'Who are you,' Abner shouted back, 'calling up the king like this?'

'You're a fine soldier!' shouted David. 'You're the finest soldier of them all! What sort of guard is this to keep over his majesty the king? Didn't you know there's an assassin prowling round? What a soldier you are! By GOD, you ought to be executed for sleeping—you're supposed to be on guard, you know! Do you want proof? See where the king's spear and his water-jug are now—not at his head!'

Saul, awake by now, recognized David's voice.

'Is that you, my son David?' he called.

'It is, your majesty,' David shouted back. 'And let me finish what I have to say.

'Why do you hunt me like this?' he went on. 'What have I done wrong? If GOD's made you do this, let us ask his forgiveness; but if it's just slander, GOD's curse be on the slanderers—they have driven me out of the fellowship of GOD's people and tried to make me a foreigner. Don't let my blood be spilt in this foreign countryside. You're hunting me like a hawk hunting a partridge in the highlands!'

'I'm in the wrong,' said Saul. 'Come back to me, my son David. I'll do you no more hurt; you treated me as the real king today. I've been a fool and done a dreadful thing.'

'The king's spear is here,' called David. 'Let one of the soldiers come over and fetch it.'

'GOD bless you, my son David,' said Saul. 'You've a great future in front of you!'

David went on his way and Saul went home.

A Highland Farmer

There was a rich farmer in Maon, Nabal by name, who owned a farm at Carmel Town. He was a farmer in a big way; he had three thousand sheep and a thousand goats. His wife, Abigail, was an able and attractive woman. The man himself was just the opposite, a rude and coarse fellow.

It was the sheep-shearing season and Nabal was at his farm.

David was out on the moors. Someone told him about Nabal and his sheep-shearing. He sent ten young soldiers to the farm.

'Go to Carmel Town,' he told them, 'and see Nabal. Give him my regards. Wish him many happy returns—and good luck to himself and his family and farm. Then give him this message: "I've heard that sheep-shearing has begun. Your shepherds have been in my neighbourhood. We didn't molest them and they lost nothing all the time they were on the moors. Ask them—they will tell you. Treat these young soldiers well; after all, it's a festival. Give them something—whatever you like—and don't forget me, your friend." '

The men met Nabal, gave him David's message and waited for an answer.

'Who's David?' was all they got. 'There are hundreds of slaves running away from their masters now-a-days. Dammit, must I take what I've got ready for my own shearers—my bread and wine and meat —and give it to any Tom, Dick and Harry? How do I know where you've come from?'

The men went back to David and told him what had happened. He mustered his men.

'Buckle your swords on,' he commanded.

He left two hundred men with the baggage and marched with four hundred to the farm.

When David's men had left the farm, one of the servants had gone to Nabal's wife, Abigail.

'Look,' he said, 'David sent some of his men to our master with his greetings, and all he could do was to shout at them. When we were out on the hills, the men were very good to us—they didn't molest us at all and we lost nothing all the time we were with them. They were like a wall round us day and night while we were looking after the sheep near them. You'd better do something about it—our master will really be in trouble if you don't. He's a brute of a fellow; nobody can talk to him.'

Abigail didn't wait a moment. She collected two hundred loaves, two skins of wine, five sheep ready for cooking, five pecks of roasted corn, a hundred bunches of raisins and two hundred fig cakes. She packed them on donkeys and told her servants to go ahead—she would follow them. She didn't say a word to her husband.

She was riding on her donkey under the cover of the hill; David and his soldiers were moving down the opposite hillside towards her. They suddenly met.

'I've been wasting my time looking after this fellow's property out on the moors,' David had been thinking. 'He's lost nothing—and this is how he repays me! GOD help me, if I leave any of his men alive by dawn!'

Abigail got quickly off her donkey, and threw herself at David's feet.

'I am the one to blame,' she said. 'Let me tell you my side of the story. Take no notice of this brute of a fellow, Nabal; he's a fool by name and a fool by nature. I didn't know anything about the soldiers my lord sent—I didn't even see them. I've brought a present for my lord; let your soldiers have it.'

'Thank GOD for sending you to me today,' exclaimed David. 'Blessings on you! You're a sensible woman. And you've saved me from an act of bloodshed, from taking GOD's law into my own hand! I can see that GOD himself has been behind all you've done. But by GOD! if you hadn't been so quick off the mark, there wouldn't have been a man left alive on Nabal's farm by dawn!'

He accepted her present.

'Go home in peace,' he told her. 'See, I've listened to your story— I've done what you asked me.'

When Abigail got home to the farm, she found Nabal still feasting—

very merry and as drunk as a lord. So she waited until next morning when he'd slept off his drunkenness. Then she told him what had happened—who the soldiers really were and what she'd done about it. At her words, Nabal had a stroke and fell unconscious on the floor. He had another stroke ten days later, and this stroke killed him.

'Blessed be GOD!' said David when he heard of Nabal's death. 'He avenged the insult Nabal gave me—and he stopped me taking the law into my own hands. Nabal got what he deserved!'

David had been very attracted by Abigail, and he now started to court her. Then he sent some of his men to her on her farm with a proposal of marriage.

When they told her who had sent them, she got up and bowed herself to the ground. Her thoughts were: 'I would be glad to be just a slave-girl in his home, let alone his wife!'

She quickly got herself ready. She mounted a donkey and five of her maids went on foot. They followed David's soldiers back to camp, and she and David were married.

(David had now two wives—he was already married to a Jezreel girl, Ahinoam. Saul had divorced him from his daughter Michal and had married her to Paltai, a Gallim man.)

Philistine Commander

Flight to Gath

'One of these days Saul will get me,' thought David. 'The best thing I can do is to cross over into Philistine territory. It's the only way to get out of his clutches. He'll give up when he knows he can't catch me in his own territory.'

David marched his six hundred men across the frontier to the Philistine town of Gath. He went over to its chieftain Achish, and he and his men settled in the town.

When news of David's flight reached Saul, he gave up his attempt to capture him.

David spent sixteen months in Philistine territory. He and his men set off, raiding the various tribes in the Negeb as far as the Egyptian border. His raids followed a similar pattern: all the tribes-people—men and women—were killed; all livestock—sheep, cattle, donkeys, camels —were driven away and all clothing seized. He brought them all back to Achish.

(He regularly killed all men and women, rather than bring them back as prisoners to Achish, to stop any information about his movements

◄ The Negeb ('dry land'), border land linked as much with Egypt as with Palestine. It rises in places to about 3000 feet; the south-west is a barren area of rocky valleys shut in by great cliffs. Men feared its dry winds and wild animals (see also p. 113)

reaching Saul. He made this his settled policy while in Philistine territory.)

To Achish's regular question, 'Where've you been raiding today?' David always gave a vague answer.

'Oh, in the Negeb,' he would say, and add 'of Judah' or 'of the Jerahmeelites' or 'of the Kenites' in an offhand way.

Achish came to trust David.

'His own people will have finished with him,' he would think. 'I can count on him as a permanent officer of my army—he'll never dare to go home.'

When some time had passed, David spoke to Achish.

'If you are satisfied with my service,' he said, 'let me be stationed in one of the country towns—you don't need me in the city here.'

Achish appointed him to the small town of Ziklag, in the south on the road to Beersheba.

Commander of the Bodyguard

At last the Philistines called out their forces for a full-scale war against the Israelites.

'I expect you to fight with my army,' Achish told David.

'Certainly!' said David. 'You'll see what kind of a soldier I am!'

'Fine!' said Achish. 'I promote you commander of my bodyguard.'

The Philistines assembled their forces at Aphek across their northern border. The Israelite camp lay at Harod in the Jezreel Valley.

The Philistines held a march-past—the chieftains with their regiments and companies, David and his men bringing up the rear under Achish of Gath.

The Philistine High Command protested.

'What are these highlanders doing here?' they asked.

'You know,' said Achish. 'It's David who deserted from Saul. He's been with me for a year or more now. He's given excellent service— I've no complaints at all.'

The Philistine officers were in an ugly mood.

'Send him packing!' they said. 'Let him get back to the town where you stationed him. He's not taking part in this battle—he'll turn traitor as soon as the fighting begins. What better way could he find of putting himself right with his king than by turning on our own troops?'

Achish called David over to him.

'As GOD lives,' he said, 'you are an honourable man, and, as far as I am concerned, you should be marching with me in this campaign. I've no complaint to make about you from the day you entered my service, but the High Command doesn't approve of you. Go back—and go without any fuss—I don't want any trouble with the other chieftains.'

'But what have I done?' asked David. 'Have I ever done anything as an officer of yours which disqualifies me from fighting your enemies by your side?'

'You are a magnificent officer,' said Achish. 'But the fact is this. The High Command have made it plain that you are not to have any part in this campaign. Your orders are to go at first light tomorrow—you and your soldiers—back to Ziklag. Don't take this badly; you know what I think of you. But at dawn tomorrow, you must be gone.'

So, at first light, David and his men marched off, back through Philistine territory, as far south as Ziklag—three days' march. The Philistine army moved north, through the Megiddo Pass, and then eastwards to Jezreel Valley.[1]

Back to Ziklag

By the time David got back, Amalekite tribes had raided the Negeb and sacked Ziklag and burned it to the ground. They had marched away all the women they found there—young and old. What David found was a burned town—wives, sons and daughters all gone. The soldiers broke down in an agony of grief.

David himself was now in real danger. His soldiers were so bitter and grief-stricken that they talked of stoning him there and then.

He turned to Abiathar the priest.

'Bring the ephod here,' he commanded.

He put a question to GOD:

'Shall I go after that mob? If I do, shall I capture them?'

'Go after them,' said GOD. 'You will certainly capture them and rescue the prisoners.'

David set out with all his six hundred soldiers. He reached Besor Ravine. Here he left two hundred men who were too exhausted to go further. He and the other four hundred men went on.

In the open country his men found an Egyptian lying half-dead on the ground, and brought him to David. They gave him something to eat—bread, a fig cake and two bunches of raisins—and some water to drink. That bought him round; he had been starving for three whole days.

'Who owns you?' asked David, 'and where do you come from?'

'I'm an Egyptian,' he said, 'and my master's an Amalekite. I was taken ill three days ago, and he left me to die. We'd been on a raid into the Negeb. We burned down Ziklag town.'

'Will you guide me down to these raiders?' asked David.

'I'll guide you,' he answered, 'but swear to me that you won't kill me or hand me over to my master.'

---

[1] For the story of the battle between the Philistines and the Israelites, see p. 33.

Above a statuette of a harp player, probably a member of the temple choir in Ashod where this statuette was found

Left clay statuette of the mother goddess in the shape of a seated woman; her body forms part of the chair

He led David down—and there they were, spread over the whole countryside, eating and drinking and dancing. They had captured a vast amount of loot in Philistine territory. David attacked them and routed them; the fighting went on from dawn to dark and into the next day. The only men to escape were four hundred young men who fled on camels.

David recovered all the loot that had been taken at Ziklag. The prisoners were all safe. His men took possession of all the livestock they found in the Amalekite camp—sheep and cattle—and drove them away to shouts of 'David's Booty!'

He returned to Besor Ravine. The two hundred men left there came out to meet him and his men. David saluted them. Some of the meaner-minded soldiers who had taken part in the fighting objected to the two hundred sharing in the loot.

Above Philistine bowl

Left Philistine stirrup-jar with black and red decorations

'They didn't fight—they don't get anything,' they said. 'Let them take their wives and children and go!'

'Not on your life,' said David. 'GOD has given us all this booty and saved our lives and given us the victory—who's going to think like you? No! The men who guard the baggage and the men who fight share alike!'

When David got back to Ziklag he sent part of the loot to the elders of his own tribe—Judah—and to his friends there, with this message: 'Here's a present for you from the loot of GOD's enemies!'

King of the South

Crowned at Hebron

David had only been two days back at Ziklag when news of Saul's death on Gilboa Mountain reached him.[1]

'Shall I leave Ziklag,' he asked GOD, 'and go up to one of the towns in the Judean highlands?'

'Yes,' said GOD.

'Where shall I go?' David asked.

'To Hebron,' said GOD.

So David marched with his men to Hebron and settled in the surrounding villages. They took their wives and families with them; David took both his wives, Ahinoam of Jezreel and Abigail, Nabal's widow from Carmel.

---

[1] See p. 35.

The men of Judah came and crowned David as their king.

The story of how the men of Jabesh-Gilead had buried Saul's body was told to David. He was deeply moved and sent a message to the town:

'Blessings on you for your loyalty to Saul and for seeing to it that he was properly buried. May GOD show steadfast love and faithfulness to you! I shall not forget; I will see that you get a proper reward for what you have done. May you always show such a brave and valiant spirit. King Saul is dead; the men of Judah have crowned me as their King!'

Meanwhile, Saul's commander-in-chief, Abner, had escorted Saul's son, Ishbaal, across Jordan River and crowned him king of the northern tribes in Mahanaim in the highlands. Only the southern tribe of Judah acknowledged David as king.

The Battle of Gibeon

Abner, the northern commander, set out from Mahanaim, with the northern army, crossed Jordan River and marched to Gibeon on the eastern edge of Saul's own tribal territory of Benjamin, northwest of the fortified Canaanite city of Jerusalem.

Joab, David's commander, marched north from Hebron, with David's army.

The two armies met at Gibeon Pool.

'Let the lads try their luck,' Abner said to Joab. 'Let's have a trial of strength.'

'Yes, let them fight it out,' said Joab.

So they counted off soldiers from each side by number—twelve Benjamites and twelve of David's men. It was bloody fighting. Each soldier seized his opponent with one hand by the hair of his head, and with his other hand plunged his sword into his side. Both fell dead together.

Fierce fighting now broke out between the armies, and David's soldiers routed the Northerners.

Joab's brother, Asahel, a divisional commander, was a famous runner who could run (as the saying went) 'as fast as a wild gazelle'. He marked down the Northern commander, Abner, and ran after him, never letting him out of his sight.

Abner rounded on him.

'Are you Asahel?' he called out.

'I am!' he shouted back.

'Then clear off and tackle a common soldier,' he said. 'Take his armour for loot!'

Asahel still kept on his track.

'I've told you to clear off,' called Abner. 'Stop following me, or I'll kill you. How could I look your brother in the face then?'

But Asahel wouldn't be put off.

So Abner struck him in the stomach with a backward blow. The spear came out at his back, and Asahel fell dead in his tracks.

Asahel's two brothers, Joab the commander-in-chief and Abishai, were hot on Abner's trail. At sunset they reached Ammah Hill on the desert road. The Northern soldiers formed a solid phalanx behind Abner on the brow of the hill.

'Is there to be no end to the fighting?' Abner called out. 'It can only bring bitterness for us all. How much longer have we got to wait for you to call off the pursuit and stop kinsman fighting kinsman?'

'By GOD!' said Joab, 'if you hadn't spoken we would have gone on fighting all night!'

Joab gave the command for the bugle to be blown. The Southern army halted; the pursuit of the Northern soldiers was over and there was no more fighting.

Abner moved that night along the Jordan Valley, forded the river and marched all morning to reach the eastern capital, Mahanaim, by noon.

At a roll-call of the Southern army, Joab listed the casualties of the fighting: on the Southern side, nineteen dead (besides Asahel); on the Northern side, three hundred and sixty dead. He and his men marched southwards all through the night and reached Hebron at daybreak. They carried Asahel's body with them and buried him in his ancestral tomb in Bethlehem town.

The war between North and South—between Saul's family and David —went on and on. David had the better of the fighting; the Northern resistance began to give way before his growing military strength.

Rebellion in the North

Abner became the most powerful man in the North—his influence grew and grew. He took a fancy to one of Saul's secondary wives called Rizpah.

'What game are you up to,' King Ishbaal asked him, 'sleeping with one of my father's wives?'

This touched Abner on the raw.

'Am I scum from the South?' he exploded, 'I—who've stood by Saul's family and saved you from David's attacks? And you go and spread scandal about a woman at this time of day!'

The king was reduced to silence; he was thoroughly scared.

Abner now sent a secret message to David at Hebron, the Southern capital.

'If you'll come to an agreement with me,' he said, 'all my influence in the North is at your disposal. I will arrange for the North to crown you king.'

'Excellent,' David's answer came back. 'I will certainly come to an agreement with you. I have only one condition. When you come to negotiate the terms of the treaty, you must bring Michal, Saul's daughter, with you.'

At the same time, David sent an official request to King Ishbaal: 'I demand the surrender of Michal my wife—I was betrothed to her.'

King Ishbaal commanded Michal to go with Abner's mission to the South. Her husband followed her for miles along the road, in great distress, until Abner ordered him home.

Now Abner had already had secret talks with leading men in the North about the future of the kingship. There was a growing movement to make David king instead of Ishbaal. Abner urged immediate action. He put the same point to the leaders of Saul's own tribe, Benjamin.

He had done all this before he set out on his mission to David to tell him about the friendly feeling towards him in the North—especially among the leaders of Saul's own tribe.

So he and the twenty men accompanying him reached Hebron. David gave them a banquet.

'I will now go back and rally the North to your side,' Abner told David, 'and get them to make a treaty with you. You can be king over as wide a kingdom as you wish.'

David sent him back under safe conduct.

Just then the Southern commander-in-chief, Joab, came in from a raiding expedition. Abner by now had set off back to the North. Joab soon learned what David had done—let Abner, the Northern commander-in-chief, visit him and go away under safe conduct.

He went straight into the king's presence.

'What have you been up to?' he blurted out. 'You've had a visit from Abner, have you? And you've given him a safe conduct home? Don't you know he only came here spying and making a fool of you? And you let him get away!'

He stormed out of the king's presence, and sent some of his soldiers after Abner, without even informing him. They overtook Abner at Sirah's Pool and brought him back to Hebron. Joab beckoned him over to the side of the town gate, as if he was going to talk to him, man to man. He stabbed him in the stomach and killed him—that would pay him back for killing his brother Asahel.

The murder was quickly reported to David.

'I and my kingdom have had no part in this. GOD knows that!' he exclaimed. 'May Joab and all his descendants suffer for it—may they be sick, lepers, lame, beggars or murdered!'

He ordered the whole court to go into mourning. Abner was buried in Hebron. King David walked behind the bier and there was loud wailing at the graveside; everyone wept openly. King David himself made this lament for Abner:

> 'That Abner should die
>> a peasant's death—
> hands not handcuffed,
>> feet not fettered!
> You died
>> at the hands of villains!'

The wailing went on.

The court tried to persuade David to take some food.

'No!' said David. 'May GOD punish me if I eat any food until after sunset!'

The people were impressed; David had done the right thing and it was clear to everybody that he had nothing to do with Abner's murder.

'A great commander has died today,' King David told his court. 'I am a crowned king, but it breaks my heart. I'll not have cruelty like the cruelty of these men. May they suffer for their crime!'

Assassination

There was panic in the North when news of Abner's murder reached there. King Ishbaal himself was a very frightened man.

One day two of his guerrilla leaders, Rechab and Baanah, entered the palace. It was early in the afternoon, the hottest time of the day. The king was taking his siesta; the woman in charge of the palace gate had been sifting wheat and had drowsed off.

Two men slipped quietly past, broke into the royal bedroom and murdered the king in his sleep. They cut his head off and made off with it. All afternoon and through the darkness of the night they hurried south by way of Jordan Valley and reached Hebron.

They sought an audience with King David.

'Here is King Ishbaal's head,' they said. 'He was your enemy—he would have killed you if he could. GOD has seen justice done on Saul's family!'

'By GOD who has never failed to rescue me when my life's been in danger,' David exclaimed, 'I know how to treat men like you! I killed the fellow who brought me news of Saul's death; he thought he'd make something out of such "good news". He did—he died. How do you think I'll treat thugs like you who murder a good man asleep in his own home? You're not fit to live!'

He called out his bodyguard and they killed them both, there and then. They cut off their hands and feet, and hung their bodies up by Hebron Pool.

The North goes over to David

All the Northern tribes now sent their leaders south to Hebron to King David.

'Look,' they said to King David, 'we come, not as your enemies, but as your kinsmen—to crown you as our king.'

And they crowned him king of the North.

The Philistine War

This startled the Philistines. They called out their army in force, marched into the hills and occupied the whole Rephaim Valley to the south-west of Jerusalem. Their plan was to drive a wedge between South and North and capture David. But when David's scouts brought news of enemy movements, he made Adullam Fort, fifteen miles south-west of Jerusalem, his headquarters.

'Shall I attack the Philistines?' he asked GOD. 'Will you deliver them into my hands?'

'I certainly will,' said GOD.

David went into the attack and routed the Philistines all the way from Gibeon north of Jerusalem as far as Gezer in the Philistine Plain.

There are many stories told of David and his officers and their exploits in the Philistine War.

Once, when David and his men were fighting, he fell from sheer tiredness. Benob, a Philistine hero, wearing a belt of honour and with a bronze spear weighing thirteen pounds, took him prisoner and was going to kill him. Captain Abishai came to his rescue and struck the Philistine dead.

David's officers were alarmed at the risks he was running. They vowed to take no chances.

'Keep out of the fighting,' they told him. 'We don't want you killed— you're the only hope of our people.'

In another battle in Gob, Sibbecai the Hashathite killed a Philistine called Saph. In another battle in the same countryside, Elhanan, an officer from David's own town of Bethlehem, slew Goliath of Gath whose spear was as big as a bough of a tree. Once, when the fighting had reached the Philistine city of Gath, Jonathan, David's nephew, killed a giant of a man (he had six fingers on each hand and six toes on each foot) when he stood up and taunted the Israelite soldiers. All these were members of the Scimitar Brigade.

Here is the roll-call of David's officers.

There were three commanders over the army. These are some of their exploits.

His commander-in-chief was Ishbaal the Hachmonite—he was famous for winning a fight against great odds, armed only with a spear.

The second-in-command was Eleazar. He was once with David in a tight corner in Pasdammim. The Philistine troops were pushing the Israelites back. But the battle was saved by Eleazar who stood his ground and fought on till his arm was almost too tired to lift and his hand felt as if it was glued to his sword. But he rallied his men to victory —all that was left was the looting!

The third commander was Shammah the Hararite. The fighting at a place called 'Jawbone' was swaying round a plot of ground, a lentil garden. The Israelite soldiers began to give way, but Shammah stood boldly in the middle of the lentil plot and refused to give ground—it turned the tide of battle.

Under the Three Commanders were Thirty Captains.

The most famous and the Commander of the Thirty was Abishai, brother of Joab, David's Commander-in-Chief. He once killed three hundred men with his spear. That made his reputation. Although he became Commander of the Thirty he never reached the rank of the Three.

Among the other captains was Benaiah, a born soldier about whom many stories were told: how he once killed two Moabite heroes; how he fought with a lion in a pit on a snowy day and killed it; how he slew a giant of an Egyptian. He had only a club, but he attacked the armed Egyptian, wrenched the spear out of his hand, and killed him with his own spear. Benaiah was a very famous soldier. David made him Captain of his Bodyguard.

The Thirty Captains came from very different places. Several came from David's own town of Bethlehem or the countryside round about it. Others came from north of Galilee Lake, the mountains east of Jordan River, from the Plain between the mountains and the sea, from south of the Salt Sea, from the old Southern capital Hebron. Two came from Saul's own town of Gibeah. Two were foreigners, one an Ammonite and one a Hittite—of whom we shall hear more.

There's a famous story about three of his Thirty Captains. It happened when David was besieged by Philistine troops in the Adullam Fort in the Rephaim Valley—about three or four miles from his home town of Bethlehem, where the Philistines had an outpost.

One day, David was very thirsty.

'What wouldn't I give for a drink of Bethlehem water from the well by the city gate!' he exclaimed.

Three of his captains overheard him. Without telling anybody, they
broke through the Philistine lines, went to Bethlehem, drew some water
from the well by the city gate, and brought it back to David.

He wouldn't drink it.

'GOD forbid that I should do such a thing!' he said. 'This is the blood
of men who took their lives in their hands—can I drink water as costly
as that?'

He poured it out as an offering to GOD, and refused to quench his
thirst with it.

King of the South and North

New Capital

North and South each had their own capital city—Mahanaim in the North
and Hebron in the South. David, now he was king of South and North, decided
to establish a new capital city for the new nation. Near the borders of North
and South lay the fortress of Jerusalem, controlling the road between them. It
was still in Jebusite hands—it had never been captured. This, he made up his
mind, should be his new capital city.

David besieged Jerusalem with his troops.

'You can't capture us!' the Jebusite soldiers laughed at them from
the city walls. 'Blind and lame men could guard our gates!'

They knew David couldn't storm the walls. But he broke into the
fortress.

David may have captured it in this way (the actual text is obscure):
Jerusalem city had no natural water supply; the citizens had to sink a deep
shaft down to the spring outside the western wall. They thought this was quite
safe, for the water rose and filled the bottom of the shaft. But for a short time
each day the water level dropped. David may have done what nobody had
ever done before—sent some of his commando troops up the shaft while the
water was low. They had just time to climb up it. They took the fortress by
surprise; before the guards realized what was happening, David's soldiers had
opened the city gates and his troops stormed in.

He made the citadel his palace—he called it 'Davidstown'—and built
the city proper inwards from the Great Tower.

David now became a powerful king; GOD was with him.

He made treaties with neighbouring kings. For example, he hired,
by treaty, Tyrian workmen—carpenters and stone-masons—to build
his palace.

Entrance to the tunnel for the Gihon Spring ('Bubbling Spring'). This led to the shaft through which the citizens of Jerusalem drew water – the shaft David's commandos may have used to break into the city (see the diagrams). It also led to the tunnel King Hezekiah made to link the spring to Siloam Pool on the western side of the city

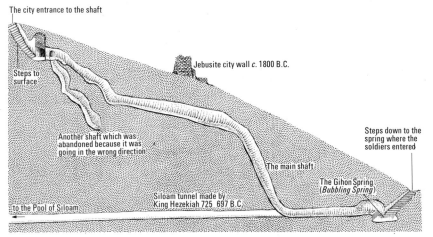

The city entrance to the shaft

Steps to surface

Jebusite city wall *c.* 1800 B.C.

Steps down to the spring where the soldiers entered

Another shaft which was abandoned because it was going in the wrong direction

The main shaft

The Gihon Spring (*Bubbling Spring*)

Siloam tunnel made by King Hezekiah 725 697 B.C.

to the Pool of Siloam

The water tunnel cut through the rock in the Jebusite city of Jerusalem (before 1000 B.C.E.). This is the water tunnel David's soldiers climbed to get inside the city. (The plan is foreshortened, which makes the shaft look steeper than it really is)

One Religious Centre for South and North

The Ark of GOD had stayed until now in the house of Abinadab on the hill—the men of Kiriath-jearim had taken it there when the Philistines sent it back.

King David now mustered his army and set out to bring it to Jerusalem. They took it from Abinadab's house and put it on a new cart. Two sons of Abinadab—Uzzah and his brother—guided the cart. Uzzah walked beside it; his brother walked in front. The king and the people formed a procession, dancing wildly and singing to the music of guitars, harps, tambourines, bells and cymbals.

They reached a certain threshing-floor. Suddenly the oxen stumbled and Uzzah put out his hand to steady the Ark. He collapsed and died beside it—GOD was angry with him for touching it. King David was vexed at what GOD had done and he was afraid of him.

'How can I do anything with the Ark now?' he asked.

He changed his mind about taking it to Davidstown and left it in the house of Obed-Edom the Philistine. Here it stayed for three months —lucky months for Obed-Edom and his family. When the king learned that nothing unlucky had happened, he decided that it would be safe to bring it to Davidstown. He set out and brought it to his city in a joyous procession.

As the Ark was being carried into the town, Michal was watching the procession from a palace window. She saw the king leaping and dancing with religious fervour; and she despised him for acting as she thought no king should.

When David came back to the palace to greet his family, she came out to meet him.

'The king has been a fine king today,' she sneered, 'walking naked for slave-girls to laugh at—like a village peasant!'

'I will dance for GOD if I think I ought to,' David retorted. 'He chose me, anyhow, instead of your father, and he made me king of his people. I will dance and make merry before him, if I want to. I'll make myself "like a village peasant", as you put it, and you can sneer at me as much as you like! But slave-girls won't laugh at me—they know what I'm doing and honour me for it!'

He treated her no more as his wife.

The Court History

David and Meribaal

'Jonathan was a sworn friend of mine,' said King David one day. 'I must carry out my promise to him. I wonder if any of his father's family are still alive.'

One of Saul's courtiers, a man called Ziba, was still living in one of the villages. He was summoned to court.

'So you're Ziba, are you?' the king asked him.

'I am,' he said.

'Tell me something,' said the king. 'Are any of Saul's descendants still alive?'

'There's a grandson,' he said, 'a lame son of Jonathan's. He was only five years old when news of his father's and his grandfather's deaths on Gilboa Mountain was brought from the battlefield. His nurse picked him up and ran away into hiding. But she stumbled as she ran and dropped him. He was hurt and has been lame ever since. He's called Meribaal.'

'Where is he now?' asked the king.

'Oh, he's living with Machir's family in Lodebar.'

King David summoned Meribaal to court.

He came, and bowed to the ground in homage.

'Meribaal!' said the king.

'Here I am, your Majesty,' he said.

'There's nothing to be frightened of,' said David. 'Your father was my friend and I must fulfil my promise to him. I am going to give you back all your grandfather's estates. I want you to live here as a member of my court.'

'Who am I, for you to treat me like this?' said Meribaal. 'I'm just a useless nobody.'

The king spoke to Ziba.

'I have given back to your master's son all the estates of his grandfather,' he said. 'These are your orders: you and your family are to take charge of the estates and bring the produce to Meribaal. He will live here at my court.'

'I will carry out your orders to the letter, your Majesty,' said Ziba.

So Meribaal lived with King David as though he were one of his own sons.

The Ammonite War

East of the River

Not long afterwards, the king of Ammon, east of Jordan River, died. His son, Hanun, succeeded him.

'The dead king was a good friend of mine,' thought David, 'I will offer my friendship to his son to show my respect for his father.'

He sent ambassadors to the Ammonite capital, Rabbah, to offer his sympathy to the new king.

The Ammonite sheiks had different views.

'You don't think David sends ambassadors here just out of respect for your father, do you?' they said to the king. 'It isn't sympathy they're bringing—it's a clever move to see the city at first hand. They are just spies, trying to find out how it can be captured.'

King Hanun insulted the ambassadors. He shaved off half their beards and ripped off their clothes below their waist and sent them packing.

The men went back embarrassed and ashamed. News of the insult went ahead of them. When David heard of it, he sent officers to meet them with orders for them to stay at Jericho—where they had crossed the river—till their beards were grown again; and then to come up to the capital.

The Ammonites knew that they were now in serious trouble. David wasn't the sort of man to let an act like this pass unchallenged. So they made a treaty with the Aramaeans in the north under which they were to take into their pay some thousands of infantry.

David called out his army and sent his commander-in-chief, General Joab, to deal with the matter.

The Ammonites drew up the main body of their troops in front of the city gates; the foreign infantry were kept as a mobile force out in the open countryside.

Joab noted their strategy: he was to be attacked both in the front and in the rear. So he made his plans. He led his crack troops against the Aramaean force in the open country; he put his brother, Abishai, in charge of the main army and posted him against the main body of the Ammonite troops in front of the city. Battle orders to Abishai were: 'You come to my help if the battle goes against me; I will come to your help if you find the Ammonite army too strong to deal with. Be of good heart. Let us play the man today, for our people and the cities of our GOD! The issue is in GOD's hands!'

Joab and his crack troops attacked the Aramaeans out in the open countryside and routed them. When the main body of the Ammonite army saw what was happening they gave way under Abishai's attack and withdrew into the city. Joab did not feel strong enough to besiege

Scribes writing the court records ▶

a fortified city; he abandoned the attack and marched back to Jerusalem.

Events now took a serious turn.

The Aramaeans resented being beaten by the Israelites. They rallied their main forces and came into the war—Hadadezer, their king, wasn't going to let troops of his be routed like this. He sent his commander-in-chief, Shobach, with a large army into Ammonite territory and they took up their position at Helam.

News reached David. He called out army and reserves, crossed Jordan River and advanced to Helam. He struck swiftly and destroyed the Aramaean army. The Aramaean casualties were heavy; Shobach, the commander-in-chief, himself died of wounds.

The Aramaean sheiks admitted defeat, sued for peace and surrendered to David. They left the Ammonites to deal with their own problems.

Next year, after harvest (when fighting was usually begun again), David sent his commander-in-chief to ravage the Ammonite countryside and to lay siege to their capital city, Rabbah. David himself stayed in Jerusalem.

A Foul Crime

Late one afternoon David got up from his siesta and strolled to and fro on the flat roof of the palace. He looked down over the neighbouring courtyards and caught sight of a woman—a very beautiful woman—bathing. He sent one of his officers to find out who she was: she was Bathsheba, he was told, the wife of one of his Thirty Captains—Uriah the Hittite—who was on active service at the siege of Rabbah, the Ammonite capital.

He sent an officer to bring her over to the palace. They slept together that night and she went home. She became pregnant and saw to it that the king knew what had happened.

He acted quickly. He sent a dispatch to the commander-in-chief at the front, ordering Captain Uriah home on leave. The captain was sent home to report to the palace. The king discussed the war with him, and then told him to go home and enjoy his leave.

Captain Uriah left the palace with the present the king gave him. But he wouldn't go home to his wife; he slept with the guard posted at the palace gate. This was reported to the king.

'My dear fellow,' the king said to him. 'You've had a long journey. Why didn't you go home?'

'The troops are under canvas,' Captain Uriah answered. 'The Ark is at the front. General Joab and your Majesty's soldiers are sleeping on

◀ Storm over Jerusalem

the bare ground. You don't think I could just go home and have a good meal and go to bed with my wife—as if there was no war on? By GOD, I am a soldier, not a civilian!'

'Well, then,' said the king, 'you can stay in the palace tonight. Tomorrow, I'll let you get back to the fighting.'

Next morning, the king invited Captain Uriah to share the royal table with him, and plied him with wine till he was drunk. He was too drunk to return to the front. He went and slept that night with the officers of the guard. He still wouldn't go home.

Next morning the king sent a dispatch to his commander-in-chief, General Joab. Here are the brutal words:

'Order Captain Uriah into the front line where the fighting is fiercest. Then suddenly fall back and leave him to his fate.'

He gave the dispatch to Captain Uriah himself to deliver to the commander-in-chief.

General Joab surveyed the siege and stationed Captain Uriah opposite the enemy's crack troops. It was at this point that the enemy then struck in force. Quite a number of officers were killed in the fighting. Captain Uriah was among them.

The commander-in-chief then sent a dispatch back to the king with a full report of the battle.

'When you've given this report to the king,' he told the officer taking the dispatch, 'he may be bitterly angry. If he says to you, "Why did you press the fighting so close to the city? Don't you know the danger of fighting right under the walls? Why did you go so near?"—just say these words: "Your officer, Captain Uriah, died in the fighting too."'

The officer left for Jerusalem and gave King David the full report of the battle—just as his commander-in-chief had ordered. The report angered him and he turned on the officer—just as the commander-in-chief expected.

'The enemy were out in strength,' replied the officer. 'They attacked us out in the open and we drove them back to the city gate. The archers on the wall shot a storm of arrows down on your troops. A number of your Majesty's officers were killed—about eighteen of them. Captain Uriah was among the dead.'

'Take this message back to General Joab,' King David told the officer. 'Tell him this to encourage him: "Don't let this incident depress you. You have to be prepared for all sorts of casualties in war. Mount a stronger attack on the city and take it by storm."'

The news of Captain Uriah's death was given to his wife, and she went into mourning for him. As soon as the funeral rites were over King David sent for her and took her into his harem. In due time she gave birth to a son.

Rembrandt: *Nathan reproving King David*

The way King David had treated Captain Uriah and his wife was wrong in GOD's eyes. He sent the Prophet Nathan to tell him so. This is how Nathan told him:

'Two farmers—one very rich and one very poor—lived in the same country town,' he said to King David as if he were reporting a case for him to deal with. 'The rich farmer hardly knew how many flocks and herds he had, he had so many. The poor farmer had practically nothing except one little ewe lamb. He had bought it and reared it; it grew up like a member of the family, sharing his food and drinking from his cup and sleeping in his arms. It was like a child to him.

'One day a traveller arrived at the rich farmer's house. And what did he do but take the poor farmer's little ewe-lamb to feed his guest—he was too mean to kill a sheep or an ox of his own.'

David was furious.

'By GOD!' he told Nathan. 'The fellow ought to die! Hadn't he a touch of pity in him? I'll see he pays back four times more than he took from the poor farmer!'

'You're the man I'm talking about,' said Nathan. 'These are GOD's words: "Why have you slighted me by doing this hateful thing—murdering Captain Uriah and stealing his wife?" '

'I have sinned,' said the king, 'and I have sinned against GOD himself.'

'GOD has forgiven you; you shall not die,' said Nathan. 'But the baby will die; you treated GOD with contempt.'

Nathan went home.

When the baby was taken very ill, King David prayed to GOD. He refused to eat anything and spent the nights lying in sackcloth on the ground. Some of the older courtiers came and tried to make him get up from the ground. But he stayed where he was and wouldn't have any meals with them.

A week later the baby died, and there wasn't a courtier who dared breathe a word about it to him.

'He wouldn't listen to us when the baby was alive and we tried to talk to him,' they said. 'Now the baby's dead, he'll do something desperate if we tell him.'

King David saw his courtiers whispering together and he guessed what had happened.

'Is he dead?' he asked.

'Yes, he is,' they said.

He got up from the ground, washed and anointed himself, changed his clothes and went into GOD's house to pray. He then went back to the palace, called for a good meal (which was quickly brought to the royal table) and ate it up.

His courtiers thought he was acting strangely.

'When the baby was alive,' they said to him, 'you ate nothing and wept; now he is dead, you get up and have a good meal!'

'As long as the baby was alive,' said the king, 'there was hope GOD would have pity on me and let him live. Now he is dead, what's the point of fasting? Can I bring him back again? I shall go to him, but he will never come back to me.'

Some time later, Bathsheba bore another son to David. His name was Solomon.

The End of the War

General Joab, acting on King David's orders, made a full-scale attack on Rabbah, the Ammonite capital. He captured the Water City, and sent an urgent dispatch back to Jerusalem.

'I have made an attack on Rabbah,' he informed the king, 'and I have taken the King's Pool by storm. Bring the rest of the army and come yourself and capture the main city. I don't want to be known as the conqueror of Rabbah—as I shall be if I storm it alone.'

So the king mustered the rest of the army, marched to Rabbah and took it by storm. The crown of Milcom, the Ammonite god, was captured —it was made of silver and gold, and set with a very costly jewel. David tried it on.

A great deal of loot was captured in the city; the citizens were organized into labour gangs with saws and iron picks and axes, and set to forced labour in the brick-kilns.

The other Ammonite cities were captured and treated in the same way. Then David and his army marched back to Jerusalem.

Southern Rebellion

A Sordid Beginning

It began with a harem intrigue.

Amnon and Absalom were half-brothers, both sons of King David but with different mothers. Amnon fell madly in love with Tamar, Absalom's beautiful sister. He was so tormented with his love for her that he made himself ill. But she was quite out of his reach; she was a virgin, and was confined to her mother's quarters in the royal harem.

Now Amnon had a friend, Jonadab, a nephew of the king and a very crafty man.

'My dear prince,' he said one day, 'you look haggard and ill. What's the matter? Won't you tell me your secret?'

'I'm just desperately in love with Tamar,' said Amnon.

'I'll easily put that right,' said Jonadab. 'You go to bed and pretend to be ill. When your father comes to see what's the matter with you, tell him you just can't eat anything. And then go on to tell him that if Tamar came and cooked some choice food in your own room, that would give you an appetite. Ask him to let her come and look after you.'

Amnon thought it a clever idea; he took to his bed and pretended to be ill.

His father came to see him.

'If Tamar came,' Amnon told him, 'and made a couple of cakes while I watch, that would give me an appetite. Let her come.'

So King David summoned Tamar to the Palace.

'Go to your brother Amnon's house,' he told her, 'and get him a meal.'

Tamar found Amnon in bed. She got him a meal of cakes. She kneaded the dough, made the cakes and baked them. Amnon watched.

Then she took the pan and served the cakes. But Amnon wouldn't touch them.

'Clear the room,' he ordered.

When everybody had gone, he told Tamar to bring the cakes into the inner bedroom.

'I'd rather have them from you,' he said.

Tamar did as she was told; and as she handed him the cakes, he caught hold of her.

'Come to bed with me, my sister,' he pleaded.

'No! No! No! my brother!' she protested. 'You mustn't dishonour me like this. It isn't right. You mustn't rape me. Where should I hide my shame? And you'll be held as one of the most vicious scoundrels in the country. Speak to the king—he'll let us marry.'

Amnon just wouldn't listen. With his greater strength, he overpowered her and raped her.

His love suddenly turned to bitter hatred; he hated her now more than he had ever loved her. He ordered her out of the house.

'No!' she said. 'Sending me off like this is worse than the wrong you've already done me.'

He ignored her and called his servant.

'Put this woman out,' he ordered, 'and lock the door behind her.'

The servant pushed her out into the street, and bolted the door.

Tamar was beside herself. She threw dust on her head, tore her royal dress, and, with her hand on her head, went screaming home.

Her brother Absalom met her.

'Has your brother Amnon been with you?' he asked. 'Well, keep your mouth shut—he is your brother—and forget it.'

So Tamar stayed in Absalom's house; she was broken-hearted.

When King David heard about it all, he was very angry indeed, but he did nothing. Amnon was his eldest son and he didn't want to hurt him.

But with Absalom it was a different matter. He never spoke to Amnon again, one way or another. He just hated him with a deadly hatred for raping his sister.

Absalom's Revenge

Two years went by.

Absalom was holding a sheep shearing at a place called Baal-Hazor, some fifteen miles north-east of Jerusalem; and he invited all the royal princes.

He sought an audience with his father.

'I've a sheep-shearing festival soon,' he said. 'It would be fine if your Majesty and the court would attend.'

'No, my son,' said the king. 'We should be too great a burden.'

Absalom pressed his father to come. He firmly refused but gave him his blessing.

'Well,' said Absalom, 'if you won't come, at least let my brother Amnon join us.'

'Why Amnon?' asked the king. 'Why should he go with you?'

Absalom wouldn't be put off. So the king let Amnon go along with the other princes.

Absalom prepared a royal banquet. But he gave secret orders to his servants.

'Make a careful note of this: when Amnon has got a little drunk, I shall call out "Down with Amnon!" Kill him. There's nothing to be frightened about—I am giving the orders. Be bold like men!'

Absalom's orders were carried out. All the other princes rose from the table, mounted their mules and escaped.

News went ahead of them and rumour had it that all the princes had been murdered—there were no survivors. The king tore his clothes and lay flat on the ground; all his courtiers tore their clothes in grief.

But Jonadab, the king's nephew, spoke up.

'Your Majesty,' he said, 'you mustn't believe a mere rumour like this. Only one prince is dead—and it's Prince Amnon. Absalom has had one grim purpose ever since Amnon raped his sister Tamar. Your Majesty mustn't get the idea that all the princes are murdered. Only Prince Amnon is dead.'

Meanwhile the sentry saw a crowd of men coming down the hill on the Horonaim road. He reported to the king.

'Look, your Majesty,' Jonadab said. 'The princes are here. It's exactly as I said.'

He had hardly finished speaking when the princes entered the palace. They were weeping; the king and the whole court broke into bitter weeping too.

Absalom himself escaped to Talmai, king of Geshur, east of Jordan River.

Back in Favour

Three years went by. The king had got over the shock of Amnon's murder and now was pining for the exiled Absalom. General Joab noticed his mood. He knew it was no good talking plainly to him; so this is what he did.

He sent to Tekoa, some ten miles south of Jerusalem, for a wise woman who lived there.

'I want you to dress up as a mourner,' he told her. 'Put on funeral clothes, and look as if you have been mourning the death of your

husband for a long time. Don't freshen yourself up in any way. Then
I want you to seek an audience with the king, and I'll tell you what I
want you to say.'

So he rehearsed with her the speech he wanted her to make.

The woman asked for an audience with the king. She fell down on
her face in homage.

'Help me, your Majesty!' she cried out. 'Oh help me!'

'What do you want me to do?' asked the king.

'I am a widow,' she said. 'My husband died a long time ago. I'm in
real trouble. My two sons had a violent quarrel while they were out
working in the field; one of them struck his brother and killed him. The
whole clan is now up in arms. They want me to hand the murderer over
to them—death is what he deserves, they say, and they mean it. But if
they kill him, my husband will have no heir. They would take my last
hope from me. My husband will have neither name nor descendant left
in the world.'

'Go home,' said the king. 'I will give the necessary orders, and you
will be all right.'

'I don't want any guilt to fall on your Majesty or your throne,' said
the woman. 'The guilt all lies on me and my family.'

'If anybody interferes with you,' said the king, 'report him to me.
I'll see to it that he causes you no further trouble.'

'Will you swear this by GOD's name?' asked the woman. 'I'm
frightened of the blood-avenger and what he might do—he might kill
my son.'

'In GOD's name,' said the king, 'not a hair of his head shall be cut
off!'

'Might I talk plainly to your Majesty?' asked the woman.

'You may,' said the king.

'I'm really talking about Absalom,' said the woman. 'Why is he still
banished—an evil for the whole country and a very wrong thing in
itself, as your Majesty has admitted in what you have just said to me?

'That's why I came with my story to you,' she went on. 'You represent
GOD. You know how to tell right from wrong. I wanted you, your
Majesty, to pass judgment on my case so that you could pass judgment
on your own. Your word is final.'

'Tell me everything,' said the king. 'I want you to give me a plain
answer to a plain question.'

'Ask me any question you like, your Majesty,' said the woman.

'Has General Joab put you up to this?' he asked.

'You have asked a plain question; I'll give you a plain answer,' said
the woman. 'Yes, he has. He told me what to say. He wanted your
Majesty to look at the whole matter of Absalom's banishment in a new

light. Your Majesty has GOD's wisdom—you know everything.'

The king summoned General Joab into his presence.

'I grant you your wish,' he told him. 'Recall Prince Absalom.'

General Joab bowed to the ground in homage.

'I thank your Majesty,' he said. 'You have granted my request; I know now how highly you think of me.'

He set off straight away for Geshur and escorted Prince Absalom back to Jerusalem.

But the king had further orders: Absalom was to be confined to his own house; he was not to set foot in the palace.

So Absalom stayed in his own house in Jerusalem; for two whole years he and his father never met.

At last, Prince Absalom sent for General Joab—he wanted him to speak to the king. Joab refused to meet him. He refused a second time, when Absalom sent for him.

'You know that field of General Joab's,' said Prince Absalom to his courtiers. 'It's the field next to mine—the field where he's growing barley. Burn it down.'

They set the field on fire.

This soon brought General Joab round to Prince Absalom's house.

'What are you up to?' he asked. 'Your men have burned my field down!'

'Well, what do you expect?' said the prince. 'I sent for you twice. I want you to see my father and tell him that I might as well have stayed in Geshur as stay confined to this house. I want justice. If I deserve death tell him to put me to death.'

General Joab sought an audience with King David and told him what Prince Absalom had said. The king summoned the prince into his presence. Prince Absalom bowed to the ground in homage, and King David kissed him. He was back in favour.

Open Rebellion

Prince Absalom was now a free man.

The first thing he did was to set himself up with a royal chariot and horses, and fifty runners to go before him.

Every morning he would go down and stand by the road leading to the city gate (where the king held his Court of Justice). He would stop everybody who was going along to the Court.

'Where do you come from?' he would ask.

'From such and such district,' the man would answer.

'What's the trouble?'

The man would tell him.

'You've got a very good case,' he would say. 'But you won't get any justice from the king.'

Or sometimes—

'If only I were appointed the supreme judge! If only everybody with a dispute or lawsuit could come to me! I'd see he got justice!'

When any man came to him to pay his respects, Prince Absalom would offer his hand and embrace and kiss him. This is how he treated everybody who came to the Court of Justice; and in this way he won the loyalty of many citizens.

This went on for four years.

Then the Prince sought an audience with his father.

'May I have permission to go to Hebron to discharge a vow I made to GOD?' he asked. 'I made the vow when I was living in Geshur; I promised GOD that, if he would bring me back to Jerusalem, I would worship him in Hebron.'

'Certainly,' said his father.

So he set off for Hebron.

At the same time, he sent secret agents everywhere with these orders:

'At the sound of the bugle, shout "Long live King Absalom in Hebron!"'

Two hundred invited guests went along with him, but they went quite innocently—they hadn't any idea what was afoot. The prince also summoned Ahithophel, the king's Counseller, to come from his town of Giloh.

The rebellion spread far and wide.

Flight from Jerusalem

News of the revolt was brought to King David—it was clear that the Southern clans had gone over to Prince Absalom. He ordered his court to escape.

'We must get out as quickly as we can,' he said. 'If we stay we shall be captured. A sudden attack by Absalom and we are finished. He'll put the city to the sword.'

'As your Majesty commands,' said his courtiers. 'We are your officers.'

So the king and his court left the city. The secondary wives were left to take care of the palace.

At the Far House a halt was made, while the king watched the march past of his Foreign Legion—Cretans and Philistines and the Gath Battalion of six hundred men under their commander Ittai.

He called Captain Ittai over to him.

'There's no need for you to come,' he said. 'Go back and take service under the new king. You are a foreigner and an exile from your country. It isn't long since you came here. Why should I make you a vagabond like myself—I haven't any idea where I'm going. Go back with your men. May GOD be kind and faithful to you!'

'Not on your life, your Majesty,' said Captain Ittai, 'I'm not going back! I am an officer under command—where you go, I go, come life, come death!'

'Very good,' said the king. 'March on!'

Captain Ittai marched on with his soldiers and camp-followers.

The crowds watching were in tears as the procession moved by. The king crossed the Kidron Valley and took the desert road.

Zadok and Abiathar, the priests, were carrying the Ark of GOD. They had set it down until everybody had marched past.

The king went over and spoke to Zadok.

'Look,' he said, 'I want you to go straight back to the city, you and Abiathar and your two sons Ahimaaz and Jonathan. Keep your eyes open and keep me informed. I will stay by the Fords and wait there for any news you can get to me.'

So Zadok and Abiathar took the Ark of GOD back to Jerusalem and stayed there.

King David slowly climbed the slopes of the Olive Hill. He was in tears. He'd drawn his cloak over his head and was walking barefoot. The men with him walked up the hill with covered heads and in tears, too.

Someone told the king that Ahithophel was among the rebels on Absalom's side.

'May Ahithophel give bad advice, O GOD!' he said.

He had just come to the top of the hill where there is a shrine when he suddenly met his old friend Hushai the Archite, with his coat torn and earth on his head.

'If you come along with me,' the king said to him, 'you'll only be a burden. But you can be a real help if you'll go back to the city. Get on the right side of Absalom. Tell him that once you were his father's courtier, and that now you will be his. You may get a chance of confusing Ahithophel's advice to my advantage. Then you can get all the palace news to me. Tell Zadok and Abiathar anything you find out. Their sons will bring it to me.'

Hushai reached the city just as Absalom was entering it.

Stories of the Flight

Over the top of the hill, the king met Ziba, Meribaal's servant. He was driving two donkeys laden with bread, raisin cakes, summer fruits and wine.

'What are all these for?' he asked.

'The donkeys are for your Majesty's family to ride on,' said Ziba.

'The bread and fruit are for the soldiers. And someone will need the wine if he faints on the desert march.'

'Where's Meribaal?' asked the king.

'Back in Jerusalem,' said Ziba. 'He thinks the country will give him back his grandfather's kingdom.'

'I see!' he said. 'All Meribaal's estate is now yours.'

'I give you the homage which is your due, your Majesty,' said Ziba. 'May you always think kindly of me.'

As the king reached Bahurim Village, a man called Shimei came running out cursing and throwing stones at him, although his Guards were marching on each side of him.

'Down with you! Down with you, you murderer, you scoundrel!' he shouted. 'You usurped Saul's throne and now GOD is avenging the murder of Saul's family! He's made your son Absalom king! You are a murderer, that's why you've come to this miserable end!'

(Shimei was a Benjamite like Saul.)

'Why should your Majesty let a wretch like this curse you?' asked Captain Abishai. 'Let me go over and knock his head off!'

'You're a violent lot, you and Joab!' said the king. 'You can't quarrel with a fellow like this and his curses—perhaps GOD himself inspired him.'

He turned to his court.

'My own son,' he said, 'the son of my own body, would kill me if he could; who can blame this Benjamite for doing what my own son does? Let him go and let him get on with his cursing—GOD has inspired him to curse me. I pray that GOD won't forget me; he may turn his curse into blessing!'

King David and his soldiers marched on along the road and ignored him. Shimei ran along with them, on the hillside above, cursing and throwing stones.

They came at last, dead-tired, to the Fords. It was good to drink the cold water.

Absalom occupies Jerusalem

Prince Absalom and the Southern rebels were now masters of Jerusalem. Ahithophel was his Chief Adviser.

David's friend, Hushai, sought an audience with the prince.

'Long live the king!' he said.

'This is a queer sort of loyalty,' said the prince. 'Why aren't you with your old friend?'

'My place is here,' he replied, 'with the king GOD and his people have chosen. Here I stay. Besides, whose officer should I be? His son's —I will serve you as I served your father.'

Jerusalem from the Kidron Valley. The walls of David's City are uncovered at the bottom of the excavated trench; 'Bubbling Spring' is just below the lower of the two small buildings

The prince summoned his Chief Adviser, Ahithophel.

'Give us your advice,' he said. 'What do you suggest we should now do?'

'Make it clear that you have completely broken with your father,' he said. 'Nothing would make this clearer than your taking his secondary wives as your own wives. He left ten of them to look after the palace. That will stiffen the resistance of your followers.'

So they set up the bridal tent on the roof of the palace. All his followers could now see that he intended to be the real king.

'There is another urgent matter,' said Ahithophel. 'Give me the army tonight and I will attack King David while he's tired and exhausted —that will put him in a panic. His troops will scatter and I can get him by himself and kill him. I will unite the whole country behind you. The fact is that there is one man—and one man only—who stands in your way. Deal with him and the whole country will be at peace.'

This seemed excellent advice to the prince and his court.

'I would like to know what Hushai would advise,' he said.

Hushai was summoned to the court and told about Ahithophel's plans.

'What do you think?' asked the prince. 'Don't be frightened to disagree—I want your own unbiased judgment.'

'I don't really think it's good advice,' said Hushai.

'I'll give you my reasons,' he went on. 'You are dealing with veteran soldiers—the Guards will fight to the death like a wild bear robbed of her cubs. Your father is a seasoned soldier—you won't find him where you think you will. He won't be with his troops tonight; he'll be in hiding in some ravine or other. You'll certainly have some casualties in the first attack. It would be easy to make that look like defeat. You've got men with lion's courage, but they know David's reputation as a hero and they know how the Guards fight.

'What I would suggest is this: attack David with overwhelming force; call upon the whole country and march yourself as their commander-in-chief. Then, whenever you attack him, you can utterly outnumber his forces and wipe them out, Guards and all. If he retires into a fortified city, you will be strong enough to storm it and destroy it.'

The prince and the whole court now voted for Hushai's plan as better than Ahithophel's.

Hushai told Zadok and Abiathar what had happened at court—Ahithophel's plans and his own proposals.

'Get the information to King David immediately,' he told them. 'Warn him not to stay at the Fords tonight but to get over to the other side of Jordan River. He is in great danger.'

Now Jonathan and Ahimaaz were hiding at Rogel Well. A girl used to go from time to time and tell them what was happening. On this occasion, a boy saw them and Prince Absalom was told about them. They left Rogel Well in a hurry and got as far as Bahurim Village, and took refuge with one of the villagers. They climbed down into the pit in the courtyard, and his wife covered it with a sheet and scattered grain on top of it—there was nothing to make anybody suspect anything. Rebel officers from Jerusalem tracked them down to the village.

'They went on through the ravine,' she said.

The officers searched everywhere in vain, and at last went back to Jerusalem to report.

When all was clear, the two men climbed out of the pit and found King David at the Fords.

'Up, and over the river!' they told the king. 'Don't waste any time.' They gave him a detailed account of Ahithophel's plans.

King David and his troops struck camp and crossed Jordan River.

By dawn they were all over on the eastern bank.

Ahithophel knew that Prince Absalom had made a fatal mistake in not taking his advice. He saddled his donkey, and went back to his home town. He put all his affairs in order, and then hanged himself. He was buried in his father's grave.

David in Mahanaim

King David marched into the eastern mountains and reached Mahanaim.

Prince Absalom and his troops crossed Jordan River, marched on into the Gilead Highlands and set up camp there. (He had made General Amasa his commander-in-chief instead of David's commander-in-chief, General Joab.)

North-west of Jordan River, the men of Ammon and Gilead rallied to David in Mahanaim. Couches, rugs, basins and earthen vessels were brought along; wheat, barley, meal, parched corn, beans, lentils, honey, curdled milk, sheep and calves were given freely.

'They must be starving after the march through the wild mountains,' people said.

Among those who gave freely were, for example, Shobi the Ammonite (he lived in Rabbah, the capital city), Machir from Lo-debar, and the Gileadite Barzillai from Rogelim.

Fighting in the Forest

King David now reviewed his troops and reorganized the command.

He formed three army corps, under three commanders—General Joab, General Abishai (his brother) and Captain Ittai, the commander of the Foreign Legion. He proposed to lead the troops himself as commander-in-chief. His generals strongly objected.

'No!' they said. 'If we are routed, they won't bother about us. You are worth ten thousand soldiers; it would be the end of us if you were killed. You must stay in Mahanaim. You can survey the course of the battle and send reinforcements when they are needed.'

'I accept your judgment,' he said.

So he took the salute, standing by the side of the city gate; the regiments and battalions marched by.

He gave special orders to his three commanders about Absalom.

'Don't be hard on the young man,' he said, 'for my sake.'

This was made clear in army orders.

The battle took place in the forest south of Mahanaim. The rebels were routed by David's veteran soldiers. There were terrible casualties.

Jordan River looking north. David and his soldiers crossed the 'fords' (at the bottom of the picture) in their flight from Jerusalem and marched north through the mountains east of the river. These mountains were heavily wooded then, and in these woods Absalom lost his life

The fighting spread over the whole countryside; more died in the forest than died on the battle-field.

In the confusion of the fighting, Prince Absalom stumbled accidentally into a body of David's soldiers. The mule he was riding bolted into the forest under the branches of a great oak tree and his hair got caught in the branches. He was left hanging between heaven and earth.

A soldier reported the incident to General Joab.

'I saw Prince Absalom hanging from an oak tree,' he said.

'You stand there and just tell me you saw him!' exclaimed the general. 'Why didn't you kill him there and then? I would have rewarded and promoted you.'

'I wouldn't lay my hands on the king's son for a thousand pounds,' said the soldier. 'You know what the king's orders are. If I'd played the traitor and disobeyed them at the risk of my life, I'd be quickly found out—and you wouldn't have lifted a finger to help me at the court martial!'

'I'm not standing here arguing with you all day,' snapped the general.

He took three darts and drove them into the prince's heart, while he was still alive, hanging from the oak tree.

He then sounded the 'Cease Fire', calling off the pursuit and withdrawing his troops. Soldiers threw Prince Absalom's body into a hole in the forest and built a pile of stones over it. The surviving rebels made off home.

David hears the News

Ahimaaz, son of Zadok the priest, spoke to General Joab.

'Let me be the first with the good news,' he asked. 'Let me tell King David how GOD has routed the rebels!'

'Not today,' said the general. 'Not today. Another day perhaps. You're not the right kind of messenger to announce the prince's death.'

He called one of the foreign soldiers of the Guards.

'Go and tell the king what you've seen,' he commanded.

The guardsman saluted and ran off.

'Let me run after him,' said Ahimaaz, 'I don't care what happens!'

'Why risk it?' said the general. 'It won't pay.'

'I don't care,' said Ahimaaz. 'I'm going!'

'All right,' said the general, 'you run!'

Ahimaaz ran off, and, taking the road through the Jordan Plain, overtook the guardsman.

King David was sitting in the open space between the outer and inner gates of Mahanaim City. A sentry, stationed on the top of the outer gate, was watching the road.

'There's a man running alone!' he called out.

'He's bringing news of the battle, then,' said the king.

As the man came nearer, running fast, the sentry saw another man running behind him.

'There's another man running after him,' he shouted down to the guard below.

'He's bringing news, too,' said the king.

'The first man looks to me like Ahimaaz,' the sentry shouted down. 'Only Ahimaaz runs like this!'

'A good man,' said the king, 'and good news.'

Ahimaaz reached the gate.

'All's well!' he shouted as he saluted. 'Praise GOD! the rebels are routed, your Majesty!'

'Is the young prince safe?' asked the king.

'There was such a hullaballoo when General Joab sent me off,' he said, 'I don't know what it was all about.'

'Step aside,' said the king, 'and stand here.'

He stood at ease and waited.

The guardsman came running in.

'Good news for your Majesty!' he reported. 'GOD has rescued you from the rebels.'

'Is the young prince safe?' asked the king.

'May all your enemies and all rebels die as he died!' said the guardsman.

King David broke down and burst into tears. He stumbled up to the guardroom over the gate; and all the way he kept saying, 'O my son, Absalom—my son—my son Absalom! I would rather have died myself! O Absalom, my son, my son!'

Angry Soldiers

General Joab was told how the king had taken the news—broken with grief for his dead son. There was no victory parade. News of the king's grief damped the spirits of all his soldiers. They walked about the city in silence; you would have thought they had lost the battle and were ashamed of their cowardice. All the time King David could think of nobody but his dead son; he had pulled his cloak over his face and kept on saying, again and again, 'O my son Absalom! Absalom, my son, my son!'

General Joab went to the palace and rebuked the king to his face.

'You have shamed your own soldiers,' he said curtly, 'soldiers who have saved your life and the lives of all your family. This is a nice state of affairs—you love those who hate you, and hate those who love you! It's quite obvious that neither officers nor men mean a thing to you. What a happy man you'd be if we were all dead and Absalom was alive! Stand up and be a man! Go out and congratulate your soldiers. By GOD, there'll not be a soldier in the city tonight if you don't! That will teach you—you've never had to face anything like that since you were a young soldier yourself!'

The king got up and took his seat at the gate.

News spread throughout the city, and the soldiers crowded round.

The March back to Jerusalem

There was chaos throughout the whole country. The rebels were back in their own homes and people everywhere were talking.

'What's happened to the king?' they were asking. 'He was our hero in the early days. He put the Philistines in their place. But his own son Absalom drove him out of the country and we crowned him king! Now *he's* dead! Why is David idling in Mahanaim? Why does nobody do anything about bringing him home?'

News of this country-wide gossip was reported to King David. He sent a message to Zadok and Abiathar in Jerusalem:

'Call a meeting of the leaders of the Southern tribe of Judah and put this to them: "Why should you—members of my own clan, my blood-relations—be so slow to get me, your king, back home?" Tell General Amasa: "We are close kinsmen. I'll see to it you are commander-in-chief instead of General Joab",' So David again won the affections of the leaders of his own clan. There was a unanimous decision to invite him and his court back to his capital city.

He set off on the march home and reached Jordan River. The Southern clansmen came as far as Gilgal to escort him across.

Shimei—the Benjamite from Bahurim Village, who had cursed David when he was escaping—eagerly joined the Southern clansmen at the head of a thousand Benjamites. Ziba, who had helped the king in his escape, was there too, with fifteen sons and twenty slaves. Indeed he had made sure of getting to the river before the king arrived and had crossed the ford to the eastern side to escort him across and see to his needs.

King David was about to cross the river when Shimei threw himself on the ground before him.

'I pray your Majesty not to hold me guilty,' he said. 'I remember with shame how I treated your Majesty when you were escaping from Jerusalem. I hope you won't hold it against me now; I know what a terrible thing I did. Today, you see, I am the first of the Northern clansmen to come and greet your Majesty.'

'He cursed GOD's anointed king,' General Abishai broke in. 'Is he going to get away with it?'

'You and your brother!' said King David. 'What bitter men you are! You're talking like my enemy! On such a day as this, it is unthinkable that any man should be put to death. I am king again—and I know it!'

He turned to Shimei.

'You shall not die!' he said. 'This is my solemn promise!'

Meribaal, Saul's lame grandson, was there too. He had gone into mourning from the day the king escaped from the city until the day of his return in safety.

'Why didn't you go with me into exile, Meribaal?' asked the king.

'Your Majesty,' he said, 'my servant Ziba betrayed me. I told him to saddle the donkey—I am lame and if I were to overtake your Majesty I had to ride. What he did was to slander me. Your Majesty is the representative of GOD. Punish me as you please. I've no right to complain—my whole family were at your mercy when you called me to share your Majesty's royal table.'

'You talk a lot,' said the king briefly. 'You and Ziba can share your estates between you.'

'He can take it all!' exclaimed Meribaal. 'I'm only too glad to have you Majesty safe home again!'

Then there was Barzillai the Gileadite. He had come up to Mahanaim from his village of Rogelim and travelled with the king all the way to Jordan River. He was an old man, eighty years of age, and a very rich farmer. He had seen to the king's needs all the time he was in Mahanaim.

'You must come along with me,' said the king to him. 'In Jerusalem I can look after you in your old age.'

'I am now eighty years of age,' said Barzillai. 'I haven't many more
years to live. I'm an old man—I can't tell the taste of one thing from
the taste of another, and I'm too deaf to hear the singers. There's no
point in my going with your Majesty and living in your palace. I
should only be a burden. I haven't done much—I don't deserve such
handsome treatment. Let me go back to my home town and die there by
my father and mother's grave. My son here can go with your Majesty
—give him what you would have given me.'

'Your son shall come with me, indeed,' said the king. 'I will treat
him as you wish. And if there's anything I can do for you, tell me and
I will do it.'

The troops began to ford the river, and the king followed. He kissed
Barzillai goodbye, and the old man went home.

The king reached Gilgal, escorted by Southern clansmen and some
Northerners.

Northern Rebellion

The Northern clansmen had already begun to make trouble. They
sought an audience with King David while he was still in Gilgal.

'Why have the Southern clansmen stolen a march on us?' they asked.
'Why should they step in and escort your Majesty and his court over
Jordan River?'

'It's obvious,' retorted the Southerners. 'He's our fellow-clansman.
What on earth is there in that to make you angry? We haven't sponged
on him. We haven't kidnapped him!'

'We have ten shares in the king to your two,' they retorted, 'and
we've an older history—we were in this land first! Why slight us like
this? Weren't we the first to talk of escorting the king back to his
capital?'

But the Southerners shouted the Northerners down.

Now there was a scoundrel of a man among the Northerners—Sheba
from King Saul's clan, the Benjamites. He sounded the war-cry—

> 'We don't belong to David!
> We've nothing to do
> with the Bethlehemite farmer!
> Back to the North!'

Some of the Northerners, led by Sheba, rose in rebellion. The
Southerners rallied to King David and escorted him from Gilgal to
Jerusalem, his capital city.

'Muster the Southern clansmen,' the king commanded General Amasa,
'and report to me in three days' time.'

Gibeon ('hill'), a wealthy and important town long before the Israelites came to the highlands. The townspeople made a treaty with the Israelites. It was by the 'Great Pool' here that the gruesome 'trial of strength' between Northern and Southern soldiers took place

At the end of three days, there was no sign of General Amasa.

The king ordered General Joab to deal with the Northern rebellion.

'Take the Guards,' he commanded, 'and hunt Sheba down. He'll do us more harm than Prince Absalom. If he wins over the fortified cities, we're in grave difficulties.'

General Abishai and General Joab called out the Guards and marched north.

At the great stone in Gibeon, they came face to face with General Amasa. General Joab was wearing his uniform. His sword was in its sheath and was fastened by a girdle over it. It fell out as he went forward and dropped on the ground. He picked it up with his left hand, as he greeted General Amasa.

'How are you?' he asked, and took the general's beard in his right hand to kiss him. General Amasa hadn't noticed the sword in his left hand. General Joab jabbed his sword in his stomach, and he died without a second blow.

The two generals went on after Sheba.

One of the guardsmen stood over General Amasa's body shouting 'Let everyone who's a friend of General Joab's and is for King David, follow the General!'

The body lay in the middle of the road in a pool of blood with a crowd round it. A soldier dragged it off the road into a field and covered it with a cloak. The soldiers marched on after General Joab.

Sheba had moved rapidly north to Abel Town, some twenty five miles north of Galilee Lake. His fellow clansmen rallied round him and occupied the town. General Joab caught him there, and besieged him. He set his soldiers to build a mound against the rampart and to batter the city walls down.

Then a wise woman stood on the outer city wall and called down to the soldiers below.

'Listen to me! Listen to me!' she shouted. 'Tell General Joab to come here. I want to talk to him.'

General Joab approached the wall.

'Are you General Joab?' she asked.

'I am,' he answered.

'Listen to me,' she said.

'I'm listening,' he said.

'There's an old proverb,' she said. 'It says: "In Abel disputes are settled". You are destroying a city where GOD's People can settle their disputes. Why destroy GOD's heritage?'

'I don't want to do that,' answered General Joab. 'I'm no destroyer or vandal. That's not the issue. There's a man inside the city who has raised his hand against King David—Sheba's his name. Hand him over and I'll withdraw.'

'Then,' said the woman, 'his head shall be thrown over the city wall to you!'

So she talked the city over to her way of thinking. They executed Sheba and threw his head over the city wall to General Joab.

The general sounded the retreat and withdrew from the city. The soldiers went home and General Joab reported to the king in Jerusalem.

Palace Plot

King David was now a very old man and needed nursing.

Prince Adonijah—born after Absalom and a good-looking man—began to talk publicly about being his father's successor on the throne. Like Absalom, he was a favourite son; David let him do what he liked.

He now set himself up as king—with a chariot and horsemen and fifty soldiers to lead his cavalcade, just like Absalom in his bid to be king. He came to an understanding with General Joab, the commander-in-chief, and Abiathar the priest, men who had been loyal to King David. He failed to win the support of the priest Zadok, the prophet Nathan and the Guards and Captain Benaiah.

His coronation was arranged. A sacrificial feast was held by the Serpent's Stone near Fuller's Well in the Kidron Valley south-west of the city. He invited all his brother princes and the royal officials, but not Nathan or Captain Benaiah or the Guards—or his brother Solomon.

The coronation ceremony began.

News of all this soon spread. The prophet Nathan went immediately to Bathsheba, David's favourite wife, the mother of Solomon.

'Have you heard what's happening?' he said. 'Prince Adonijah is being crowned king—without his Majesty knowing anything about it. Your life and Prince Solomon's are in danger. Let me give you some advice. Seek an audience with the king and say this to him: "Didn't your Majesty promise me that your son Prince Solomon should succeed to the throne? Why, then, is Prince Adonijah being crowned king?" I'll wait till you've started talking to him and then come hurriedly into the room and support what you are saying.'

Bathsheba went into the king's bedroom where the nurse was looking after him. She bowed in homage.

'What do you want?' he asked.

She said what Nathan had told her to say.

'You don't know what's happening,' she went on. 'You swore that my son Solomon should succeed you. But the coronation of Prince Adonijah is taking place at this moment. All the princes are there—and Abiathar the priest and General Joab. But Prince Solomon hasn't been invited. The whole country is waiting to know whom your Majesty will announce as your successor. As things are going, I and Prince Solomon will just be treated as rebels on your death!'

It was at this point that the prophet Nathan came into the room.

'Nathan the prophet asks for an audience with your Majesty,' the king was told.

Nathan bowed before him in homage.

'Has your Majesty made a royal proclamation that Prince Adonijah shall succeed to the throne?' he asked. 'He is holding his coronation ceremony at this very moment. The princes and General Joab and Abiathar the priest are attending the coronation banquet. The whole company have raised the cry "Long live King Adonijah!" I haven't been invited—nor has Zadok nor Captain Benaiah nor Prince Solomon. Has your Majesty commanded this coronation ceremony without a word to us, your officers?'

'Call Bathsheba over to me,' said the king.

She came and stood in front of him.

'In GOD's name who has always come to my rescue,' he said 'what I promised to do I will do—and I will do it now.'

Bathsheba bowed in homage.

'Long live your Majesty!' she said.

'Call Zadok and Nathan and Captain Benaiah into my presence,' he commanded.

The three men stood before him.

'Order my officers on parade,' he said. 'Escort Prince Solomon, mounted on my royal mule, to Bubbling Spring in the Kidron Valley. Let Zadok and Nathan crown him. Let the bugles blow and let everybody shout "Long live King Solomon!" Escort him to the throne-room and let him take possession of my throne. He shall be my successor and king of the whole country, North and South. This is my will.'

'As your Majesty commands,' said Captain Benaiah. 'May GOD confirm your Majesty's decision. As GOD has blessed your Majesty, may he bless King Solomon. May his reign be greater even than your Majesty's!'

Zadok, Nathan, Captain Benaiah and the Guards escorted Prince Solomon, riding on the king's mule, to Bubbling Spring. Then Zadok the priest anointed Prince Solomon king. The bugle was blown, and the soldiers and the crowds shouted 'Long live King Solomon!' With flutes playing, the Guards escorted the new king back into the city. The noise was tremendous.

Prince Adonijah and his guests further down the valley heard the shouting—the feast was almost over.

'What does the shouting mean?' asked General Joab.

While he was asking the question, Jonathan, Abiathar's son, burst in.

'Come in!' Prince Adonijah called out. 'A good man like you must be bringing good news.'

'I'm not,' he said. 'The shouting you heard was the shouting at Prince Solomon's coronation. King David has made a royal proclamation. Zadok and Nathan and Captain Benaiah and the Guards have carried it out. The noise you heard was the royal procession going back into the city. What is more—Solomon has taken his seat on the royal throne. All King David's officers are now congratulating him on his decision, and he is acknowledging them. He has confirmed his proclamation.'

The guests were terrified and were soon gone. Prince Adonijah was so frightened that he ran to the royal shrine and clung to the altar there.

'King Solomon must first promise not to murder me!' he kept saying.

All this was reported to King Solomon.

'If he keeps straight,' he said, 'he's safe enough. One slip, and he'll be a dead man.'

King Solomon ordered Prince Adonijah into his presence.

He was brought from the altar and he bowed in homage before the new king.

'Go home,' said King Solomon.

Not long after, the old king died.

Memories of the Past

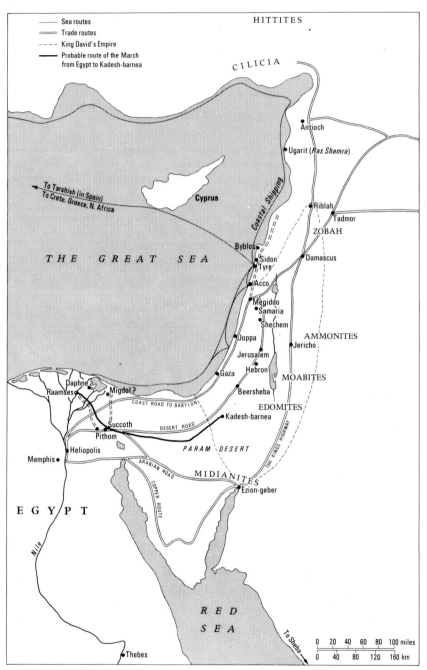

The route of Moses' march across the desert

Introduction

The Israelites came into the highlands with firm convictions about their destiny: they were 'GOD's People'.

Many of them held these convictions strongly; they knew what they believed. Many others had only a vague idea of what it was all about. Some held no deep convictions at all. This variety of attitude and conviction is what we find in all societies, even in the closely-knit societies of the ancient world. But there was a peculiar strength about the common convictions of the Israelite people in these early days of their history which marked them off from their neighbours. This strength stemmed from the insight and greatness of Moses and the profound meaning which he helped them to find in their dramatic escape from Egypt.

The story of their brief hour of glory which we have just read has only given us glimpses of these profound common convictions; we must turn now to look at them in greater depth.

We find them embodied in their 'tribal traditions' which were recited regularly at their religious festivals by the guardians of the sanctuaries at Shiloh and Hebron (afterwards at Bethel and Jerusalem). These traditions were gathered together and written down in King Solomon's time.

Tribal traditions, handed on by word of mouth from generation to generation, are not like written contemporary records; but we know now that they can give us a reliable picture, in broad outline, of the decisive events through which the people who cherished them have lived. They also have a value which written records can never have. The form in which we have them has been given to them through their being recited again and again in worship; they express, therefore, the common convictions of a whole society—the recital year by year at their religious festivals was a public statement of their faith. For at these festivals they were not merely celebrating important events that had happened in the past; they were declaring their enduring meaning —a meaning which still gave purpose to their own lives.

The Israelite people believed that, under GOD, they owed their convictions to one man, Moses—one of the greatest men who has ever lived, to judge by his influence over the later history of the world. These central convictions were two: that they owed everything to GOD and what he had done for them; and that they were to be his 'People' and live in his Way.

It was only when their city was in ruins and their national life destroyed that they really discovered on what strong foundations these convictions were built. As we read these old traditions about their escape from Egypt, their march across the desert, what happened at 'GOD's

Mountain', and their settlement in their new homeland, we must keep
our eyes open for the 'growing points' of this old story, and remember
that we are watching the beginnings of a faith that three thousand years
later will grow into the faith of a Martin Buber or of a William Temple.

In the very early days, before they became a people or a nation, the
ancestors of the Israelites belonged to many different tribes with many
different names. They had no one common name—except the con-
temptuous name given them by their powerful neighbours: 'Hebrews'
—'freebooters'. This is the name we will use in this part.

This is a brick-kiln near Baghdad. Kilns like this were used in Egypt; the Hebrew
labourers probably worked on such kilns

Escape From Egypt: Moses

Moses was the founder of Israelite religion. He dominates the traditions his people handed down of their escape from Egypt and their march to their homeland. His great achievement was to weld the very mixed company of tribesmen he led out of Egypt into a people with common religious convictions. The traditions do not hide from us the fact that he had to face disaffection and even rebellion. But he is one of the outstanding leaders in world history. His courage and vision stand out in these stories his people told of him. His courage he shared with many of his soldiers; his vision was something new which we look for in vain in the worship of the surrounding peoples of his time.

His vision can be put quite simply. From the point of view of the historian, the story of the Hebrew labourers was just the story of an escape across the frontiers. It must have been so common a story that no mention of it is to be found in Egyptian records. It would have passed unnoted and unrecorded— but for Moses. To him this was not just an escape—it was a deliverance. Here was a god who came to a people who were at the lowest level of human society—slaves in the Egyptian labour gangs—and acted for them though they never expected help and had not even asked for it. This is the key to the importance of these old stories: it is the first step towards the adult and mature faith of the Israelite prophets and of Jesus. So GOD for Moses was Deliverer and Saviour of his people: and this faith of his was embodied in the 'Covenant' established at 'GOD's Mountain'.

There is much in these stories which, as we might expect, is crude and far from what Jesus was to believe. Their idea of GOD, for example, as the friend of the Hebrews but the enemy of the Egyptians was too naïve—but something that we should not be surprised to find among rebel slaves. But their central convictions that they owed everything to GOD was not mistaken. Moses saw that if GOD rescued them like this, he must be master of history and nature. He did not see this with all the fulness with which the prophets, some five hundred years later, were to see it. But he saw it and saw it clearly. He transformed an apparently insignificant border incident into a turning point in the religious history of the world.

Egyptian Labour Corps

A new Pharaoh had risen to power in Egypt—a Pharaoh who cared nothing for the fact that the Hebrew Joseph, more than a hundred years before, had been viceroy of Egypt.

'We'd better beware,' he said one day to his ministers. 'There are too many of these Hebrews about—they are far too strong for us to feel safe. If we're ever at war, they'll go over to the enemy and make good their escape.'

So orders were given to break their spirit. They were conscripted into labour gangs (as if they were prisoners of war) and forced to work on the building of new store-cities in the Nile Delta near the Bitter Sea. But this hard slavery made no difference; their numbers kept on growing, and they even emigrated into other parts of the country. The Egyptians loathed them.

Pharaoh gave brutal orders.

'Throw their baby boys into the river,' he ordered. 'You needn't bother about the baby girls—they can live.'

Incident on a Building Site

Moses had been brought up at the royal court, away from his fellow-countrymen.

He went out one day to see what was happening to the men in the labour gangs. He soon found out how savagely the Egyptians were treating them—he actually saw an Egyptian officer strike down one of his fellow-countrymen. He looked round to see if anyone else was in sight—they were alone. He killed the officer and buried his body in the sand.

Some time later, he went out again to see what was happening and found two Hebrew labourers fighting. One was obviously a bully.

'What are you beating him up for?' he asked.

'Hello, who made you boss round here?' the man sneered. 'Are you going to murder me as you murdered the officer?'

That scared Moses.

'Everybody knows about it,' he thought.

He got out of Egypt as quickly as he could and went as far as the tribal territory of the Midianites. He came to an oasis and sat down by the well.

Seven shepherd girls, daughters of the priest there, brought their sheep to the well to water them. They were filling the trough with water when some shepherds came along and began to drive them off.

Moses went to their rescue and helped them to water their sheep.

'You've got back early today,' said their father when they got home.

'An Egyptian rescued us from the shepherds,' they said. 'He even drew the water and helped us to water the sheep.'

'Well—where is he?' he asked. 'You haven't left him at the well, have you? Go and fetch him at once—we can at least give him hospitality.'

Where the Midianites lived. Their territory lay on both sides of the Aqaba Gulf (seen in the distance). Here Moses fled from Egypt; and near the gulf Solomon built his ship-yards and copper refinery

That's how Moses came to stay in the Midianite encampment. He stayed there a long time; he married one of the priest's daughters, and his son was born there.

The Mountain Experience

This is the story of how GOD called Moses to his great work. We must remember that it is a tribal tradition, not a contemporary record; and that it was a story the Israelites were to think about and live by through the centuries.

The story is how the name of the Hebrews' God was revealed to Moses as 'Yahweh'. The Midianites (among whom he was now living) and some Hebrew tribes had always used this name for God; others had not known it—it was a new name to them. We do not know what the name 'Yahweh' originally meant (perhaps it was 'Storm God'); but it was given a new meaning for the Hebrews through their experience of being rescued from Egypt. Later, as in the story below, they were to explain it as 'I AM WHO I AM' (or 'I WILL BE WHAT I WILL BE') because in Hebrew the words 'I am Yahweh' and 'I am who I am'[1] sound somewhat alike.

What is important for us is not what the name originally meant but what it meant to the people who used it. And to Moses it meant a new idea of God as the 'Living God' who made himself known in the ordinary experience of men. Moses saw God in action in the rescue of the small, insignificant and hopeless group of slaves from Egypt. He was not just a tribal god (as he was for their tribal ancestors) and he was not like the gods of the surrounding nations, a nature god. He was Lord of history and of nature. We have put this in our own language; the tribes whose stories we are reading put it in their cruder, more limited way. It was a new idea of God; this is what lies behind this story of how GOD revealed his name to Moses.

Moses spent his time looking after his father-in-law's sheep. One day he found himself in the western part of the desert.

He looked—a bush was on fire, but the fire went on burning brightly.

'I must have a look at this remarkable sight,' thought Moses. 'I wonder why the bush doesn't burn out.'

GOD saw that he went out of his way to have a look at it.

'Stay where you are,' he said. 'Take your sandals off. You are standing on holy ground. I am your ancestors' God.'

Moses hid his face; he was frightened at meeting GOD like this.

'I have seen the brutal treatment of my people in Egypt,' GOD went on. 'I have heard their cry for help under their savage foremen. I know what they are going through and I have come down to rescue them. I'm going to send you back to rescue them from the Egyptians.'

'But—I'm not the man to rescue them,' said Moses.

'I'll stand by you,' said God. 'And this will prove to you that I myself have given you your orders: when you've escaped from Egypt, you shall worship me here on this mountain.'

'But if I go back to Egypt,' said Moses, 'and tell the Hebrew labourers that their ancestral God has sent me to them, they'll only say "Well, you tell us what his name is, then". What shall I say?'

'I AM[2]—that is my name,' said God. 'Tell them that I AM has sent you to them. Go and get the heads of the great families together. Tell them that the God of their fathers has appeared to you, and that he told you to tell them this: "I have been watching. I have seen what you are going through in Egypt. I promise to rescue you from this savage suffering".'

[1] The words 'I am' in Hebrew are much stronger than our 'I am'; they mean 'I am present and active'.

[2] In the earliest form of the story, this would probably read 'I am Yahweh' ('I am GOD'). Later editors put 'I AM' (what, for them, was the meaning of the name) in its place.

Egyptian traders ▶

'They won't believe a word I say,' said Moses. 'They won't even listen to me. They will say "GOD never appeared to you!" '

'What's that in your hand?' asked GOD.

'A staff,' said Moses.

'Throw it on the ground,' said GOD.

Moses threw it on the ground—it became a snake. He jumped away from it.

'Stretch your hand out,' said GOD, 'and take it by the tail.'

He stretched his hand out and caught hold of it—it was a staff in his hand again.

'Put your hand inside your shirt,' said GOD.

He put his hand in his shirt. He pulled it out—it was snow-white with leprosy.

'Put your hand inside your shirt again,' he said.

He put his hand in. When he pulled it out, it was his ordinary healthy hand.

But Moses hadn't finished.

'O GOD,' he said, 'I'm a poor speaker. I always was, and I still am—even though you have spoken to me. I never know what to say.'

'Who made man's mouth?' asked GOD. 'If a man is dumb or deaf, seeing or blind, who makes him so? Is it not I who am GOD? Go—I'm your mouth, I'll give you the words you must speak. Back to Egypt! The men who wanted to kill you are all dead.'

So Moses took his wife and son, put them on a donkey and went back to Egypt.

Audience with Pharaoh

When Moses got there he called all the heads of the great families of his people together.

He told them what GOD had said to him, and proved that GOD had really spoken to him by the signs of the 'staff' and the 'hand'.

They took him at his word.

When they heard what GOD had said—that he had come to his people and seen all they were going through—they bowed their heads in worship.

Some days later, Moses and some of the Hebrew leaders went to Pharaoh.

'These are the words of GOD, the God of the Hebrew labourers: "Let my people go—they must hold a religious festival in the desert",' Moses told him.

'Who's he?' sneered Pharaoh. 'Why should I take any notice of him and let them go? I know nothing about him. I'll not let them go.'

◀ Pharaoh

'But our GOD has met us,' said Moses. 'Let us go forty or fifty miles into the desert and offer our sacrifices to him—terrible things might happen to us if we don't.'

'You are just stopping the people working!' Pharaoh said. 'Mind your own business!'

'They're a lazy lot,' he thought to himself, 'and you'd give them a holiday, would you?'

So, that same day, he gave new orders to the Egyptian officers in charge of the labour force.

'No more straw for the brick-making,' he said. 'I won't have that any more—let them get their own straw. But I want the same number of bricks as before—no slackening off! They're a lazy lot—that's why they want to go off to the desert. Make them work harder. Take no notice of their lies.'

The officers went out.

'New orders of the day from Pharaoh,' they announced. ' "No more straw. Get it yourselves where you can find it. But no change in the number of bricks to be made!" '

The labourers had to go all over Egypt trying to find stubble for straw.

The officers kept shouting at them—'Today's work's got to be finished today, just as before!'

They beat up the Hebrew foremen.

'Why haven't you got the right number of bricks today? You used to get them made all right!'

The foremen appealed to Pharaoh.

'Why are you treating us like this?' they pleaded. 'You give us no straw but tell us to make bricks. We are beaten up. It's all your officers' fault.'

'Lazy, lazy, lazy!' said Pharaoh. 'That's why you want to go off to the desert. Get back to work! No straw—but bricks as usual!'

The foremen saw that they had an impossible task—the number of bricks demanded was beyond all reason.

As they came out from the palace, they met Moses waiting for them.

'GOD will put you in your place,' they said. 'We're now the scum of the earth to Pharaoh and his officers. You've just given them the chance they wanted—they'll soon have us all dead men.'

Moses prayed to GOD.

'Why have you treated these men so brutally?' he said. 'And why did you ever send me? We've had nothing but disaster ever since I came here with your message. You haven't rescued us at all!'

'You'll see how I'll deal with Pharaoh,' said GOD. 'It won't be a matter of "letting the people go"—he'll make them go!'

Sunset on the Nile, the great river of Egypt which figures in 'Egyptian Disasters' and in the hymn included with Amos's poems (p. 245)

Egyptian Disasters

We do not know what actually happened in Egypt; all we can say is that some natural disasters struck Egypt and Moses saw in them GOD coming to the rescue of the Hebrew labourers.

'Pharoah's a stubborn man,' GOD said to Moses. 'He just won't let the people go. Tomorrow morning, meet him on the river bank as he is going to bathe. Tell him this: The God of the labourers sends me to you with this message: "Let my people go to hold a pilgrimage festival in the desert. You have not done what I told you. You shall learn that I am GOD. I will strike the Nile water. The fish will die; the water will stink—nobody will be able to find any to drink"'.'

GOD struck the river. The fish died; the water stank—nobody could drink it.

Pharaoh went into his palace—he wasn't at all troubled. The Egyptians had to dig in the ground for water; they couldn't stomach the river water.

A week passed.

'Go to Pharaoh,' said GOD to Moses. 'Tell him: These are GOD's words: "Let my people go to worship me. If you still say No, I will infest the whole countryside with frogs. You'll have frogs everywhere—in your palace and royal bedroom and on the royal bed, and in the houses of your ministers and citizens and in ovens and kneading bowls. They'll come swarming out of the Nile".'

And so it happened.

'Ask GOD to take the frogs away,' said Pharaoh to Moses, 'away from me and my people. I'll let the labourers go on their pilgrimage.'

'When?' asked Moses. 'What are your orders?'

'Tomorrow,' said Pharaoh.

'As you command,' said Moses. 'You shall learn that there is no one like our GOD. The frogs will leave you and your houses.'

Moses left the palace. He did what he had promised and prayed to GOD about the frogs. And GOD did what Moses asked him.

The frogs died out—in house, courtyard and field. They were piled up in heaps and there was a terrible stench.

Pharaoh saw it was all over, and he was as stubborn as ever.

'Get up early tomorrow morning,' said GOD to Moses. 'Wait for Pharaoh as he's going down to the river to bathe. Tell him: These are GOD's words: "Let my people go to worship me. If you won't, I'll send swarms of insects everywhere—in the houses, on the ground, to your ministers and your common people alike. There shall be no insects where the labourers live; that will prove to you that I am GOD even here in Egypt. This shall all happen tomorrow".'

That's just what GOD did. The insects came—into the palace and into the houses of his ministers. Everywhere the insects ruined the land.

Pharaoh summoned Moses to the palace.

'You can go and worship,' he said, 'but you must stay in Egypt.'

'No,' said Moses. 'At our religious festivals we sacrifice animals. Egyptians would stone us if we did that sort of thing here. We must go right out into the desert; it is there we must do what GOD commands.'

'Well, I'll let you go to the desert for your festival,' said Pharaoh, 'but you mustn't go far. Now pray to GOD for me.'

'Look,' said Moses, 'I am leaving your presence; I will ask GOD to get rid of the insects tomorrow. But we don't want any double-dealing from you. We don't want to find you saying No to us again.'

Moses went out from the palace and prayed to GOD. And GOD did what Moses asked and got rid of all the insects—there was not an insect left.

But Pharaoh was just his old stubborn self. He wouldn't let the people go.

'Get up early tomorrow morning,' said GOD to Moses. 'Stand in the presence of Pharaoh. Tell him: These are GOD's words: "Let my people go to worship me. You are still being proud and stubborn—refusing to let them go. So tomorrow I will send a violent hail-storm, a storm more terrible than any you Egyptians have ever known in all your history. You had better get your livestock—and everything else you've got out in the fields—under shelter. Nothing out of doors will survive this storm".'

Some Egyptian ministers had begun to take GOD seriously; they quickly got animals and slaves indoors. Those who dismissed the whole thing as nonsense, of course, left their slaves and animals out in the open.

Then the thunder and lightning began. The hailstones were bigger than anybody had ever seen; they struck everything down—man and animal, plant and tree. Only where the Israelite labourers lived was there no storm.

Pharaoh sent for Moses.

'I'm a guilty man,' he said. 'Your GOD is in the right; we are all in the wrong. Pray to him—the storm has lasted long enough. I will let you go. You can get out right away.'

'When I've left the city,' said Moses, 'I will pray to GOD. The thunder and hail will stop. The earth is GOD's—remember that! But I know you and your ministers—you don't yet take GOD seriously.'

Moses went out of the palace and out of the city, and prayed to GOD. The thunder and hail stopped and there were clear skies.

But Pharaoh and his ministers hadn't changed at all. They were as stubborn as ever—when the storm was over.

'Go into the presence of Pharaoh,' said GOD to Moses.

So Moses went to the palace.

'These are the words of GOD, the God of the labourers,' he said ' "How long are you going to be stubborn? Let my people go to worship me. If you still say No, I will bring swarms of locusts into Egypt—you won't be able to see the ground you walk on. They'll eat up everything —everything the hail left, every tree left standing. They will swarm into your palaces, and into the houses of your ministers and common people alike. Neither your fathers nor your grandfathers ever saw a plague of locusts like it".'

Moses turned on his heel and left the palace.

Pharaoh's ministers now spoke up.

'How long is this man going to be a menace to us all?' they asked. 'Don't you know that Egypt is ruined already? Let the labourers go to worship their GOD.'

They brought Moses back to the palace.

'You can go to worship your GOD,' said Pharaoh. 'But who's going?'

'All of us,' said Moses, 'young and old, sons and daughters, flocks and herds. We must hold a proper festival.'

'Not on your life!' said Pharaoh. 'Children indeed! What scheming idea have you got into your heads? Let me be plain: only the labourers themselves can go to worship their GOD. That's what you wanted, isn't it?'

Moses was roughly dismissed from the royal presence.

An east wind blew all that day and night. And next morning the locusts were everywhere. Dense swarms settled over the whole land. Nobody had ever seen anything like it. The countryside was dark with locusts, everywhere everything was eaten up—plant, fruit, tree and grass, every bit of green.

Pharaoh sent hurriedly for Moses.

'I stand guilty—in GOD's sight and in yours,' he said. 'Forgive me, I beseech you, this once. Ask GOD to take this deadly plague away.'

Moses went out of the presence of Pharaoh and prayed to GOD.

GOD changed the wind into a very strong west wind which blew the locusts into the Sea of Reeds. There wasn't a locust left in Egypt.

But Pharaoh was as stubborn as ever.

'I will send a great darkness over the whole land of Egypt,' said GOD to Moses.

The whole sky went black. Nobody could see anybody else; people had to stay indoors. But it was daylight where the labourers lived.

Pharaoh sent for Moses.

'Go and worship,' he said, 'and you can take your children with you. But you must leave your livestock behind.'

'We need them,' said Moses, 'we need them for the festival sacrifices. We must take them all; we shan't know what we need until we get there. We won't leave an animal behind.'

'Get out,' said Pharaoh, 'and see that you never come into my presence again. I'll have you executed if you do.'

'As you say,' said Moses. 'I won't.'

The Last Night

This is a story of an epidemic which was so widespread that it reached the Pharaoh's palace itself. The death of the Crown Prince was for Egyptians a terrible disaster, for he was thought by them to be a divine being.

'There's yet one more plague for Pharaoh and the Egyptians,' GOD said to Moses. 'He will let you go after this one. And when he does, he'll make you go—and make you go in a hurry. Give the people these orders: Every man and every woman must borrow gold and silver jewelry from their Egyptian neighbours.'

The Egyptian people began to feel some sympathy for the Hebrew labourers. Indeed the man Moses was accepted as an outstanding leader by both Egyptian ministers and ordinary people.

Moses gave the people further orders from GOD.

'These are GOD's words,' he told them. ' "At midnight I will deal with the Egyptians. The plague will be so widespread it will reach even the palace. It will infect the cattle too. There shall be wailing all over Egypt—wailing such as was never heard before and will never be heard again".'

Moses called the heads of the great families together and gave them their orders.

'You must carry out these orders family by family,' he said. 'Kill a lamb. Take a bunch of the hyssop plant, dip it in the blood and smear it on the outer door of your house—on the lintel and the two doorposts. And stay indoors all night. GOD will be passing through the whole of Egypt bringing death to the Egyptians. When he sees the smear of blood on your door, he will pass by and forbid the Destroyer to bring death to any in your house.'

The people bowed their heads in worship.

At midnight it happened. The Crown Prince of Egypt died—and many others. Cattled suffered too.

Pharaoh, ministers and common people got up out of bed, and there was wailing all over Egypt. Death was everywhere.

In the darkness of the night, Pharaoh summoned Moses to the palace.

'Get up and get out,' he said, 'out from among my people. Go and worship GOD, as you said you wanted to. Take all your cattle, if you want to, and get out. And bless me too.'

The people of Egypt were in a panic to get rid of the labourers.

'If they stay here,' they said, 'we'll all be dead!'

It all happened so suddenly, that the Hebrews couldn't finish baking their bread—they had to pick up the unleavened dough, wrap up the kneading bowls in their cloaks and carry them on their shoulders. They had already carried out Moses' orders and borrowed silver and gold and clothing from their Egyptian neighbours. There had been no trouble about that—their neighbours had been very friendly.

They set out from Rameses and got as far as Succoth. They were a mixed crowd—labourers who were not Hebrews escaped with them. And there were large herds of cattle.

1

The Egypt the Hebrew labourers knew

1. The Step Pyramid at Saqqara (c 2600 B.C.E.),
   one of the earliest of the massive royal tombs

2. A statuette of the god Amon-Ra, the king of
   the gods in the times of the ancient Egyptian
   empire; he was often pictured as having a
   human head (sometimes a ram's head), with
   long ostrich plumes rising from his headdress

3. A statuette of the god Osiris ('many-eyed'), one
   of the chief gods of Egypt. He was believed to
   have died and risen again, and thus to be the
   god of the dead and the after-life

4. A wall painting from a tomb showing ordinary
   Egyptian peasants at work in the harvest fields

4

2   3

The Sea of Reeds

The Hebrew name for this sea is 'Yam suph'; the second word is from an Egyptian word meaning 'reed' or 'papyrus'; and the first word can mean 'sea' or 'marsh'. The Sea is not the Red Sea, but a reed marsh or lake not far from the Mediterranean coast. We owe the use of the name 'Red Sea' for this sea to the Greek translation of the Old Testament.

They left Succoth and set up camp at the border fortress of Etham on the edge of the desert.

They travelled day and night. GOD guided them—a column of cloud by day, a column of fire by night. The cloud and the fire were always ahead of the moving people.

Pharaoh now changed his mind.

'What on earth have we done?' he said. 'We've lost our labour gangs.'

He ordered his chariot force out in pursuit.

The Hebrews were in a panic. They turned on Moses, talking like the slaves they were.

'Weren't there graves enough in Egypt,' they said, 'that you'd got to bring us out here to die in the desert? Is this what all your talking about "rescue" means? Didn't we tell you in Egypt to let us alone? Living as slaves in Egypt is better than dying in the desert.'

'Don't panic,' said Moses. 'Stand firm. GOD will rescue you—and rescue you today. You see that Egyptian army over there—you will never see it again. GOD's on your side—you've only got to stand your ground.'

The column of cloud moved from ahead of them and stopped behind them—between the camps of the Egyptian army and the escaping people. The cloud remained dark. Thus the camps were out of touch with each other throughout the night. GOD drove the sea back by a strong east wind, the sirocco, all night.

The Egyptians followed them far into the water.

Just before dawn next morning, GOD looked down from the column of cloud towards the Egyptian army and threw it into panic.

'GOD's on their side!' the Egyptian soldiers shouted to one another.

When daylight came, the sea fell back to its steady flow. The Egyptian troops were caught and GOD swept them away.

That's how GOD rescued the Hebrew labourers from the attack of the Egyptian army. They saw the dead bodies of Egyptian soldiers lying on the seashore. They held GOD in awe and put their trust in him and Moses, his messenger.

And they made this song:

> Sing to GOD—
>> he marches in triumph;
> horse and rider
>> he has sunk in the sea.
> He shall reign
>> for ever.

Stories of the Desert March

The marchers went on into the desert which lay to the east of Egypt—marching for three days across a waterless stretch of salty ground.

They came at last to the water hole called 'Bitter Springs'. The water was undrinkable.

The people soon began to grumble again; they still showed how slavery had sapped their courage. And, of course, they blamed Moses for everything.

'What are we going to drink?' they asked.

Moses prayed to GOD.

GOD showed him a tree and he threw it into the water; that sweetened it.

They came to another waterless stretch of the desert where there was a great rock. Again the marchers blamed Moses.

'Get us water to drink,' they said.

'Why do you go for me?' asked Moses. 'Why do you argue with GOD!' Moses prayed to GOD.

'These people will lynch me,' said Moses. 'How am I to handle them?'

'Go ahead of the people,' said GOD. 'Take some of the heads of the great families with you—and the staff you used when you struck the waters of the River Nile. See—I will stand in front of you on the rock there. Strike the rock. Water will gush out—the people can drink that.'

That's what Moses did.

One day they were attacked by wandering Amalekite tribesmen.

'Pick some of the men,' said Moses to Joshua, 'and go out and fight these tribesmen. Tomorrow I will stand at the top of the hill.'

Joshua attacked the Amalekite tribesmen; and Moses, with two of his leaders, climbed the hill.

The fight went first this way and then that. The Hebrews beat the tribesmen back whenever Moses lifted his hand; whenever he dropped it, the tribesmen drove them back.

At last Moses got very tired. So the two leaders with him got a large stone for him to sit on, and they stood on each side of him and held his hands up.

They stood like that, holding his hands steady, till darkness fell.

The fight ended with the defeat of the tribesmen.

At the Mountain: the Covenant

Here we come to the story of the event which embodies Moses' second great conviction: that GOD, who rescued the tribes from Egypt, had called them to be his people. At a great religious assembly on 'GOD's Mountain' he made this clear.

We do not know where the mountain was. It has two names—Horeb and Sinai—in the Hebrew stories. It was a mountain associated with the Midianites and their worship, the people among whom Moses had his great experience. The Midianites were roving people; the mountain may have been in their old territory east of Aqabah Gulf or nearer Kadesh Oasis. It is not likely to have been the present Mount Sinai.

The idea of a Covenant between God and Man was a new idea and it expressed Moses' new conviction about God and what he is like. He is a God who comes into personal relationship with those who worship him, offering them his friendship and asking for their trust—and their trust in him must be expressed by living in his Way. This is the fact that lies behind these popular stories. We cannot now know what actually happened in this decisive religious event, but the new insight into God's nature and God's Way is the foundation of all later understanding for both Jews and Christians. Everything rested on their conviction that GOD had rescued them from slavery.

The Covenant was, on GOD's part, the offer of his love and care—'I am your God; I rescued you from Egypt'. On man's part, it meant trusting him and living in his Way. 'Living in GOD's Way' was embodied in the 'Ten Words' ('Ten Commandments').

News about Moses and what GOD had done for him and his people reached his father-in-law, the Midianite priest. He had been taking care of his wife and his two sons. He now came to meet Moses in the desert and brought them with him. He found him camped at the Holy Mountain, 'GOD's Mountain'.

'Your father-in-law is on the way here—and your family is with him,' Moses was told.

Moses went out to meet him and received him with proper courtesy. They asked after each other's health, and went into the tent together. He told his father-in-law how GOD had rescued them from Egypt and about the rough time they'd had on the desert march.

'Blessed be GOD,' said his father-in-law. 'Now I know what our GOD is really like—he is the God who rescues his people and defeats the proud Egyptians. Now I know he is the greatest of the gods.'

And there, at the Holy Mountain, his father-in-law led their worship of GOD. They offered a sacrifice and shared in a sacred meal together.

Next day, Moses held a law-court in the presence of the people; he was busy from dawn to darkness.

His father-in-law sat watching.

'What do you think you are doing?' he asked Moses. 'Why do you tackle this by yourself—the court sessions just go on and on.'

'It's the people,' said Moses. 'They keep on coming to me for justice. When there's a dispute, they bring it to me and I have to pronounce judgment and show them what God's law is.'

'This is no way to do it,' said his father-in-law. 'You'll just get worn out. It's too big a job—you can't do it alone.

'Listen to me,' he went on. 'I'll tell you what to do. This is how God's work should be done. Share the work out with able and trust-worthy men—the sort of men who can't be bribed—and give them various ranks. You will represent the people before God—and make God's Way clear to them, how day-to-day life must be lived. They will carry on the ordinary day-to-day court work. All really important matters will be referred to you. That will make it easier for you, and they can share the work with you. If you deal with the work in this way, God will give you the strength you need, law won't break down and the people will go home knowing justice has been done.'

Moses reorganized the work of the law-courts as his father-in-law suggested.

He said goodbye to him, and his father-in-law set off home.

The Hebrews set up camp facing the Holy Mountain, and Moses climbed up to the top of it. GOD called to him.

'Tell the people: I am Lord of the whole earth,' said GOD. 'They shall be my own people—if they listen to me and walk in my Way.'

Moses told the people what GOD had said.

'We will do all he tells us,' they said.

Moses went back up the mountain with their answer.

'Go down again to the people,' GOD said. 'They must wash their clothes and be ready to come into my presence in two days' time. Set boundaries round the mountain. These are my orders: "Do not climb the mountain—or even walk on the edge of it. Anybody found on the mountain will be executed. He must be executed by stoning or shooting

—he himself must not be touched. Animals must be dealt with in the same way".'

Moses came down the mountain, back to the camp. He got the people ready to go into GOD's presence.

'You must be ready in two days' time,' he said. 'While you are getting ready, there must be no sexual intercourse.'

On the second morning, a storm broke over the mountain. The lightning flashed and the thunder boomed; smoke rolled over it, like smoke belching out of a kiln. And there was an earthquake. GOD was coming down in fire.

GOD called Moses to the mountain top.

'Go down to the people,' he said. 'If they cross the boundaries of the mountain to see what is happening, many of them will die.'

'They can't climb the mountain,' said Moses. 'We have had your strict orders.'

'But go down again to them,' said GOD. 'None of them must try to come into my presence and risk violent death.'

So down Moses went and made it quite clear to the people.

These are the Ten Words GOD gave the people:
'I am your GOD. I rescued you from Egypt where you lived as slaves.

> 'You must worship no other gods;
> 'You must not make any images to worship;
> 'You must not use my name in wrong ways;
> 'You must do no work on the Sabbath;
>
> 'You must never despise your father and mother;
> 'You must not kill;
> 'You must not commit adultery;
> 'You must not steal;
> 'You must not bear false witness against anybody;
> 'You must not covet anybody else's family property'.

Moses came down from the mountain and gave the people the 'Ten Words'.

'What GOD commands, we will do,' they said. They were all agreed.

Moses wrote down GOD's 'Ten Words'.

He rose at dawn next day. At the foot of the mountain he built an altar and set up twelve pillars. Then the Covenant between GOD and the people was confirmed. There was a great sacrifice, carried out by the young men. Moses took half the blood in bowls, and half the blood he splashed on the altar. He read the 'Ten Words' so that all the people could hear them.

'All GOD commands, we will do,' said the people. 'We will obey him.'
Moses splashed the blood in the bowls on the people.

'This is the blood of the Covenant,' he said, 'the Covenant GOD has
made with you and set out in the "Ten Words".'

The March to the River

Hobab, a leader of the Blacksmith Tribes, was camping nearby.

'We are striking camp,' Moses told him. 'We are setting out for the
homeland GOD has promised us. March with us. You won't lose by it—
you can share with us in the good things GOD will give us.'

'No,' said Hobab. 'I'm not going with you. I'm going home to my
fellow tribesmen.'

'Please don't leave us,' said Moses. 'You know we have to cross the
desert—you can be our guide. If you'll act as guide, we'll treat you as
GOD has treated us.'   ,

So they left the Holy Mountain and went out into the desert on the
first lap of their journey. The Ark of GOD was carried ahead of the
march to make clear which oasis should be their camping place.

There was a hard core of trouble-makers in the camp—strangers who
had joined them. They had got thoroughly tired of desert food; and
everybody—Hebrews and all—just dreamed of gorging themselves
with meat.

'Oh for a piece of meat to eat,' they grumbled. 'We can still taste
the fish we had in Egypt—the cucumbers, the melons, the leeks, the
onions, the garlic! But it doesn't make a bit of difference. We are as
hungry as hunters—and all we've got to look at is this wretched
manna!'[1]

Moses heard all this—the men were standing at their tent-doors—
and he didn't like it. GOD was angry too.

Moses prayed to GOD.

'Why have you led me into all this trouble?' he asked. 'What have I
done that you let me carry the heavy burden of looking after all these
people alone? I'm not their mother! I'm not responsible for them. You
treat me like a nurse-maid—"Carry them in your arms" is what it all
comes to! Where do you think I can get meat to give them? "Get us

---

[1] 'There is still manna today in the inland region of the Sinaitic peninsula, and it is even called
mann by the nomadic inhabitants of this region. It is a sort of drop-like formation on the leaves of
the tamarisk tree or shrub, . . . formed of the secretions produced by the sting of the tree louse.'
(North, *Exodus* p. 132).

meat, get us meat!'' is what they are forever saying!'

'I'll deal with the matter,' said GOD. 'Tell the people: These are GOD's orders—"Get ready to come into my presence tomorrow; and you shall have meat to eat. I know what you've been saying—'We had a grand time in Egypt, but there's nobody to give us one here.' But now you'll eat meat till you are sick of it!'' '

'But where are you going to get the meat from?' asked Moses. 'Kill all the livestock? All the fish in the sea wouldn't be enough!'

'Do you think I've lost my power?' asked GOD. 'You will find out whether I can do what I say or not!'

So Moses went out to tell the people.

A great wind blew up and drove quails in from the sea. A mass of them dropped on the ground all round the camp.

All that day and night and all next day the people were out gathering quails. Even the man who gathered least gathered as much as a donkey could carry on ten journeys!

But as soon as they ate the quail meat, plague broke out and many people died.

The place where it happened had a sinister name—it was called 'Boundary Graves'.

One day, on the march, Moses sent some of his men on ahead.

'Go up into the Negeb over there,' he told them, 'and explore the highlands. Find out what the country is like—whether the soil is rich or poor, what kind of people live there (their strength and numbers), what their settlements are like (camps, like ours, or walled towns), if it is wooded country. Be bold. And bring back some samples of the plants they grow.'

The men went north into the Negeb, as far as the old fortified town of Hebron on the summit of the highlands, where the descendants of the legendary giants—'necklace' people—lived. They found a rich valley. It was the beginning of the grape harvest; so they cut a branch with a single cluster of grapes, and two of the men carried it on a pole. They picked pomegranates and figs as well.

Then they went back to the Hebrew encampment.

'We carried out your orders,' they reported. 'It is a rich and fertile land—this is the sort of fruit which grows there. But the people are a different matter. They are big men—descendants of the giants of old; their towns are large and strongly fortified.'

Caleb—one of the scouts—reassured the people.

'Let us march there at once and capture the territory,' he said.'We could take it in our stride.'

The Negeb, showing the wide valleys (where some cultivation could take place) and the desolate hills (see also p. 48)

'That's not true,' said the others. 'We can't capture it—they're far too strong for us.'

The people were in a panic.

'Let's choose another captain of our own,' they said, 'and be off back to Egypt!'

'How long will these people go on despising me?' asked GOD. 'None of them shall ever see his new homeland. Caleb's a different sort of man —he's got the right spirit and his whole heart's in the march to the new land I'm giving you. I'll give him the countryside he's just explored— he and his descendants shall live there. But now, here are your orders: "Tomorrow you all go back—back to the desert and the Sea of Reeds".'

When Moses told the people GOD's orders, they were very dismayed.

They got up at dawn next day and marched to the highlands.

'We have done wrong,' they said to Moses. 'Here we are—we'll capture the highlands GOD has promised us.'

'Why are you now defying GOD's clear command?' said Moses. 'You can't win. Stop this march; you'll only be beaten back by the high-landers—GOD is not on your side. The highlanders stand across your path; you will just die fighting. You are defying GOD; he is not on your side.'

But they stubbornly went on, though neither the Ark of GOD nor Moses left the camp.

They were badly defeated. The highlanders rushed down from the hills and swept them as far south as Hormah, east of Beersheba.

Two men, Dathan and Abiram, rebelled against Moses and spread rumours in the camp.

Moses sent for them.

'We are staying where we are,' they sent back word. 'You add one thing to another. You brought us from a rich and fertile country, and all we get is death in the desert. And then you play the tyrant over us. You promised to guide us to another rich and fertile land and make us owners of fields and vineyards—and see where you've got us. You're just hood-winking the people. We stay here.'

Moses was very angry.

He protested to GOD.

'Don't take any notice of their complaints,' he said. 'I'm innocent—I've never robbed anybody or done anybody any harm.'

He went into the camp, with other leaders, to deal with Dathan and Abiram face to face.

'Have nothing to do with these men,' he told the people. 'If you do, you will suffer their fate as well.'

The crowd moved away. Dathan and Abiram, with their families, stood outside their tent-doors.

Moses spoke to the crowd.

'This will prove that I've done what I have done because GOD told me to,' he said. 'I've done nothing of my own accord. If these men die an ordinary death, the common fate of us all, GOD has not sent me to be your leader. But if GOD makes a great hole swallow them up, then you will know what kind of men they are.'

He had scarcely finished speaking, when there was an earthquake.

Dathan and Abiram and all their families fell to their death in a great hole in the ground and vanished from sight.

The crowd scattered in panic. They feared the same fate.

Moses sent a messenger to the court of the king of Edom, east of Jordan River.

The King's Highway. This road, now macadamised in places, was the road Moses wanted to travel along on the march to the Jordan River

'We are your kinsmen,' ran the message. 'You will have heard of the hard times we have had. Our ancestors settled in Egypt. The Egyptians treated us brutally; but GOD heard our cry for help and rescued us. We are now encamped at Kadesh, on the edge of your territory. May we have your permission to pass through? We will keep clear of fields and vineyards; we will leave the wells alone (rain-water will be enough for us). We will march by the King's Highway, and keep to it until we are out of your territory.'

'You'll keep out of our territory altogether,' was the Edomite answer. 'If you try to enter it, we will call out our army.'

The Hebrews tried again.

'We will stick to the King's Highway,' said their second message. 'All we want is your permission to march through your territory. Nothing more.'

'No,' was the answer—and the calling out of the army.

That settled it. The Hebrews set off from Kadesh but they had to find another way round.

The Death of Moses

They reached the edge of the Jordan Valley—the high hills which look down on Jericho, the City of Palms. They had made themselves masters of the territory between the rivers, the Arnon and the Jabbok.

From the top of a high mountain GOD showed Moses the land on the other side of the valley.

'This is the land I promised your ancestors,' he said. 'I have let you see it from a distance. You yourself will not cross the river.'

Moses died there. He was buried in a valley in Moabite territory. His grave is unknown.

Moses was a great man. No prophet has ever been as great as he was —he talked to GOD face to face.

'To a prophet
  I, GOD, show myself
  in vision or speech or dream,'
    says GOD.
'But with my servant Moses
  I am different—
my people's destiny
  is in his hands.
I speak with him face to face,
  never in riddles.
He sees me
  as I really am.'

◀ The Arnon Gorge, near its approach to Jordan River. This is the kind of territory the Hebrews had to cross on their march north from the Kadesh Oasis

In the Highlands

In the central highlands (where little fighting is recorded) Hebrew tribes who had not been in Egypt were already in occupation; here the invading Hebrews, after overwhelming a few fortified towns, joined up with their kinsmen in the Shechem area and established themselves in the hills round Shechem City. Fighting took place in the south, and fortified cities like Lachish were destroyed about this time; the attack here seems to have been made, not by Joshua but by other Hebrew tribes from the south. There was fighting in the north, too; the fortified city of Hazor was destroyed about this time.

Many of the stories in *Joshua* seem to be late popular accounts which were told when people had forgotten what really happened; the earliest accounts which told of hard and scattered fighting or of peaceful penetration seem to have been discarded. An early account survives in the first chapter of *Judges*, and we give it first.

We give, secondly, the account of the great assembly of the Hebrew tribes in the central highlands when they renewed the Covenant together.

The old tribal stories in *Judges* show how slow and difficult settlement in their new homeland was; we give some of them here.

The Settlement

The Hebrews asked GOD what he wanted them to do now.

'Which of us must attack the highlands first?' they asked.

'The men of Judah,' said GOD. 'See, I am giving them the country to rule over.'

The men of Judah discussed the situation with their kinsmen, the men of Simeon.

'Help us to invade the territory given to us,' they said. 'If you will share in the attack, we will help you in your fighting.'

Hebron, in the Negeb, was attacked and captured. Then they moved on to Debir whose old name was Kiriath-sepher ('Book City'—perhaps 'The City of the Writers' Guild').

Caleb was fighting alongside the men of Judah.

'Whoever attacks and captures Kiriath-sepher,' he said, 'can marry my daughter, Achsah.'

His nephew, Othniel, captured it and married her.

When they met her father, Othniel urged Achsah to ask him for some fields as part of her dowry.

She got down from the donkey she was riding.

'What do you want?' asked her father.

'You have given me some dry Negeb countryside,' she said. 'Give me some springs as well.'

So Caleb gave her the Upper Springs and the Lower Springs.

Hobab, the Smith, who had been Moses' guide, fought alongside the men of Judah. He came up from the City of Palms with them and was fighting for them to the south of Hebron. Then he went off to live with the Amalekites.

The men of Judah and Simeon went off and captured Hormah.

GOD helped the men of Judah in their fighting in the highlands. But the fortified towns of the plain were too strong for them—the soldiers of these towns fought with iron chariots.

Nor could the men of Benjamin capture Jerusalem where the Jebusites lived.

The men of Joseph marched against Bethel, twelve miles north of Jerusalem. GOD helped them too.

When they reached Bethel, they sent scouts out to reconnoitre the town. They saw a man walking out of the town into the countryside.

'Show us how to get into the town,' said the scouts, 'and we'll look after you.'

He told them what they wanted to know, and they sacked the city. The informer and his family were given their freedom, and went off to live in Hittite territory.

The men of Manasseh went north, to the valleys between the Jordan and the sea.

The fortified cities of Bethshan (in the Jordan Valley), of Taanach (seventeen miles west of Bethshan), Dor (on the coast) and Megiddo (in the Esdraelon Valley)—all these held out against them.

Nor did the men of Ephraim drive out the citizens of the fortified city of Gezer—they all settled down together.

The same thing happened with the men of Zebulun when they attacked the towns of Kitron (near Acco) and Nahalal (which was about three miles west of Nazareth).

The men of Asher could not capture the fortified towns of Acco and Sidon—nor Ahlab, Achzib, Helbah, Aphik and Rehob. Like their kinsmen in the south, they settled down together with citizens of these towns. They were not strong enough to drive them out.

The men of Naphtali fared the same way when they attacked the fortified towns of Beth Shemesh ('House of the Sun') and Beth-anath ('House of Anath').

Above the view looking down from what remains of the ramparts of Megiddo, the fortress which guarded the road from Egypt to Damascus and beyond, where it crossed the hills into the Esdraelon Valley

Right a stone sculpture from Egypt showing Canaanites defending a fortified city. It gives an idea of what the ramparts of Megiddo might have looked like to the Hebrew attackers

Left the figure of a Canaanite girl on a plaque probably from a piece of furniture, found in the ruins of Megiddo

The Amorites drove the men of Dan into the highlands—they were masters of the plains and they held on to their towns.

(So the Hebrews settled in the sparsely-populated highlands; the fortified cities of the plains remained unconquered.)

The Meeting at Shechem

Joshua, who had served under Moses as one of his commanders, became the great hero of the settlement in Palestine. He was the leader of the tribes who penetrated the central highlands by way of the Jordan Valley. He later came to be thought of as the hero of all the Hebrew tribes throughout the whole of the occupied territory in the south and north as well as in the central highlands. His greatness lies in the fact that he was the man who saw to it that the vision of Moses was not lost.

The meeting at Shechem is a renewal of the Covenant, a call to the tribes to take up, under their new conditions, the work of Moses and to be 'GOD's People' in their new homeland.

When the worst of the fighting was over, Joshua called a great meeting of the Hebrew tribesmen—the heads of the great families and tribal leaders—in Shechem.

He recited the history of the tribes—what GOD had done for them—from the days when their ancestors had lived beyond the Euphrates River. He reminded them of the hard times in Egypt, GOD's rescue of them, the march across the desert and the fighting with hostile tribes. Now they were in the homeland GOD had given them—land on which they themselves had never laboured and towns they themselves had not built.

'You must now choose,' said Joshua, 'whom you are going to worship—your ancestral GOD or the gods of the land here. I know what I'm going to do—I and my family will choose GOD and be loyal to him.'

'We, too,' said the people, 'will be loyal to GOD—he is our God.'

'You can't serve GOD and the gods of the peoples around you as well,' said Joshua. 'If you worship GOD, you must worship him alone.'

'It's GOD we want to be loyal to,' said the people.

'You are your own witnesses,' said Joshua, 'that you have chosen GOD to give your loyal service to him.'

'We are witnesses,' they said.

'If there are any foreign gods worshipped among you,' said Joshua, 'get rid of them now. You must give your whole hearts to GOD.'

'We will serve GOD,' said the people. 'What he commands we will do.'

So that day Joshua and the people renewed the Covenant with GOD.

Tribal Stories

The Ballad of Kishon River
Let the whole world listen—

I will sing—I will sing to GOD,
I will praise the God of his people.

When GOD came out of the southern highlands,
marching from the Edomite mountains
through earthquake and drenching rain and cloudburst,
the mountains quaked before him,
before GOD, the God of his people.

Caravans were gone from the high roads,
travellers were taking the byways,
villages were deserted, deserted—

until you arose, O Deborah,
arose a mother among GOD's people.

There was not a blacksmith to be found,
not a soldier left in the city—
not a shield or a lance
among the forty thousand of GOD's people.

My heart goes out to the captains,
the volunteers in the villages.

Bless GOD! Tell the good news!
You, riding on tawny asses,
you who sit on rich carpets
and you who travel on foot!

Above the chattering at the well
GOD's triumphs will be told
the triumphs of his villagers!

To the city gates marched GOD's people:
'Awake, awake, Deborah!
Awake, awake, strike up the song!
Up, Barak, seize your prisoners,
Son of Abinoam!'

Those that were left marched down like nobles,
GOD's people marched down like heroes.

The men of Ephraim surged into the valley,
'We are with you,' came the Benjamin battle cry!

From Manasseh came down the commanders,
From Zebulun came down the marshals!

The chieftains of Issachar followed Deborah,
The men of Naphtali rallied to Barak,
into the valley they stormed at his heels!

The men of Zebulun recklessly courted death,
the men of Naphtali were in the thick of the fighting.

There was a lot of arguing in Reuben—
lounging among the sheepfolds,
listening to the shepherds piping!

The men of Gad stayed beyond Jordan River,
the men of Dan idled by Galilee Lake,
the men of Asher lounged by their Great Sea landings!

The kings came and fought!
the Canaanite chieftains fought;
but at Taanach, by Megiddo streams
they seized no loot of silver:
from the sky the stars were fighting,
the wheeling stars against Sisera.

The Kishon River swept them away,
the raging torrent, the Kishon River.

March on my soul, march on!

Loud hammered the hoofs
of the galloping, galloping horses.

'Curses on the town of Meroz,' said GOD's messenger,
'bitter curses on all who live there.
They did not come to GOD's help,
to GOD's help like heroes.'

But happiest of women be Jael,
of Bedouin women the happiest!
Water he asked,
but she would no more have given him water

than milk in a royal bowl.
She picked up a hammer,
with her right hand a workman's hammer;
she struck Sisera a blow,
she crushed his head—
she shattered and smashed his temple.
At her feet he sank, he fell,
lifeless he lay—
at her feet he sank, he fell
dead where he fell.

Through the window she peered,
gazed, Sisera's mother, through the lattice window.
'Why is his chariot so slow,
why linger his chariot's hoof beats?'
Her knowing ladies-in-waiting tell her—
indeed she keeps telling herself—
'They're finding and sorting the booty, of course!
A girl or two for each soldier!
Loot of dyed cloth for Sisera,
    dyed cloth embroidered;
two pieces of dyed cloth embroidered
    for my shoulders!'

So perish all your enemies, O GOD!
But let your friends conquer
    like the rising sun!

Gideon

At Ophrah, in the Jezreel Plain, there was an oak tree. It belonged to a man called Joash whose son was called Gideon. The Midiantites—camel-riding nomads from the desert—were raiding the Hebrew villages.

Gideon was threshing wheat, but not openly on the village threshing-floor. He was beating a few sheaves of wheat down on the floor of the winepress, to keep it out of sight of the raiders. GOD's messenger came and sat down under the tree.

'GOD is with you, brave hero,' he said.

'Then tell me,' said Gideon, 'if GOD is on our side, why has there been all this raiding?'

GOD turned to him.

'You're a leader,' said GOD. 'Go and rescue your fellow countrymen from the raiders. Am I not sending you?'

'Tell me, sir,' said Gideon, 'how can I rescue my fellow countrymen? We're the poorest clan in Manasseh; and I carry no influence at all in my clan.'

'I will be on your side,' said GOD. 'You shall wipe out the raiders to the last man.'

'Don't go away, I beg you,' said Gideon. 'Wait here till I come back with my present for you.'

'I'll stay till you come back,' he said.

Gideon went inside. He prepared a kid and made unleavened cakes with some flour. He put the meat in a basket and the broth in a pot. He brought them back to the oak tree and offered his present to his visitor.

GOD's messenger lifted his staff and touched the meat and the cakes. A flash of fire from the rock burned them all up. Gideon then knew for certain that he was GOD's messenger.

'O GOD!' he said. 'I have seen you face to face—I'm a doomed man!'

'You are quite safe,' said GOD. 'Don't panic, you won't die.'

Gideon built an altar on the spot. He was filled with GOD's spirit and mustered his clan to follow him. They got up early and set up camp near Harod Well. The raiders' camp lay to the north of them, by Teacher's Hill in the valley of Jezreel.

That very night, GOD spoke to him.

'Get up and go down to the camp. It's yours,' he said. 'If you are too scared to go alone, take your servant Purah with you. Listen to the raiders talking. That will give you courage enough to attack the camp.'

They both crept down to the camp and got close to the tents of the outposts. A man was talking.

'I've just had a strange dream,' he was saying. 'I saw a loaf of barley bread come tumbling into the camp. It smashed a tent flat.'

'I know what that means,' said his comrade. 'It's Gideon's army. It means we're beaten.'

When Gideon heard that, he said a prayer to GOD and went back to his own men.

'Up!' he said. 'GOD's giving the raiders into our hands!'

He divided his three hundred men into three companies and gave them jars with torches inside.

'Watch me,' he said. 'When we reach the tents, make sure you do just what I do. And when I blow the trumpet, shout "For GOD and for Gideon!"'

They reached the camp about midnight, just after the guard had been changed. They surrounded it, smashed the jars with a loud noise, waved the torches in their left hands and held their swords in their right hands.

'For GOD and for Gideon!' they shouted.

The camp awoke and stampeded down the valley and over the Jordan. Gideon had only three hundred men, but they followed the raiders across the Jordan and into the eastern highlands. They reached the town of Succoth, dead-tired.

'Give us some food,' Gideon said to the townspeople. 'We're tired out with chasing the Midianite chieftains.'

'Have you caught them,' they sneered, 'that we should feed you and your soldiers?'

'All right,' he said, 'when I've caught them, I'll thrash you with thorns and thistles!'

The same thing happened at Penuel.

'When I've come back in triumph,' he told the townspeople there, 'I'll tear down the tower of your town!'

He followed the caravan road and caught the raiders off their guard. The chieftains escaped. He went after them and caught them; and the raiding army melted away. He turned for home.

He passed by Succoth and captured a Succoth boy out in the fields. He asked for the names of the town's officers and wrote down a list of them—seventy seven of them, all told. He entered the town.

'Here are the Midianite chieftains,' he said. 'What about your sneering now?'

He arrested the town officials, got hold of some thorns and thistles and taught them a lesson. He didn't forget the townspeople of Penuel, either. He tore down their tower and executed their officials.

Then he turned to the two Midianite chieftains.

'What about the men you murdered at Tabor in the Jezreel Valley?' he asked.

'They were like you, every one of them,' they said. 'They had a royal look about them.'

'They were my brothers,' he said, 'sons of my own mother. By GOD! —if you had let them live, I wouldn't be executing you now!'

'Kill them!' he said to his eldest son.

The boy was frightened; he was only a boy and he wouldn't draw his sword.

'Kill us yourself,' said the chieftains. 'It needs a man's strength.'

Gideon killed them both, and he took the crescents from the necks of the camels.

'I've one thing to ask,' he said to his soldiers. 'Let each of you give me the ear-rings of the men he's captured.'

'That we will,' they said.

They spread out a cloak on the ground and threw the ear-rings into it. There was a great weight of gold. Gideon made an idol of it and set it up in his own town of Ophrah.

Abimelech

Abimelech was one of Gideon's sons—born to him by a Shechem slave-girl, a Canaanitess.

He went to Shechem to meet his relatives and the members of his mother's clan.

'Start this rumour going round the city,' he said. ' "Is it better to have a lot of Gideon's sons ruling over you or to have just one man your ruler?" and don't forget that Abimelech's a member of our clan.'

This is how his relatives talked; the citizens thought it wasn't a bad idea.

'After all,' they said, 'he's one of us.'

The town treasury was kept in the temple of the local god, 'The Lord of the Covenant'. The officials of the town took money from the temple and gave it to Abimelech who hired some devil-may-care ruffians with it. He went to Ophrah, his father's home town not far away, and murdered his half-brothers on the self-same stone.[1] Only Gideon's youngest son, Jotham, managed to hide himself and escape.

The citizens of Shechem gathered at the Great Tower of the city and crowned Abimelech king by the oak tree of the Sacred Pillar.

Shechem city lay in a valley between two mountains; Gerizim Mountain lay to the south. When Jotham—the one son of Gideon to escape—heard the news he climbed the mountain and shouted down to the citizens below.

'Citizens of Shechem!' he called. 'Listen to me—and GOD may listen to you. Here's a story:

> Once upon a time the trees set out to elect their king.
> They said to the olive tree—'Be our king!'
> 'Do you think I've no rich oil left,' said he, 'the oil that adorns both gods and men, that I should go swaying over trees?'
> So the trees asked the fig tree.
> 'Do come and be our king.' they said.
> 'Do you think I've no sweet rich figs left,' he said, 'that I should go swaying over trees?'
> So the trees asked the vine.
> 'Do come and be our king,' they said.
> 'Do you think I've no wine left,' said he, 'the wine that cheers both gods and men, that I should go swaying over trees?'
> At last, the trees had to go to the thorn-bush.
> 'Do be our king,' they said.

[1] To give his act the look of a legal execution (or possibly a sacrifice).

The road through the desert ▶

'Well,' said the thorn-bush, 'if you're serious about it, come and shelter in my shade. But, if you're not, let the thorn-bush burst into flames and start a forest fire!'

'You see the point?

'If you're serious about Abimelech, well and good—have a happy time together. But if you're playing a game, Abimelech will burst into flames; and you'll all be burned—citizens, fortified tower and Abimelech himself!'

Jotham then made off. He settled at a place called 'The Well'—out of reach of Abimelech.

Three years later there was trouble in Shechem; the citizens fell out with Abimelech. They didn't hesitate to do him whatever mischief they could. Important roads crossed at Shechem. So they set men in ambush on the hilltops, robbed the passers by and kept the money for themselves—that touched Abimelech's pocket. He soon learned about their treachery.

He rounded up his men, divided them into three companies and lay in ambush in the fields. He waited until he saw the people coming out of the city. He and his company made a dash for the city gate and captured the entrance square. The other two companies attacked the people in the fields.

It was a hard fight all day. But Abimelech captured the city, killed its citizens, razed the walls and buildings to the ground and sowed the place with salt—all but the strong Great Tower in the Temple of the 'Lord of the Covenant' outside the city.

Crowds had packed in here to escape the havoc within the walls. When they heard what Abimelech had done, they crowded into the underground crypt of the tower. Abimelech and his men climbed the hill, cut down the brushwood, carried it back on their shoulders and put it on the crypt. Then they set it all on fire. About a thousand people died.

Abimelech went on to Thebez, besieged it and captured it.

The Great Tower there was inside the city. It was crowded with citizens. They barred the doors and climbed on to the roof.

Abimelech attacked it. He went towards the tower door to set it on fire; a woman on the roof pushed over a heavy millstone and it caught him on the head and broke his skull.

'Draw your sword and kill me,' he said to his armour-bearer. 'I don't want people to say that a woman killed me.'

His armour-bearer carried out his orders.

When his soldiers saw that he was dead, they went home.

◀ Jericho and the daunting face of the Highlands

Danite Stories

The Danite tribes were settled in the neighbourhood of the Philistine 'Five Cities' and had become their vassals. Later they were to march north and capture, with great brutality, a town north of Galilee Lake. The stories about Samson are really 'tall stories' of the tribe's imagined prowess in dealing with the Philistines—when they were far enough away to tell them! They are popular stories —Samson was a legendary hero. Later historians were a little doubtful even then about some of these stories (to get over the difficulty they tried to think of Samson as a sort of 'Man of GOD'—we have not given their later account of this).

If we are tempted to dismiss these stories out of hand, let us remind ourselves of the brutalities of our own century—even in our 'Christian' west. A good world has to grow out of the world as it is; we shall see that the Israelite prophets saw this quite clearly. Their greatest men were later to condemn this violence and inhumanity in unambiguous words (see pp. 236, 276).

Tall Stories of the Plain

Samson lived in a Southern village near Zorah, fifteen miles west of Jerusalem, on the borders of the plain where the Philistines, the Sea Peoples, lived.

He went one day down to the Philistine town of Timnah, four miles across the valley, and a Philistine girl caught his eye. When he got home he told his father.

'I saw a Philistine girl in Timnah,' he said. 'I want to marry her— make the arrangements.'

'Can't you find a girl in your own clan or people, that you have to go off and marry a girl from these heathen foreigners?'

'You get her for me,' said Samson. 'I like her.'

Samson went back to Timnah. Just as he came to the town's vineyards, a young lion sprang at him with a roar. GOD's spirit filled him with tremendous strength. He had nothing in his hands, but he tore the lion to pieces as though it had been a kid. He said nothing about what he had done to anybody, but went on down into the town and met the girl again. He really liked her.

On a later visit to the town, he went out of his way to see what had happened to the lion's carcase; there was a swarm of bees inside—and honey! He scraped the honey out with his hands and ate it as he walked along. When he got home, he gave some to his parents, but he didn't tell them where he got it from.

He went down to Timnah for his wedding feast. The people there chose thirty friends to attend him.

'Let me ask you a riddle,' he said. 'The feast lasts seven days. If you can solve it before it ends, I'll give you thirty fine linen sheets and thirty gold dresses. If you can't, you'll give the same to me.'

'Out with your riddle,' they said, 'let's hear it.'

'Here it is,' he said.

> 'From the eater came something to eat,
> from the strong came something sweet.'

For three days they tried to solve it, but it beat them.

'Coax your husband to give you the answer,' they said to his wife. 'If you don't, we'll set the whole house on fire. Did you invite us here just to ruin us?'

His wife tried tears.

'You don't love me,' she sobbed. 'You just hate me. You haven't told me the answer!'

'I haven't told it even to my parents,' said Samson, 'why should I tell it you?'

She went on badgering him for the rest of the feast. At last he could stand it no longer and he told her.

On the last night, just when the marriage ceremony was about to be completed, the guests gave him the answer—

> 'What's sweeter than honey?
> What's stronger than a lion?'

'If you hadn't ploughed with my horse, you wouldn't have solved my riddle,' said Samson.

Off he went to the Philistines at Ashkelon—twenty four miles there and twenty four miles back. He killed thirty men, looted the gold dresses he wanted and gave them to the wedding guests. Blazing with anger he strode off home.

Her father gave his wife to his best man!

It was wheat harvest.

'I think I'll visit my wife,' said Samson, and he went down to Timnah with a kid to give her. He had no idea what had happened after he strode out of the wedding feast. He thought the marriage ceremony had been completed.

Her father stopped him.

'I thought you'd finished with her,' he said. 'I gave her to your best man. Take her younger sister—she's a more attractive girl!'

'I'll be quits with these Philistines this time,' Samson told himself. 'I'll give it to them hot!'

He caught three hundred jackals. He tied each pair of jackals tail to tail, fastened a torch between their tails and lit the torches. He turned the lot loose into the standing corn of the Philistine farmers. What a fire!

'Who's the villain who's done this?' asked the farmers.

'Samson,' was the general opinion. 'You know what happened at his wedding.'

So off they went into the town, and burned his father-in-law's house down with the girl and her family inside.

'If this is the sort of thing you'll do,' said Samson, 'I'll not leave you alone until I've got my own back!'

He rushed at them, hitting left and right with his great strength and killed many of them. Then he went off and lived in a cave at Etam Rock.

The Philistines raided a town of the Judah clan.

'Why are you treating us like enemies?' asked the Judeans.

'We want Samson,' they said. 'We are going to give him a bit of his own medicine.'

So a large company of the citizens went down to Etam Rock.

'This is Philistine country—you know that,' they said to Samson (who was not of their tribe), 'why harm us?'

'I only treated them as they treated me,' he answered.

'Well, we're not having it,' they said. 'We're going to take you prisoner and hand you over to the Philistines.'

'Promise me you won't kill me yourselves,' said Samson.

'We promise,' they said. 'We just want to get hold of you and hand you over. We don't want to kill you.'

The bound him with two new ropes, and took him up from the cave in the Rock.

Outside the town, the Philistines rushed at him shouting.

GOD's spirit seized Samson and he broke free—in a flash he'd snapped the ropes like burning flax and his handcuffs like melting wax. He saw a fresh jawbone—a donkey's. He picked it up and felled a thousand Philistines with it. Hence the saying—

'With a red donkey's jawbone I have reddened them red,
    with a red donkey's jawbone I have felled a thousand men.'

He threw the jawbone away.

Samson fell in love with a girl in the Sorek Valley—Delilah.

The five Philistine chieftains came to her.

'Coax him,' they said, 'and find out the secret of his great strength—how we can master him and bind him and make him helpless. We'll pay you well—£50 each.'

'Do tell me why you're so strong,' she said to Samson, 'and how you can be bound helpless.'

'Seven fresh undried bowstrings will do it,' he said. 'That'll make me as weak as an ordinary man.'

The Philistine chieftains got seven fresh undried bowstrings for her, and she tied him up with them. Men were lying in ambush in the inner room.

'Samson! Samson!' she shouted. 'The Philistines are here!'

He snapped the bowstrings as a strand of tow snaps at the touch of fire—he was as strong as ever.

'You're just playing with me,' said Delilah. 'You're lying to me. Go on—tell me how you can be tied up!'

'Try new ropes—really new ones,' he said. 'That'll make me as weak as an ordinary man.'

She tried new ropes.

'Samson! Samson!' she shouted. 'The Philistines are here!'

Again, men were waiting in ambush in the inner room.

He snapped the ropes like thread.

'You're just playing with me,' said Delilah. 'You go on telling me lies. Now, how can you be tied up?'

Samson had long hair.

'Weave the seven locks of my hair into the loom there,' he said, 'and beat them in with the loom pin. That will do it.'

While he was sleeping, that's what Delilah did.

'Samson! Samson!' she shouted. 'The Philistines are here!'

He started up and pulled up the loom with his hair.

'You don't trust me at all,' said Delilah. 'How can you say you love me? You're just laughing at me—and you've done it three times now! I still don't know why you're so strong—you won't tell me.'

She went on badgering him and getting at him till he was sick of the whole thing and told her his secret.

'I've never had my hair cut off,' he said. 'I'm under a vow. I should be just like an ordinary man if my hair were cut off—my strength would vanish.'

Delilah knew that he was now telling the truth. She went for the the Philistine chieftains.

'Come back once more,' she said. 'He's told me the truth this time.'

They came back; and this time they brought the money with them.

Samson went to sleep with his head on her lap. She beckoned one of the men and had his hair cut off.

'Samson! Samson!' she shouted. 'The Philistines are here!'

He woke up.

'I'll escape,' he thought, 'as I've escaped so many times before. I'll shake myself free.'

He did not know that GOD had left him; the Philistines got hold of

A primitive wheat-mill such as the blinded Samson, in the Danite story, had to push round (this is from Iraq)

him, put his eyes out, took him down to Gaza and bound him with bronze fetters. He spent his time grinding corn in the prison mill. His hair, however, began to grow again.

The Philistine chieftains gathered in the temple for a great sacrifice to their god Dagon, and to celebrate the capture of Samson with public games.

'Dagon has captured our enemy, Samson, for us!' they shouted.

When the crowd saw their god Dagon they sang his praises:

> 'Dagon has captured him—
> Samson our enemy,
> destroyer of our land,
> murderer of our people!'

They were in high spirits.

'Bring him in to entertain us!' they went on shouting.

Samson was brought from prison, and entertained them with exhibitions of his strength.

Then they put him to stand between the pillars. A boy was holding his hand.

'Let me feel the temple pillars,' he said to the boy. 'I want to lean against them.'

The temple was crowded with men and women. The chieftains were there, and about three thousand climbed on to the roof to watch the entertainment.

'O GOD,' prayed Samson, 'remember me. Give me my strength again—just once again, O GOD. I want to get my revenge on the Philistines for the loss of my two eyes!'

He grasped the two central supporting pillars with both his arms and threw his weight against them.

'Let me die with the Philistines,' he said.

He pulled with all his strength and the temple fell in on chieftains and crowd. The death roll was greater than all those he had already killed.

His relatives came and took his body away. They buried him in their ancestral tomb, between Zorah and Eshtaol.

The March to the North

A prosperous farmer, Micah, lived in the central highlands. He had his own shrine; he had carved an idol and household gods, and made his son his priest.

A young man from the south was wandering through the country. He belonged to the Southern tribe of Judah, his home town was Bethlehem and he was a member of the priestly clan. He was looking for somewhere to live. He came one day into the highlands and stopped at Micah's farm.

'Where are you from?' asked Micah.

'Bethlehem,' he said. 'I'm a priest from Judah. I am wandering about the country to settle down where I can.'

'Just the man I'm looking for!' said Micah. 'Stay with me, and be a father and a priest to me.'

Micah treated him like one of his own sons. He became his priest and one of the family.

'I know GOD will be good to me now,' said Micah. 'I've got a real priest.'

At that time the Danites wanted to get away from Philistine country and find a home of their own. They sent five of their bravest men to explore the north country and find out what it was like.

They came into the highlands and lighted on Micah's farm—a good place to spend the night. They recognized the southern accent of the young priest.

'Who brought you here?' they asked. 'What are you doing here?'

'The farmer took me on as his priest,' he said.

'Pray to GOD for us, then,' they said. 'Find out whether our expedition will be a success.'

'Go in peace,' he said. 'Your expedition is in GOD's care.'

The five men left the farm and went on to the north of Galilee Lake and found a quiet and unsuspecting town, Laish, a remote place, far from anyone, and especially from their overlords, the Sidonians. It had everything men could ask for. The men went back home.

'How did you get on?' everybody asked.

'Come with us,' they said. 'We've found the very place. Let's attack it.'

They all set out for the north, women and children and livestock going on ahead, six hundred soldiers bringing up the rear. They climbed the hills and camped at Kiriath-jearim. Then they pushed on into the central highlands and made for Micah's farm.

'Do you know, there's an idol on this farm,' said the five scouts to their comrades, 'and household gods. Don't waste this piece of good luck.'

They went toward the buildings and found the young priest's house and greeted him. The soldiers stood at the open gate while the five scouts seized the idol and its belongings.

'What are you up to?' the priest protested.

'Sh-sh,' they said. 'Keep you mouth shut. Come along with us and be father and priest to us. A whole tribe's better than one man's family, isn't it?'

The priest was delighted. He picked up the idol and its belongings and went off with them.

The soldiers turned round and marched off. They had gone some distance along the road before Micah could muster the men in the nearby houses and overtake them. He shouted to them to stop.

The soldiers turned round.

'What's the trouble?' they asked. 'And why this mob?'

'You take my gods—gods I made myself—and my priest,' shouted Micah, 'and you walk away and leave me with nothing—and then ask what the trouble is!'

'Keep your voice down,' said the soldiers. 'Some of us might lose our tempers—and then you and your men would lose your lives!'

The soldiers marched on north—with the god and the priest. Micah knew he was beaten and went home.

The countryside near Dan and the sources of Jordan River: the 'lonely valley' where the Danites burned down the town of Laish

The Danites came at last to Laish in its lonely valley. They killed the people who lived there and burned the town to the ground—there was nobody to stop them. They then rebuilt it and made it their headquarters. They changed its name to Dan.

The Death of Two Cities

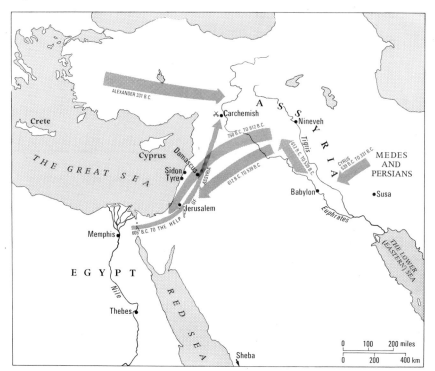

The Near East, 8th to 2nd centuries B.C.E.

Introduction

We must now take the story up again, at the point where we laid it down at the end of *Brief Hour of Glory*

We have seen what kind of people the Israelites were, and how they became a nation; and we have seen something, too, of the religious convictions that sustained them.

The vision of Moses and King David is not in doubt. But is this the way it is to be worked out? The next four hundred years provided the answer. We turn now to see what happened.

At first glance, the story that follows reads as if it might have come from the pages of any national history: military dictatorship; bitter hostility between North and South; civil war; invasion and the death of cities and villages; and all through, intrigue, assassination, exploitation, rebellion. Why is this story a special story? Perhaps that is the point—it isn't; it is, so far, a recognizable, human story provoking the question 'Why?' as appalling suffering always does. Here, in their own words, is their own account of these fateful years—contemporary narrative, official document, prophetic history, popular story.

But there *is* something special about the story. It reads like the story of the end; in fact, it is the story of a new beginning. Within fifty years of the final disaster in 586 B.C.E., a handful of men and women returned to rebuild the ruined city and begin life again as 'God's People'. How did this happen? What kept the vision of Moses and David alive?

The Death of Two Cities is, as a matter of fact, only part of the story. There is another part yet to be told: the rise of the great prophets, only glimpsed in the histories. These men, lacking political power, were critics of king and people; they saw, when statesmen were blind, the coming political disaster, but they interpreted it, not as the defeat of Moses' vision but as GOD's judgment on his own people for betraying it. To get the full picture of what happened, we must read both *The Death of Two Cities* and *Making Sense of the Story*.

New King   New Ways

A Brutal Beginning

Prince Adonijah came to Bathsheba, King Solomon's mother, and bowed in homage before her.

'Do you come as a friend?' she asked.

'Yes,' he said, 'as a friend. I want to talk to you.'

'Go on,' she said.

'I ought to have been king, you know,' he said. 'I am King David's eldest surviving son, and the whole country expected me to succeed him. All that's changed now. My younger brother is king—so GOD determined it. I've got one thing to ask you—don't say No.'

'Go on,' she said again.

'Ask King Solomon if he will let me marry Abishag. He won't refuse you if you ask him.'[1]

'All right,' she said, 'I'll do what you want.'

She sought an audience with the king.

He stood up to receive her, bowed and then ascended the throne. A throne was brought for Bathsheba and she sat at his right-hand.

'I've something to ask you,' she said. 'I hope you won't say No.'

'All right, mother,' he said, 'I won't say No. Tell me what you want.'

'Let Abishag be given in marriage to Prince Adonijah,' she said.

'Why Abishag to Prince Adonijah?' said the king in anger. 'You might as well tell me to give him the whole country! You know he is my elder brother. This is a plot—Abiathar the priest and General Joab have got a finger in it! By GOD! Adonijah shall pay for this with his life! And he shall die today!'

He ordered Captain Benaiah of the Guards to execute Prince Adonijah immediately; the order was carried out.

The king then dealt with Abiathar the priest.

'Home to your village of Anathoth!' he commanded. 'I'd have you executed too—but for two things: you carried GOD's Ark in my father's time and you stood by him in his darkest days.'

He deprived him of his priestly office.

When General Joab heard what had happened to Prince Adonijah and Abiathar the priest, he fled to the Tent of GOD and clung to the altar.

---

[1] Abishag was one of King David's wives. Prince Adonijah was still thinking of keeping his claim to the throne alive.

'Go and kill him.' the king commanded Captain Benaiah, when he heard what he had done.

'In the name of the king, come out!' Captain Benaiah commanded the general.

'If I'm to die,' said General Joab, 'I'll die here.'

The captain hesitated to kill him in the very Tent of GOD itself, and went back to report to the king.

'Let him die as he asks!' said the king. 'Kill him and get him buried! He was a bloody man in his day; I don't want the guilt of his reckless crimes put on me or my father's house. He murdered General Abner and General Amasa in cold blood without a word to my father. He must pay for his own bloody deeds. I'm not having the peace of my father's dynasty put to risk.'

Captain Benaiah went back and killed General Joab where he was. The general's body was buried in his own desert home.

King Solomon made Captain Benaiah his commander-in-chief; and appointed Zadok the priest to take Abiathar's place.

He then turned to deal with the Benjamite Shimei.

'Live here in the city,' he ordered, 'and stay here. You are under house-arrest. One step outside across the Kidron Brook—and you are a dead man. Do you understand?'

'Fair enough,' said Shimei. 'You command, I obey.'

Three years went by.

Then, one day, two of Shimei's slaves escaped to the Philistine city of Gath. When Shimei heard of their escape, he saddled a donkey and went off to Gath to get them back.

It was reported to the king that Shimei had been to Gath and back. He called Shimei into his presence.

'You swore to me by GOD that you would stay in your house,' he said, 'and I made it clear that one step outside would mean your death. You gave your word—why haven't you kept it? You were my father's bitter enemy—you know that. Now you'll pay for the wrong you did him.'

He turned to General Benaiah.

'Execute him,' he commanded.

That is how King Solomon established his authority and made certain there would be no such internal rebellions as his father had had to deal with.

Border Rebellions

King Solomon, however, had some trouble on his borders.

Prince Hadad, of the royal house of Edom, was one who caused trouble. When General Joab had won the Edomite War in King David's days, he and his troops had stayed in the country for six months, carrying out mopping-up operations and exterminating every able-bodied man they could find. Prince Hadad and a number of royal officers had escaped to Egypt—he was only a small boy at the time. They marched south through Midian, crossed the Paran Desert west of the Gulf of Aqabah (where they enlisted some tribesmen) and reached Egypt. The Pharaoh welcomed Prince Hadad and gave him a house and land and a food allowance. They got on so well together that he married a princess, Queen Tahpenes' sister. His son Genubath grew up in the palace with the royal princes.

When Prince Hadad heard of King David's death and the murder of General Joab, he judged it the right moment to make a bid for Edomite freedom.

'Let me go home,' he said to the Pharaoh.

'Why go home?' asked the Pharaoh. 'You don't lack anything here, do you?'

'No,' he said, 'but I must go home.'

He went and made himself master of Edomite territory in the east towards the desert. He was a dangerous enemy all King Solomon's days.

Another trouble-maker was King Rezon in the north. He had escaped from his overlord, King Hadad of Zobah, and become a guerilla leader, roaming the northern highlands. He went back to Damascus City, made it his headquarters and was crowned king. He, too, was a trouble to King Solomon throughout his reign.

Oriental Despot

King David had built his empire on the old tribal league; he respected the ancient loyalties of his people. But both the rebellions he had to face arose from old tribal suspicions. King Solomon learned from his father's experience. He made up his mind to break with the past and build a new kind of empire. He and his son were to find out that tribal loyalties ran more deeply and more strongly than they thought.

Government Reorganization

The king set about reorganizing the whole empire. These were the officers he appointed:

In charge of the Calendar—Azariah, Zadok's son;

Adjutant-general—Ahijah;

Secretary of State—Jehoshaphat;

Commander-in-chief—General Benaiah;

Priests—Zadok and Abiathar;

Chaplain and Adviser—Zabud, the prophet Nathan's son;

Director of the Labour Corps—Adoniram.

These were posts of cabinet rank which King David had established. To these King Solomon added two new posts:

Chief of Provincial and District Administration—Azariah;

Prime Minister (or Vizier) and Mayor of the Palace—Ahishar.

The king further reorganized the districts into which the whole country was divided, cutting across the old tribal boundaries. There were to be twelve new districts (as there had been twelve tribal districts), each under a District Officer, each to be responsible for one month a year for the maintenance of the palace (seeing that the king had all he needed) and the entertainment of royal visitors and delegations. The districts were also responsible for the supply of barley and straw for the new courier-service, arranging for it to be delivered at the various courier-stations.

Foreign Alliances

Political alliances were often confirmed by a royal marriage. Two powers above all others were important to Solomon—Egypt to the south; and the Phoenicians who controlled all the coast to the north-west and whose sea trade was expanding (they were later to found colonies in Cyprus, Sicily and Sardinia and beyond).

Egypt

King Solomon had a marriage-alliance with the Pharaoh of Egypt and married an Egyptian princess. Since he was still building his new palace and the temple and the new city wall, he housed her in Davidstown, the old city where King David had lived. For dowry, the Pharaoh gave the princess Gezer Town; he attacked the city for this purpose, captured it, burned it to the ground and killed its inhabitants. King Solomon later built a special palace for her.

The City of Tyre. The ancient city was built on an island linked by a causeway to the mainland (see colour plate facing p. 224). Ships from this city sailed all over the Mediterranean Sea and beyond

Tyre

On hearing of King Solomon's coronation, King Hiram of Tyre sent his congratulations to him by the hand of royal officers—he had always been a good friend of his father's. King Solomon returned his compliments and proposed a commercial treaty between the two countries. He wanted timber from the great cedar and pine forests of Lebanon and he offered to pay for it with an annual consignment of wheat and oil.

He also needed to hire skilled craftsmen—one of the most famous he later hired was Hiram (his father was a Tyrian who had married an Israelite widow), an outstanding worker in bronze.

So the two kings signed a treaty between their two countries.

National Defence

Key Cities

After King Solomon had finished the building of his capital city—his new palace, the temple, the citadel and the new city wall—he fortified six chariot cities as key cities for the defence of the heart-land of his empire:

Hazor, north of Galilee Lake, facing north;

Megiddo, guarding the pass through the Carmel mountain range (both these cities lay on the great trade route which ran from Egypt, along the plain, past Megiddo and then on across the Esdraelon Plain, along the shore of Galilee Lake, through Hazor and on to Damascus City);

Gezer (which King Solomon rebuilt), Bethoron and Baalath which guarded the western approaches to Jerusalem from the plain between the central highlands and the sea;

Tamar, south of the Salt Sea, facing Edomite territory.

The royal army was stationed at these points. It could be quickly organized to meet invasion, internal rebellion or troublesome border vassals.

The Chariot Force

The chariot was a military weapon King David had never tried to develop. It had been used by the Philistines and the Canaanite cities. Now the old Israelite tribal territory and the Canaanite fortified cities were welded together into one country, King Solomon made his chariot force the main arm of his army.

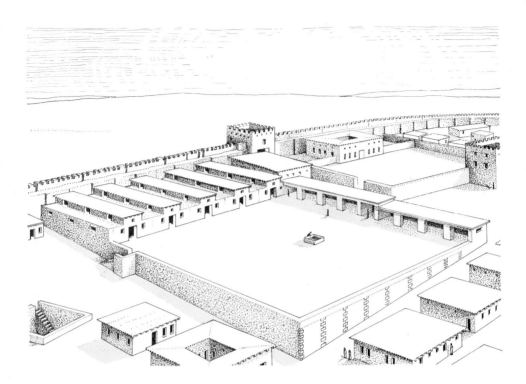

King Solomon raised a strong striking force of 1400 chariots and 1200 cavalry; they were stationed in the six chariot cities and in the capital city, Jerusalem.

Trade

King Solomon's genius was for trade and industry. His country lay across the roads from Egypt to Northern Syria and from Syria to the Red Sea; he saw how important these roads were. The city of Tyre was expanding its trade across the Great Sea; King Solomon sought to have good relations with it.

Red Sea Trade

King Solomon built a fleet of ships, hiring craftsmen from the Tyrian shipbuilding yards. He built ships at the port of Ezion-geber, on the east shore at the top of the Aqabah Gulf of the Red Sea (in Edomite territory) and they were manned by Tyrian and Israelite officers and men—the Tyrians bringing their wide experience of the seas. The fleet went on regular trading voyages—sailing as far as Ophir, on the north-east shores of Africa—and brought back large cargoes of gold, sandal-wood and precious stones.

Above the stables for the cavalry horses at Megiddo (the horse troughs are still in position in the centre), as archaeologists have uncovered them

Left the Megiddo stables as they once looked

Below a grain storage pit from Megiddo

Both King Solomon and King Hiram had fleets trading along the coasts of the Red Sea. King Solomon also had a fleet of 'refinery' ships sailing from the copper refinery of Ezion-geber. Once every three years the fleet of 'refinery' ships would come back laden with gold, silver, ivory, apes, and peacocks.

The Arabian Trade

King Solomon was interested not only in the sea routes down the Red Sea, but also in the overland caravan trade with the south. His interests went as far south as the south-eastern tip of the Arabian peninsula where the Sabeans lived—nomads who had settled down as a kingdom on the trade route which led from the shores of the Indian Ocean to Palestine. The story that was told of the Queen of Sheba's visit to Solomon's court reflects the popular interest in these far-flung adventures of his.

The Queen of Sheba (the Sabeans), so the story goes, was so impressed by King Solomon's fame, that she came with a great retinue of her officers to Jerusalem City, with camel trains carrying spices and gold and precious stones. It was his wisdom that drew her. They talked together, and she spoke freely to him, asking questions and listening to his answers—he seemed to know everything. All she saw, too, took her breath away—his new palace, the rich food at the royal table, the seating of his officers, the attendance and dress of his waiters and his cup-bearers, the sacrifices he offered in the temple. She was overwhelmed by it all.

'The reports I heard in my own country,' she told him, 'were reliable reports. But I didn't believe them—until I came here and saw with my

A camel caravan carrying grain. Solomon used such caravans in his extensive trading operations

own eyes. And now I know they weren't even half the truth—your wisdom and your wealth make a mockery of them. How happy your wives and your ministers! And how blessed is your GOD!'

She gave the king a splendid present—gold and spices and precious stones. The king never again received so splendid a gift.

He returned her kindness and gave her all she asked for. Then she and her retinue went back home.

The Copper Industry

Copper was plentiful in the territory to the south of the Salt Sea, and mines had been worked there from earliest times. King Solomon developed this and built in Ezion-geber the largest refinery that we know of in the Ancient Near East. He opened mines and built furnaces, and the copper was refined and worked into ingots in the great refinery. He must have had the help of Tyrian craftsmen. He built a 'refinery' fleet, as we have seen, ships like the Tyrian ships built for the transport of smelted metal. King Solomon needed the copper for use at home and to exchange for foreign goods.[1]

The Trade in Horses and Chariots

King Solomon built up, as we have seen, a powerful chariot force. But he neither manufactured chariots nor bred horses; Egypt made the finest chariots and Cilicia bred the best horses. Hence he had to buy chariots from Egypt and horses from Cilicia. Since he controlled the trade route between Egypt and Cilicia, he became a middle man in the trade; this business was an important source of his wealth.

King Solomon imported horses from Cilicia. His merchants would buy them at their market price and bring them to the king. A chariot bought and delivered from Egypt cost 600 silver shekels and a Cilician horse 150 silver shekels. These were sold through the agency of Israelite merchants to the kings of the Hittites and the Syrians.

New Buildings

The Palace

The palace took thirteen years to build.

There were four main buildings. 'The House of Lebanon Forest' (so called because it was built with cedar wood from Lebanon) was 150 feet long by 75 feet wide and 45 feet high. It was built in three rows of

---

[1] These paragraphs are based on J. Bright, *A History of Israel*, p. 195. But see *The Pelican Guide to Modern Theology*, vol. 3, p. 57, where it is claimed that recent excavations show that copper was produced only for Solomon's building projects, not for export.

An Assyrian relief showing timber from the Lebanon forests being transported by sea. Solomon used labour-gangs for this work. Notice the different sea creatures shown, including the mermaid halfway up the lefthand side

cedar-wood columns, fifteen in a row, on which were laid forty five cedar-wood beams. The beams were covered with cedar-wood. Window faced window and door faced door on each of the three storeys— windows and doors having square frames. 'The Hall of Pillars'—75 feet long and 45 feet deep—had a porch in front of it, with pillars and canopy in front of the pillars. 'The Hall of the Throne' (used also as the Court of Justice) was finished with cedar-wood from floor to rafters. The same wood was used in building the king's own domestic quarters in the court at the back of the palace; and similar quarters were built for his wife, the Egyptian princess. The buildings themselves were built of heavy blocks of stone, sawn to fit, and set in a large encircling court. The throne was made of ivory overlaid with gold, and all the utensils used in the palace were of gold. The throne itself had six steps, with a lion at each end of each step; a lion stood by each arm-rest, and on the throne was a calf's head.

The Temple

The temple was built by a Tyrian architect on the pattern of Syrian temples. First there was the vestibule, then the main hall (the 'Holy Place', a large rectangular room lit by small windows under the roof); then a small windowless room shaped like a cube ('The Holiest Shrine').

Two free-standing bronze columns, 27 feet high, dominated the porch. The capitals mounted on the columns were made of molten bronze. The southern column was called Jachin, and the northern Boaz. There was a large 'bronze sea', resting on the backs of oxen facing north, south, east and west (representing the underground fresh-water ocean on which, it was believed, the earth rested); and there was the central altar, on which sacrifices were made (representing the 'mountain of the gods').[1]

The temple was both the Royal Chapel (its chief priest was appointed by the king and was a member of his government) and the national shrine of the whole people. Here future kings were crowned and the great public festivals were held. Although the temple was built for the Israelite worship of GOD, its Tyrian architect embodied many pagan features in its structure; here lay a real danger for Israelite religion as Moses understood it.

The Labour Corps

To carry out all these immense building operations, King Solomon organized a conscript army of labourers, especially to work in Lebanon

---

[1] This is a short summary of the historian's very long and elaborate account of the temple and its furniture. It was a magnificent building—very different from the building his father worshipped in.

felling and transporting trees. Conscripts served one month in every three on active service.

A Note on Religion

King Solomon had a large harem, and many of his wives (as we have seen) were pagan women. He was not as loyal to the worship of GOD as his father had been. He built hill-shrines for Chemosh, the Moabite god (on the top of the mountain facing Jerusalem City itself), and for Molech, the Ammonite god. He built many altars to pagan gods for his foreign wives.

King Solomon's reign was a long and prosperous one. The population grew and the standard of living rose. The cities expanded; Jerusalem City spread beyond the great wall he built.

Outwardly there was peace and prosperity. But underneath the peace and prosperity there was growing resentment and unrest—especially in the North. His death was the signal for revolt.

Northern Rebellion (922 B.C.E.)

The story of the rebellion begins while King Solomon was still alive.

He was building the Great Tower and extending the walls of Jerusalem City. He had a very able young officer, a Northerner called Jeroboam, and he liked the thorough way in which this officer carried out his duties. He promoted him and made him the officer commanding the northern labour force—a Northerner in charge of Northern conscripts.

One day Jeroboam took the road leading north out of Jerusalem City, and as he was walking along he met the prophet Ahijah, a Northerner like himself. Ahijah stopped him, and the two of them left the road and talked together alone in a field.

Ahijah was wearing a new cloak. He tore it into twelve pieces—representing the twelve tribes of the old tribal league—and gave ten pieces to Jeroboam.

'Take ten pieces,' he said. 'This is GOD's word: "King Solomon has abandoned me and has not lived in my Way. I am going to tear the kingdom from him and give you the ten northern tribes. I appoint you king over the North. If you live in my Way, I will be with you".'

Jeroboam began to plan the rebellion of the North. King Solomon got to know about it and sentenced him to death. But he escaped to Egypt into the protection of Pharaoh Sheshak, and stayed there until King Solomon's death.

No sooner had King Solomon died than rebellion broke out in the North. It happened in this way.

King Rehoboam had already been crowned king of the South. He had now to meet the assembly of the Northern Israelites at Shechem, the meeting place of the old tribal league, to be crowned king of the North.

The assembly spoke plainly.

'Your father was a tyrant,' they told him. 'Put an end to the hard labour and the heavy burdens he laid on us, and we will be your loyal citizens.'

King Rehoboam wanted to talk the matter over with his advisers first.

'Give me three days,' he said. 'I will then give you my answer.'

'What do you suggest I do?' he asked the elder statesmen.

'A real king is the servant of his people, not a tyrant,' they said.

'If this is the sort of king you want to be, meet the people's requests; they will be your loyal subjects ever after.'

He didn't like this kind of advice, and turned to his young companions, the friends he had grown up with at court.

'Put the people in their place.' they said. 'Tell them your little finger is thicker than your father's loins! Tell them you'll add to your father's "heavy burdens", that you'll use lashes instead of your father's whips if there's any trouble. That's how to deal with them!'

The king met the assembly on the third day.

The Northern Israelites saw that it was a waste of time arguing with him. Their mood is shown in this Northern song:

> 'We don't belong to David!
> The Bethlehem farmer's no good to us!
> Home you go, men of the North!
> Let David look after himself!'

They went angrily back to their tents.

King Rehoboam ordered the Labour Force Commander, Adoram, to pacify them. The crowd stoned him and killed him.

That frightened King Rehoboam. He climbed into his chariot and made off for Jerusalem. Never again were North and South one country.

Jeroboam had already come home from Egypt. When news of King Solomon's death had reached him, he had set off for his native town of Zeredah in Ephraim territory, where he bided his time. The Northern leaders now summoned him from his village to meet the Northern Assembly and crowned him king of the North.

He rebuilt Shechem as his royal city and made it his headquarters. As a precaution, he also fortified Penuel in the highlands east of Jordan River.[1]

He also established the worship of GOD at Bethel and made it the great religious centre of the North. GOD's throne in the temple there was supported on two golden bulls instead of winged sphinxes as in the temple at Jerusalem.

'You have worshipped in Jerusalem long enough,' he told the people. 'This is the old temple where GOD who brought us out of Egypt is to be worshipped.'

---

[1] Some time later, he made Tirzah his capital city. Tirzah remained the Northern capital until King Omri built Samaria (p. 158).

Stories of the North (922–721 B.C.E.)

Attack on the South (c. 900 B.C.E.)

War broke out between North and South, and it lasted for more than twenty five years.

King Baasha of the North began it. He declared war on King Asa of the South and built and fortified Ramah Town, five miles north of Jerusalem City, to stop anybody crossing the borders between the two countries.

King Asa replied by making a treaty with King Benhadad of Syria, the country to the north of King Baasha's territory. He took silver and gold from the temple and the palace treasuries and sent them, in charge of his officers, as a gift to the Syrian king in his capital, Damascus City.

'We are allies,' he said in his message to the king, 'as our fathers were before us. I send this gift to you. King Baasha is attacking me. Cancel your treaty with him and make him withdraw his forces.'

The Syrian king willingly agreed and ordered his army south to attack the Northern cities in the Jordan Valley near Galilee Lake. King Baasha had to stop fortifying Ramah and withdraw to his fortified capital city of Tirzah seven miles north-east of Shechem. King Asa immediately issued an order to pull the fortifications of Ramah down. The Southerners carried its stones and timbers away and used them to fortify two other cities to the north of the site of Ramah—Geba and Mizpah—to guard their northern frontier.

Civil War

King Elah—King Baasha's son who had now succeeded him—had been on the throne barely two years when he lost his life in an army revolt. Captain Zimri, one of his senior chariot officers, plotted his death. The king was drinking himself drunk in the house of the mayor of the palace in Tirzah City. Captain Zimri with his soldiers broke into the house and murdered him, and proclaimed himself king. He murdered all the members of the old royal family.

But he himself was king for just one week.

Northern troops were at the time besieging the Philistine city of Gibbethon, some twenty miles north-west of Jerusalem City in the low hills between the mountains and the sea. When news of the king's murder reached them, the troops in the field immediately elected Captain Omri as king and marched from Gibbethon back to Tirzah City. They broke into it. When Zimri saw that it was lost, he went into the palace citadel, set the whole place on fire and died in the flames.

The country was now torn by civil war. Another claimant to the throne, a man called Tibni, raised the standard of revolt. Half the country supported him, and half supported Captain Omri. For four or five years fighting went on, until Captain Omri proved the stronger man. Tibni died fighting. Captain Omri was then crowned king of all the North.

He proved a strong king. During his reign of eight years, he built a new capital city. Tirzah City—the old capital city—faced the Jordan Valley; King Omri wanted a city which could control the whole country and command the roads to the north and to the east. So he bought a hill from a landowner named Shemer, built a strong city there and called it 'Samaria' after its original owner.

The wall of Samaria City – the actual wall King Omri built on land he bought from a farmer

King Ahab (869–850)

Syrian Invasion

King Benhadad of Syria invaded the North. He mustered his army—cavalry and chariots—and troops from allied countries and cities. He marched through the country and besieged the capital city, Samaria. King Ahab, King Omri's son, had stayed in the city with his people.

King Benhadad sent messengers to King Ahab. What he had to say was short and to the point.

'All your wealth is mine,' he told him.

'If you say so,' was all that King Ahab answered.

The Syrian messengers came back again.

'You don't seem to understand,' said King Benhadad's second message. 'My first message was a command to surrender to me all your wealth—and your harem. My soldiers will show you what I mean. Tomorrow, about this time, they will ransack the city—your palace and your ministers' quarters. They'll take what loot they want.'

King Ahab called a meeting of his government.

'You see what the situation is, who the aggressor is,' he told them. 'He has now asked me to surrender my family. I didn't give him a direct No when he demanded my silver and gold.'

'Stand up to him,' they answered. 'No surrender.'

King Ahab then sent this reply to King Benhadad.

'I was ready to meet your first demand,' he told him. 'But I'm not surrendering my family.'

King Benhadad's reply was an angry one.

'By God!' he said. 'I've so many troops that they will each have less than a handful of dust to take away from the rubble of your city when I've finished with it.'

King Ahab's reply was just as brief:

'Tell him to remember the proverb: Boasting's for the end of the day, not its beginning!'

King Benhadad was drinking in the Royal Tent with the kings who had come with him when King Ahab's reply was handed to him.

He turned to his officers.

'To arms!' he ordered.

While this was happening, one of the Northern prophets sought an audience with King Ahab.

'These are GOD's words,' he said. ' "Cast your eyes over this vast rabble round the city. I am about to put it at your mercy. You will know that I am really GOD!" '

'By whom will he do it?' asked King Ahab.

'By the young commandos,' the prophet answered.

'Who is to take the offensive?' asked the king.

'Your Majesty,' answered the prophet.

The king called out his troops. The commandos made a surprise attack on the Syrian camp at noon.

King Benhadad and his royal friends were drinking themselves drunk in the royal tent at the time.

Patrols reported the attack of the Northern soldiers.

'Let them come!' said King Benhadad carelessly. 'If it's peace they want—or if they want a bit of a fight—just take them all prisoners.'

The commando attack—with the main troops coming up behind them —routed the Syrian army. Every soldier got his man. King Benhadad escaped on a horse with some of his cavalry, leaving King Ahab to capture the main body of cavalry and chariots. The Syrian casualties were very heavy; those who escaped were chased back over the border.

A Syrian Council of War was held. The generals had their own explanation why they had lost.

'The enemy's gods are mountain gods,' they argued. 'That's why they beat us. Our gods are gods of the plain—we can beat these men if we fight them on the plain. And more: the kings who are our allies are no generals. Replace them with veteran captains and muster another army, horse for horse and chariot for chariot like the one we lost. Then fight the enemy in the plains; we'll defeat them.'

The king accepted his generals' advice.

The next spring he mustered his army, marched to Aphik Town, north of Galilee Lake, and attacked the Northerners there. The Northern army was drawn up facing them. The Syrians seemed to be everywhere; beside them, the Northern troops looked like two small flocks of goats.

For a whole week the two armies just watched each other. Then the fighting started. The Northerners routed the Syrians—their casualties in the first day's fighting were very heavy. The survivors fled back into Aphik Town. But the city wall collapsed in the siege and the town was taken. King Benhadad himself had to hide in the small inner room of the citadel.

'Your Majesty,' said his officers, 'the Northern kings are known to be merciful men. Let us, we pray you, dress in sackcloth with ropes on our heads and surrender to him. It may be he will spare your life.'

They did just that, and asked for an audience with King Ahab.

'King Benhadad, your Majesty's servant, surrenders,' they reported. 'He asks for his life to be spared.'

'Is my royal cousin still alive?' asked King Ahab.

The officers were watching the king closely to see which way the

Solomon's treasure ships ▶

wind was blowing; they weren't slow to catch his meaning.

'Yes,' they said, 'King Benhadad—your Majesty's royal cousin.'

'Bring him to me,' he said.

King Benhadad came, and King Ahab called him up into his chariot.

'I will give you back the cities my father captured from your father,' King Benhadad told him. 'My father established bazaars in Samaria City; you may establish bazaars in my capital city of Damascus.'

'I will accept a treaty on these terms,' said King Ahab. 'You are free to go home.'

The Last Battle (850)

For three years there was peace. But King Benhadad did not keep his promises; he did not hand back the cities as by treaty he had agreed to do.

One day King Jehoshaphat, king of the south, paid a state visit to King Ahab. He was present at a meeting of the Council when King Ahab reminded his officers that one of the towns had not been handed back—Ramoth-Gilead, thirty miles east of Jordan River.

'The town is ours and it is still not in our hands, you know,' said the king, 'and here we sit doing nothing. It's about time we took it by force.'

He turned to King Jehoshaphat.

'Will you be my ally?' he asked.

'Of course, I will,' said King Jehoshaphat. 'Count my soldiers as your soldiers, my cavalry as your cavalry.'[1]

The two kings marched on Ramoth-Gilead.

'I'll disguise myself,' said King Ahab, 'and fight like a private soldier. You can wear your royal armour.'

So he fought in disguise.

Now King Benhadad had given strict orders to his chariot captains.

'There's one man you've got to go for—and one man only,' he told them. 'That man's King Ahab. Don't waste your time over anybody else.'

The chariot captains spotted King Jehoshaphat and surrounded his chariot.

'We've got King Ahab all right!' they shouted.

King Jehoshaphat shouted back at them. They realized that they had got the wrong man, and wheeled their chariots round.

An unknown soldier took a chance shot with an arrow into the mass of Northern troops—and it struck King Ahab between his scale armour and his breastplate.

---

[1] A story about the prophet Micaiah has been inserted at this point. It did not belong to the original story and takes an unfriendly view of Ahab. We have used it later (p. 230).

◀ Cedars of Lebanon

Samaria City, as seen today from the Shechem Road

He called to his charioteer.

'Wheel round,' he commanded. 'Drive me out of the fighting. I am badly wounded.'

Bitter fighting went on all day. The king kept himself standing upright in his chariot facing the Syrians, as an example to his men. He managed to keep himself standing like that till darkness began to fall. Then he collapsed and died.

As the sun set, news of his death spread through the army.

'The king's dead!' the cry went round. 'Every man to his home!'

His soldiers drove the chariot with the dead king back to his capital city, Samaria, and buried him there.

King Jehu (842–815)

Army Revolt

King Joram of the North had been badly wounded in a battle for Ramoth-Gilead; he had retired to his royal city of Jezreel to recover from his wounds. King Ahaziah of the South went to visit him.

Elisha,[1] the Man of GŌD, sent for one of the younger members of his prophetic guild.

'Get ready to go to the army at Ramoth-Gilead,' he told him. 'Hitch up your cloak and take this flask of oil with you. When you get there, find Captain Jehu. Ask for a private interview with him in an inner room, away from his fellow-officers. Take the flask of oil and pour it on his head. Say: "These are GOD's words: I anoint you king of the North!" Then open the door and get out—as quickly as you can.'

The young man crossed Jordan River to Ramoth-Gilead. When he got there, the officers were holding a staff meeting.

'Captain Jehu,' he said, 'I've a message for you.'

'For me?' asked the captain, 'or for one of the other officers?'

'For you yourself, Captain,' he said.

Captain Jehu got up and went into an inner room. The young man poured oil on his head.

'These are GOD's words,' he said, ' "I anoint you king over my people, over the North!" '

He opened the door and vanished.

Captain Jehu went back to the staff meeting.

'Is everything all right?' they asked. 'What did that madman want with you?'

'What do you think?' he retorted. 'You know how these fellows talk!'

'Go on,' they said. 'You can't get away with that! Tell us what he said.'

'Well,' said Captain Jehu. 'He just said this: "These are GOD's words: I anoint you king over the North".'

His brother officers turned the stone steps up to the house into a throne, spreading their military cloaks on them. They sounded a fanfare of trumpets and shouted 'Long live King Jehu!'

Captain Jehu ordered his chariot out and rode to the royal city of Jezreel where the two kings were—King Joram still a sick man and King Ahaziah still on his visit.

The sentry on the top of Jezreel Tower noticed something moving along the eastern road.

'I can see riders coming!' he shouted.

---

[1] Many legends were told about Elisha as miracle-worker and adviser of kings.

'Send a cavalryman to see if there's anything wrong,' commanded King Joram.

A cavalryman rode out to meet the chariot.

He challenged the charioteer.

'In the name of the king, is it peace?' he asked.

'Peace be damned!' shouted Captain Jehu. 'Fall in behind me!'

'The cavalryman's staying with the chariot!' shouted the sentry on the tower.

King Joram ordered a second cavalryman out.

The same thing happened.

'He's staying too!' the sentry shouted down. 'The charioteer's driving like a madman—only Captain Jehu drives like this!'

'To arms!' commanded the king.

The royal chariots were driven out, and the two kings met Captain Jehu at Naboth's farm.

'Is it peace, Captain?' asked King Joram.

'Peace indeed!' said the captain. 'How can there be peace with all this paganism the Queen Mother's spreading throughout the land?'

The king wheeled his chariot round.

'We're betrayed, Ahaziah!' he shouted.

Captain Jehu shot him through the heart with an arrow, and he collapsed in his chariot.

'Throw his body on farmer Naboth's field!' he ordered.

King Ahaziah saw what his fate would soon be, and drove his chariot along the southern road. Captain Jehu followed him and caught up with him seven miles along the road in the valley near Ibleam.

'Get him!' he shouted. 'Pin him to his chariot!'

The soldiers hit him, but he drove his chariot on to Megiddo Fortress. And there he died.

Captain Jehu turned back to Jezreel and rode into the city. When the news was brought to Jezebel, the Queen Mother, she dressed as if for a royal party—painted her eyes and adorned her hair—and sat looking out of a palace window.

As Jehu rode through the palace gates, she called down to him.

'Is it peace?' she sneered. 'You Zimri! Murderer of your King!'

Captain Jehu stopped and looked up at the window.

'Who's for me?' he shouted up at the palace officials. 'Who's on my side?'

Two or three officials were looking down.

'Throw her out of the window!' he shouted.

They threw her out. Her blood spattered the wall and her body was trampled by the horses' hoofs.

Captain Jehu went on into the palace to celebrate.

'She was a king's daughter, wicked woman though she was. Give her a royal burial,' he ordered.

By the time the officers found her body, the street dogs had been scavenging around—only her skull, her feet and the palms of her hands were left.

Brutal Reform

King Jehu—as he now was—made sure that all the descendants of King Ahab were got out of the way. He arranged the murder of all who remained in the capital city of Samaria or in the royal city of Jezreel, and so got rid of any possible claimants to the crown. He left none alive —members of the royal family, relatives and friends, even priests who had favoured the old régime.

He was on his way from Jezreel to Samaria. Rechab's son, Jonadab, a fighter for the old religion of the North and an enemy of Ahab—an extremist like himself—was coming along the Jezreel road to meet him.

'Are you an out and out friend of mine,' Jehu asked, 'as I am yours?'

'I am!' said Jonadab.

'Grand!' said King Jehu. 'Give me your hand!'

Jonadab gave him his hand and the king helped him to climb up into his chariot.

'Come with me,' he said. 'I will show you how much I care for the true worship of GOD!'

When he reached Samaria City, he first of all made sure that all the relatives of King Ahab were dead.

Then he called a public meeting of all the citizens.

'King Ahab worshipped Baal,' he told them. 'But his worship of Baal will seem as nothing beside my worship of Baal. I am holding a great religious service in Baal's temple here, and I command all his prophets and worshippers and priests to attend it—and I mean all of them. Those who are absent will face the death penalty.'

All this was a deliberate trick on King Jehu's part—his real aim was to murder everybody who had anything at all to do with Baal worship.

'Arrange a temple sacrifice,' was his royal command.

A proclamation was made to the whole country. Worshippers of Baal came from near and far and packed the temple from wall to wall.

The king ordered the wardrobe-master to bring out all the sacred vestments for the worshippers to wear. Then he and Jonadab entered the temple.

'We want no worshippers of GOD here,' he told the congregation. 'Just make sure that none of them have slipped in unnoticed.'

He then began the service, offering sacrifices and burnt offerings.

Meanwhile he had stationed eighty soldiers outside.

'You are under orders,' he said. 'Make sure nobody escapes—or you'll pay for it with your lives.'

When the burnt-offering had been made, the king turned to his guards.

'Go in and butcher them,' he ordered. 'See that nobody gets away.'

The guards went in and butchered the whole crowd and threw their bodies out into the courtyard. They broke into the inner room and tore down the sacred pillar and took it outside and burned it. They demolished the whole building and turned it into a lavatory.

That's how King Jehu stamped out pagan religion in the North.

Six Kings and Four Rebellions (746–721)

Zechariah, Jeroboam II's son, was king for only six brief months. Shallum, a usurper, murdered him on the road between the royal cities, near Ibleam.

Tirzah—the capital city of the North for the forty years before King Omri built Samaria City—had become the headquarters of rebels led by a man called Menahem. He marched on Samaria City, murdered Shallum and seized the throne. (Shallum had been king for barely a month.)

Menahem was a cruel man; he destroyed the whole town of Tappuah (fourteen miles south-west of Tirzah) because they had once refused to open their gates to him. In his anger he murdered all the pregnant women with horrible brutality.

King Menahem reigned for about ten years, but only because he became a vassal of the Assyrian Emperor, Tigleth-pileser III. This emperor invaded the North and King Menahem only saved himself by paying an enormous sum of money as tribute. He had to make all the wealthy farmers pay a heavy tax—each of them had to give as much money as would buy a slave. Only on these conditions did the invading armies go home.

King Menahem's son was king for only two years. Pekah, his aide-de-camp, rose in rebellion with fifty men from east of Jordan River and murdered him in the palace fort. King Pekah reigned for four or five years. The Assyrians again marched west when King Pekah made an alliance with King Rezin of Damascus and rose in rebellion against them. They captured many cities and most of the territory in the North. Many

◄ The god Baal, a picture from a stone pillar found at Ras Shamra on the coast north of Tyre

The Assyrian emperor Asshurbanapal (669–633 B.C.E.) on a hunting expedition.
At this time, Assyrian power was declining. In 612 their capital city, Nineveh, was
sacked by the Babylonians

of the leading men were deported to Assyria, and all that was left of the
North was a small area of land round Samaria City itself.

A usurper called Hoshea murdered King Pekah with the help,
probably, of Assyrian soldiers. He reigned for nine years, but he too had
to suffer an Assyrian invasion of his country. He became an Assyrian
vassal and had to pay an annual tribute.

The end came suddenly. King Hoshea thought he could safely defy
the Assyrian armies. He sent messengers to the vizier of Egypt to come
to his help and he stopped sending tribute to Assyria. The Assyrian
emperor moved quickly. He marched west, captured and imprisoned

him—and besieged Samaria City. It held out for three years. When the Assyrians captured it, they deported thousands of its inhabitants to the east.

The story of the North was over.

The Assyrian emperor now settled people from the other parts of his empire—from Babylon and its neighbourhood, and from the country through which the Orontes River flows—to colonize Samaria and the villages which had been left empty when the Northern prisoners were deported.

Stories of the South
(922–586 B.C.E.)

Egyptian Invasion (917)

King Rehoboam had been king for only five years when Egyptian armies attacked and captured his capital city, Jerusalem. The city escaped destruction by the payment of an enormous tribute. All the treasures of the temple and the palace were ransacked—among them King Solomon's gold ceremonial shields. All King Rehoboam could do was to make bronze shields to take their place. These were kept in the guard-room of the Palace Guards, whose officers were personally responsible for their safety. They were taken out, as the old gold ones used to be, on the king's official visits to the temple. After each ceremony, they were taken back to the guard-room.

King Asa (913–873)

King Asa was a good king, and tried to rule the country in the spirit of his ancestor David. He banished all the male temple prostitutes and destroyed the images of pagan gods his father and grandfather had set up there. His mother, now the Queen Mother, had ordered a private image of the goddess Asherah to be made; he took away her rank as Queen Mother and burned the image in Kidron Valley. She had removed the gifts he and his father had dedicated to the temple; he had them brought back and set up again.

It was in his day that civil war broke out between North and South (see p. 157).

Edomite Rebellion (c. 845)

King Joram had to face trouble beyond Jordan River in the eastern highlands. The Edomites had long been subjects of the Southern kings, but when King Joram ascended the throne, they rose in revolt and were strong enough to make their country independent. King Joram mustered his chariot force and crossed the river. He was surrounded at the town of Zair and only escaped by breaking out of the besieged town in the darkness of the night. The Edomites never again lost their independence.

A statuette of the Mother Goddess found in Beth-Shemesh. She was widely worshipped in Palestine, even by Israelites: King Asa's mother worshipped her. Asherah was one of her names

Ruthless Queen (842–837)

News of the murder of King Ahaziah,[1] her son, reached Athaliah, the Queen Mother, in Jerusalem City. She at once made herself the sole ruler of the country. She got rid of all her possible rivals by murdering the royal family—all of them except a little baby boy, Joash, son of the dead King Azariah. When the princes were being hunted out, King Ahaziah's sister, the wife of Jehoiada the priest, kidnapped the little baby, pushed him and his nurse into a bedroom, hid him there and saved him from the fate of all the other princes. For the six years the Queen Mother ruled the country, he was kept hidden in a room in the temple.

A revolt against the Queen Mother and all she stood for was now brewing. It was led by Jehoiada, the priest of the true worship of GOD, the man who had helped to keep King Azariah's little son hidden. When the boy was seven years old, at the New Year Festival, Jehoiada sent for the officers of the royal guards and took them into the temple. He showed them the boy—the murdered king's son and rightful king—and made them swear an oath of loyalty to him. Then he gave them their orders:

'You will strike when the guard is mustered at full strength—that is, on the Sabbath at the changing of the guard when two companies are being marched in force into the temple. At this moment the two companies will form up, with drawn swords, as the young king's bodyguard. Anyone approaching the bodyguard will be killed on the spot. Remember—the king's life is in your hands.'

The officers carried out their orders. The whole guard—those off duty and those on duty—reported to Jehoida the priest and took up their positions, with swords drawn, right across the court from the south wall to the north wall, in front of the altar and the king's rooms. Jehoiada brought the boy out, put the crown on his head and the bracelet on his arm, and anointed him.

The guards and the crowd clapped their hands and shouted 'Long live King Joash!'

The Queen Mother heard the noise of the shouting and went across from the palace to the temple. She stared at the crowd—the new king standing by the column (as was the custom at a coronation), the captains and the trumpeters standing by his side, the common people shouting and blowing trumpets.

'Treason! Treason!' she shouted, tearing her clothes.

'March her out under guard,' commanded Jehoiada, 'and kill her.'

---

[1] See p. 164.

(He had already given orders that her execution should not take place in the temple courts.)

The guards arrested her and killed her as she went through the Cavalry Gate.

The crowd rushed off to the temple of Baal. They smashed the altar and the idols, killed the temple priest in front of the altar and razed the building to the ground.

Jehoiada stationed sentries in the temple. He and the guards' officers escorted the king down from the temple, through the Guards' Gate into the palace, and seated him on the royal throne. The common people welcomed the young king's coronation and there was no violence in the city streets.

Brilliant King (783–742)

King Uzziah was sixteen years of age when he became king. He reigned for fifty-two years in Jerusalem City and made the South into a powerful state.

He put an end to Philistine rebellion. He destroyed three of their great cities—Gath, Jabneh and Ashdod—and built fortified cities in their territory to keep it in order.

He then dealt with the Arabs who lived to the south-east and forced the Ammonites east of Jordan Valley to pay him tribute. He became master of all the country down to the Egyptian border.

He then turned his attention to the questions of defence, water supply and agriculture. He built fortified towers in the capital city itself—at the Corner Gate, the Valley Gate and the Angle—and on his desert borders. He had large herds both in the western plains and in the eastern highlands; he built many cisterns to keep them supplied with water. He was a lover of the soil and had farms and vineyards in the hills and wherever the land could support them, and many farmers to look after them.

He built up a large standing army with the help of one of his commanders, General Hananiah, and of his Civil Service. He overhauled the army's equipment, the soldiers' armour and weapons (shields, spears, helmets, coats of mail, bows and stones for slinging) and engines of war for shooting arrows and throwing heavy stones (these he stationed on his fortified towers and at the corners of the city walls in Jerusalem).

His fame spread far and wide. He was a good king and ruled in the spirit of King David.

But one thing overshadowed his reign. He became a leper and he suffered from it until his death. This forced him to live alone in a separate part of the palace; his son, the Crown Prince Jotham, took charge of the palace and the affairs of state.

Northern Attack (734)

Invasion

King Ahaz had been king for only a year when the two kingdoms, the North and Syria, rose in revolt against the Assyrian empire. They formed an alliance and tried to make him join them. They marched south and attacked Jerusalem City, but he kept them at bay.

Meanwhile he had sent to the Assyrian emperor for help.

'I am your vassal state,' he sent word. 'Come and rescue me from the alliance of Syria and the North. They are besieging me in my capital city.'

He sent a costly present to the emperor—silver and gold from the temple and palace treasuries. The Assyrian emperor was quick to move. He marched west and captured the Syrian capital city, Damascus. The Syrian king had had to march north to defend his own country. He lost his life in the fighting and his people were deported to Mesopotamia.

King Ahaz paid a state visit to the Assyrian emperor in Damascus City. He noted the altar in the pagan temple there and sent a sketch and plan of it to his priest in Jerusalem, Uriah, with orders to make an exact model and have it installed before his return home. When King Ahaz got back from his state visit to the emperor, he inspected the altar and worshipped at it. He had the old bronze altar (which had been left standing between his altar and the shrine) moved out of the way over to the north side. He gave orders that his new altar was to be used for morning and evening worship and for all public sacrifices. He kept the old altar for his own personal use when he wanted to pray to GOD himself. He made other large alterations to the temple.

A Remembered Story

This happened in the early days of the Northern invasion of the South.

The Northerners took many of their Southern kinsfolk prisoner—women and children; they looted the Southern villages and took the loot to Samaria City.

But the prophet Oded met the returning army on the road to the city.

'GOD was angry with our Southern kinsfolk,' he protested. 'That's why you've won; but butchering them was just your ungovernable anger—and that GOD hates. Now you are treating them as if they are your slaves. Have you done nothing wrong yourselves? Send them back home! GOD's as angry with you as with them!'

Four of the Northern leaders stood up to the returning soldiers too.

'We're not having any Southern prisoners here,' they said. 'We don't want any further guilt laid at our doors.'

The soldiers handed over the prisoners and loot to the leaders and representatives of the people.

The four Northern leaders who had led the protest against the brutality of the soldiers took charge of the prisoners. From the loot they clothed those who were naked, put sandals on their feet, fed them and anointed those who were wounded. They put lame people on donkeys and took all the prisoners back to their kinsfolk at Jericho, the City of Palms. Then they themselves went back to their Northern capital, Samaria City.

Besieged City (701)

Earliest Account

King Hezekiah had been king in the South for fourteen years when his country was invaded by the emperor Sennacherib of Assyria. The emperor's army overran all the fortified cities in the country, and he himself established his headquarters in Lachish, a Southern fortified town, thirty miles south-west of Jerusalem City.

King Hezekiah sent a message to the emperor.

'I have done wrong,' he said. 'Withdraw your forces; I will pay whatever tribute you impose upon me.'

The emperor required King Hezekiah to pay a very heavy tribute to him in gold and silver. It was so crippling a fine that King Hezekiah had to hand over all the silver in the temple and palace treasuries—and even break up the temple doors and columns which he himself had decorated with gold.

Assyrian Account

Hezekiah, the Jew, did not submit to me. I besieged forty-six of his strong cities, walled forts and the many small villages around them. I captured them; I built earth-ramps and used battering rams against their walls which the sappers mined and broke through, and then sent my infantry in. I drove out 200, 150 people, young and old, male and female, together with horses, mules, donkeys, camels and cattle beyond counting. All this was my booty.

A relief from the palace of Sennacherib (705–681 B.C.E.) in Nineveh, showing the
surrender of Lachish City in 701 when Assyrian armies reached the Egyptian border.
Contemporary pictorial representations of Old Testament events are extremely rare

King Hezekiah himself I shut up in Jerusalem, his royal residence,
like a bird in a cage. I surrounded him with earth-works in order to stop
anybody leaving the city. His towns (which I had plundered) I took
away from his country and gave them (over) to the kings of Ashdod,
Ekron and Gaza. I reduced his territory but increased his annual tribute.
Later Hezekiah himself . . . sent to me in Nineveh, my royal city, gold and
silver, precious stones, antimony, large cuts of red stone, couches and
arm-chairs (inlaid with ivory), elephant hides, ebony wood, box wood
(and) all kinds of valuable treasures, his (own) daughters, concubines
and male and female musicians. In order to deliver the tribute and do
obeisance as a slave he sent his personal messenger.[1]

Later Account

The Assyrian emperor sent his Chief Administrator with a large army
from Lachish to King Hezekiah in Jerusalem City. He stood by the con-
duit of the Upper Pool on the road to the Fuller's Field.

[1] Based on *Ancient and Near Eastern Texts*, p. 288.

Three officers of state—the Prime Minister, the Secretary of State and the Royal Herald—came out to meet him.

The Chief Administrator spoke to them: 'Tell King Hezekiah: These are the words of the emperor—"Why this boldness? Is mere gossip enough to go on when you're waging war? Whose help gave you courage to rebel against me? Egypt's—that broken stick! Or was it your GOD's help? Why, King Hezekiah has been destroying your GOD's hill shrines and altars all over the country and making people worship only at the altar in this city! Come, I'll make a bet with you— I'll give you two thousand horses if you can find riders for them! But if you're relying on Egyptian horsemen, how do you think you could stop even one of my master's lieutenants?" '

And so he went on.

The Southern officers of state begged him to speak in the official language, Aramaic, not in the local Hebrew dialect.

'We don't want the people on the wall to hear what you say,' they said.

'I wasn't sent to talk just to you and your king,' retorted the Chief Administrator, 'I was sent to talk to the men sitting on the wall—they are the ones who're doomed to starvation.'

The Chief Administrator shouted in the local Hebrew dialect:

'Listen to what the emperor says!' he called. 'These are his words: "Don't let King Hezekiah trick you." He can't rescue you from the emperor's armies. And don't believe him when he talks about trusting GOD to save the city. Take no notice of what he says. "Make peace with me," the emperor tells you, "and surrender. You can go on living as you do now until I come to take you to a richer land where there's grain and wine, bread and vineyards".

'King Hezekiah is talking nonsense when he says GOD will rescue you. Has any other land's god rescued it from Assyrian armies? Where are the gods of Hamath and Arpad now? And where are the gods of Samaria? Did they rescue Samaria? What happened to all these gods gives you no hope that GOD can rescue you!'

There was dead silence on the walls; nobody said anything. King Hezekiah had given orders that nobody should answer.

The three officers of state went back to Hezekiah, with their clothes torn, to report what the Chief Administrator had said.

The king tore his clothes in grief and went into the temple. He sent the Prime Minister, the Secretary of State and some older priests to the prophet Isaiah.

'This is a day of distress, rebuke and disgrace,' was the king's message to the prophet. 'The people are starving to death. Perhaps GOD, whose prophet you are, has heard what the Chief Administrator has been saying (the emperor sent him to mock him) and perhaps he will deal with him. Offer a prayer for those of us who are left.'

'Take this message back to the king,' said Isaiah. 'These are GOD's words: "Don't be frightened at the blasphemy of the emperor's officers".'

The Chief Administrator went back to the emperor and found him besieging the fortress town of Libnah—news had already reached him that he had left Lachish Town and marched north.

Then, suddenly, the emperor raised the siege and marched back to Nineveh.

Last Days

Brave King (640–609)

For more than forty years King Manasseh ruled the country. He had no love for prophets; because he was a puppet of the Assyrian emperor he celebrated pagan religions even in the temple itself. As a later historian summarized it:

'He built again the hill shrines which his father, King Hezekiah, had suppressed and altars to Baal. He made an image of the Canaanite Mother-Goddess, and worshipped the sun, moon and stars. All this went on in the very temple itself.'

His son, King Amon, had a brief reign of two years. His officers assassinated him. But the common people rose against the court conspirators, put them to death and crowned Josiah—the king's son, grandson of King Manasseh and great-grandson of King Hezekiah—as king to take his father's place.

About this time the Assyrian empire began to break up. First Egypt revolted and claimed her independence. Then, away to the north and east of the empire, Medes and Babylonians revolted too, and sacked the capital city of Nineveh in 612. King Josiah could thus make a bid for the independence of his country.

King Josiah was only eight years old when he became king. Eighteen years later—when he was twenty-six—he made up his mind to call his people back to the true worship of GOD. The first thing he did was to repair the temple in Jerusalem. He gave orders to his Secretary of State, Shaphan.

'Go to Hilkiah the priest,' he told him. 'He can use the money in the temple treasury to pay the workmen who are repairing the temple.'

'I have found a law book in the temple,' Hilkiah told Shaphan.

He gave the book to him to read. Shaphan went back to make his report.

'We have taken the money out of the treasury,' he told the king, 'and have paid the workmen with it.'

'Hilkiah gave me a book,' he added, and he began to read from it.

The king listened, and, as Shaphan went on reading, he was deeply disturbed.

'Go back to the temple,' he ordered Hilkiah and four of his officers. 'Pray to GOD for me and the people of this country. Ask him about this book. He must be angry, for our ancestors have taken no notice of what it commands.'

So the five men went to Huldah the prophetess who was living in the Second Quarter of the city and talked to her.

'The king is right,' she said. 'What GOD has to say is this: first to the whole nation—"The neglect of this book and its laws will bring a great disaster upon the whole people"; then to the king himself— "Because you were penitent and humble enough to listen carefully to all the book says, I have heard you. The disaster shall not fall in your time".'

They reported her words.

The king called a great assembly of all the priests and prophets and of the people from the country villages and the city. The Book of the Covenant—the book found in the temple—was read aloud in their presence. Then the king stood by the great bronze pillar and renewed the Covenant with GOD, promising to live in GOD's Way. All the assembly confirmed the Covenant.

Then he commanded that all signs of pagan religion should be removed from the temple. The wooden image of the Mother-Goddess was carried out to Kidron Valley and burned and the ashes scattered over the common graveyard. The rooms occupied by the temple prostitutes were torn down—rooms where the women used to weave vestments for the image of the Mother-Goddess and her worshippers. He closed all the local village hill-shrines throughout the whole country and brought their priests to the city. He destroyed the hill-shrines of the goat-demons which stood outside the entrance of the City Governor's house, on the left as you came in by the city gate. The country priests, however, when they came up to the city, were not allowed to share in the temple sacrifices; they became 'second-class priests', eating unleavened cakes with their kinsmen.

He also destroyed 'The Place of Fire' where child-sacrifices had been made to the Ammonite god, 'The King'—there were to be no more child-sacrifices. He stopped the worship of the Sun God, destroying the statues of horses at the Temple Gate (they stood near the rooms of the chamberlain, among the summer houses) and burning the 'Chariots of the Sun'. He pulled down the roof-shrines on King Ahaz's upper rooms and the altars King Manasseh had built in the two temple courts. He broke them down and scattered their dust in Kidron Valley. He got rid of the pagan shrines which stood east of the city and south of the Olive Hill and which King Solomon had built for the worship of the Mother-Goddess, the Moabite god Chemosh and the Ammonite god 'The King'. He broke down their sacred pillars and sacred poles and filled their places with human bones.

He then issued a royal edict.

'Let us keep the Passover Festival,' he ordered, 'as the Book of the Covenant sets it out. GOD saved us from the Egyptians; he has saved us again today!'

A Passover like this had not been held for a very long time—a great service of the whole country in the temple in Jerusalem City. It was the climax of King Josiah's reformation of the religion of his people.

In 609 the Egyptian Pharaoh marched north to help the Assyrian emperor against the rebels. King Josiah threw his army across his path, blocking the Megiddo Pass. In the battle that followed, King Josiah was killed. His officers carried his body in a chariot from Megiddo to Jerusalem City and buried him in his own grave. The citizens crowned his son, Jehoahaz, king in his place.

Fall of the City (609–586)

The new king, Jehoahaz, was only twenty-three, and he had been king only a few months when the Pharaoh had him deported to the north, to prevent his being a real king in his own country and causing trouble there. He demanded a heavy tribute from the South and crowned Eliakim—another son of King Josiah, an older brother of the deposed king—in his place, changing his name to Jehoiakim. Then he moved Jehoahaz to Egypt where he died a prisoner.

King Jehoiakim paid very heavy tribute to the Egyptians—so heavy that he had to use a graded tax to raise the money from farmers and merchants; the money in the palace and temple treasuries was not enough. He was Pharaoh's vassal until the new Babylonian empire (which had succeeded the Assyrian empire) defeated Egypt at the battle of Carchemish three years later (605).

Then the Babylonian armies marched south to secure their hold on the plain between Jerusalem City and the Great Sea. For three years King Jehoiakin was forced to be the vassal of the Babylonian emperor. Then he revolted. But he was attacked by raiding guerrilla bands from the

Above Babylon in ruins: the palace of Nebuchadnezzar, the Babylonian emperor (605–562 B.C.E.), now only an expanse of littered brick

Below Babylon in splendour: a reconstruction of the Ishtar Gate of the city

surrounding countries, sent by the Babylonians to harass him until they could strike with their regular armies.

Then King Jehoiakim died and was succeeded by his son, King Jehoiachin, a young man of eighteen. He had only been three months on the throne when the Babylonian armies marched south again and besieged Jerusalem City. The Babylonian emperor himself joined his armies while the siege was on. So Jehoiachin surrendered (597).

The emperor deported him, the Queen Mother and the harem, the court officials and leading citizens, seven thousand soldiers and a thousand craftsmen to Babylon. To act as regent in the deposed king's place, he chose the king's uncle, Mattaniah—a young man of twenty one—changing his name to Zedekiah.

King Zedekiah had been regent nine years when, pressed by extreme nationalists, he too rebelled against his Babylonian overlords.

In January 587 the Babylonian armies marched south to attack Jerusalem City. They camped outside the city and built a siege wall all round it, to prevent anybody leaving or entering it. The siege lasted till July 586. At the end of the siege, no food was left; starvation stared everybody in the face.

On 9 July the city walls were breached. In the darkness of the night, the king and his troops slipped through the King's Garden, out by the gate 'Between the Two Walls' (near Siloam Pool) and made for the Arabah Valley south of the Salt Sea. The Babylonian troops were busy occupying the city. But when they discovered the king's escape, they went after him and caught him in the flat country near Jericho City in the Jordan Valley. They took him before the Babylonian emperor in Riblah in the far north where he was court-martialed. The king's two sons were executed in his presence, he himself was blinded, handcuffed and deported to Babylon where he remained a prisoner for the rest of his life.

On 7 August the Babylonian commander-in-chief entered Jerusalem City and burned down the temple and the palace and every important house. He then ordered the soldiers to break down the city walls. He deported all the people who mattered—survivors of the siege and deserters to the invading forces alike. He left only the peasants to look after vineyard and field.

He then looted the temple; the bronze columns (known as 'Jachin' and 'Boaz'), the stands, and the great bronze bowl (called 'The Sea') were all broken up and the metal carried away. He melted down pots, shovels, snuffers, incense dishes, all the bronze vessels used in worship, and took away the gold and silver (of which the firepans and bowls were made) as ingots. Everything was looted.

He then rounded up representative citizens—from the priesthood and the army and the common people—to be executed as a warning to the whole nation: the two most important priests, Seraiah and Zephaniah, and three doorkeepers, the chamberlain in charge of the troops, five members of the King's Council who were discovered still hiding in the city, and the Army Secretary in charge of mobilization; and sixty common citizens found at random in the city. He deported all these to Riblah, where the emperor had them flogged and executed.

Some thousands of Southerners were exiled to Babylon, far from their own country.

Murder of the Governor[1]

The Babylonians appointed Gedaliah as governor—many people, of course, were still left in the South. He set up his headquarters in the small town of Mizpah, 'Watch Tower', some eight miles north of the ruined city. Army officers and their men who had escaped to the hills as guerrillas came to swear allegiance to their new governor.

'Don't be frightened of the Babylonian officials here,' he told them. 'We have to live as vassals of the empire. If we go quietly about our work, everything will be all right.'

But peace was soon shattered—by a man called Ishmael, a fanatical member of the exiled royal family. He broke into the governor's residence and assassinated Gedaliah—and fellow-citizens and Babylonian officers who happened to be with him. Then, in panic, army officers and citizens fled to Egypt—they knew the sort of revenge the Babylonian authorities would take.

King in Exile

In March 561—after thirty seven years of imprisonment—King Jehoiachin's fortune changed. In that month a new emperor ascended the Babylonian throne. He summoned King Jehoiachin into his presence, and spoke kindly to him. He allowed him to live in the palace. So King Jehoiachin changed his prison dress for royal robes. From this time on, he dined at the royal table; he was given regular daily allowances from the Babylonian treasury.

---

[1] See the fuller account on p. 257.

The New Lawbook

We have already read of the finding of a lawbook in the temple (p. 179). We know something of what it contained, for it was used in the writing of *Deuteronomy*, which was an expansion of it.

The last hundred years before the fall of Jerusalem had been a frustrating time for all who cared for the traditions of Moses—and a dangerous time too. The North was an Assyrian province; the South, in all but name, was an Assyrian province too. King Manasseh had given up any attempt to carry on the old traditions. Loyal followers of the old worship of GOD were suppressed.

A group of loyal worshippers of GOD went into hiding, and began to plan for the time when there would again be a loyal king on the throne. They drew up a 'Plan of Reform' which they hoped would one day become the law of the land. The 'Plan' itself had perhaps a long history behind it; a rough sketch of it may have been drawn up in the North in the dark days before the fall of Samaria, its capital city, when true worshippers of GOD there were facing as grave a situation as the South were now facing under King Manasseh. When Samaria fell, a copy was taken to the South, and there it became the 'Plan of Reform', the law book, which was later found in the temple when King Josiah began to restore it to something of its old glory. The selections from it which follow show what kind of 'Plan' it was—a recall of the people to the Covenant of Moses.

To make this very clear, the planners wrote their 'Plan of Reform' as speeches put into the mouth of Moses, imagining him making them to the Hebrew people before they crossed Jordan River on their way to the highlands. This was their way of saying 'We are not telling you anything new; we are calling you to be real followers of Moses'.

You must love GOD

Listen, you who are GOD's People: GOD, our God, is one GOD: you must love him with all you are—with your heart, your soul, your strength.

Don't despise GOD's kindness

GOD is leading you to your homeland—and a fine big country it is. Rivers and streams and springs gush out in the valleys and on the mountainsides; everywhere there is wheat and barley, grapes and figs and pomegranates and olives and honey. There will be no desert rations there—you won't lack anything. There's iron in the rocks and copper in the hills. You will eat as much as you want and thank GOD for giving you such a wonderful country.

And that's the danger point. Take care that you don't then forget GOD or begin to disobey him. When you live in your fine houses, remember all he has done for you—rescuing you from Egypt; leading your march across the vast and frightening desert, with its poisonous snakes and scorpions and its dry and waterless tracks; getting you water from the flinty cliffs and feeding you with desert 'manna' (your ancestors never knew such food). All through these years he was caring for you, keeping you humble and testing you. Don't start being proud and talking about your capturing this wonderful country 'in our own strength'. Remember that GOD gave you whatever strength you needed. He gave his promise to your ancestors; today he is keeping his promise. I warn you: if you forget GOD and start worshipping other 'gods', you will meet with disaster—the same disaster that has overtaken the tribes who were living here before you. And disaster will have only one cause—your disobedience.

Only one centre of worship

The people who lived here before you worshipped their 'gods' on high mountains and beneath trees—you must not copy them. You must wipe all this out—break the altars down, smash the stone pillars, burn their sacred poles and cut down the images of their 'gods'. Not even a memory of all this must remain.

When you worship GOD, you must only worship him in the one place he will choose, from all the tribal centres, as his home, where his name is to be known. You must bring all your sacrifices there; and there, together with your families, you must eat the sacred meal in GOD's presence, happy in the celebration of any success he may have given you.

You must not worship GOD as we are now worshipping him here in the desert, where every man does what he thinks right. For here we are not yet living in our homeland. But when you have crossed Jordan River and settled down in your homeland, and the war, with all its dangers, is over, it will be very different. You must bring your sacrifices (note what I am telling you) to the one place GOD chooses as his home, and there you shall enjoy yourselves in his presence—you and your families and your farm-workers and the priests (these, unlike you, have no land of their own). You are not to offer sacrifices to GOD at just any place that catches your eye. You must, as I am now telling you, offer your sacrifices only at the one place in your homeland GOD chooses.

You must carry out these orders to the letter. You must not copy the customs of the country which will be your home. You have not taken their place just to start doing what they do, asking how they worshipped their 'gods' and copying them. That's not the way to worship GOD—he detests all that goes on in the old temples. Why, they even burn their own children—and think that that is real religion!

There must be no sacred pole standing by GOD's altar, nor any stone pillar. That's the very sort of thing he loathes.

Look after the poor

At the end of every seven years, there must be a cancelling of debts—GOD's 'Cancellation of Debts'. This is what you must do: if a man has lent money to a fellow-citizen, he must cross the debt out—he mustn't try to get him to pay up. He can make a foreigner pay up; he mustn't make a fellow-citizen do so. Indeed, there shouldn't be any poor people at all in the country—GOD has given you enough for everybody (that is, if you listen to what he wants and do what he tells you). GOD will give you prosperity, just as he said he would. You can lend money to foreigners, if you want to, but there's to be no borrowing from them. You can govern others; you are not to be governed by them.

But if there happens to be a poor man among you—one of your own countrymen, for example, in one of your own towns—you mustn't be selfish or mean; you must be open-handed, lending him whatever he needs. And there's to be no jiggery-pokery, either—turning mean just when the seven years are nearly over and refusing to give a needy fellow-citizen any help at all. He will appeal to GOD, and you will be known for what you are—a rebel against GOD. Help him, and help him generously and don't begrudge him anything. It's treating people like this that will make your country really prosperous. There will always be some poor people about, of course; that's why I'm telling you to be generous to your fellow-countrymen—to any who are needy or poor.

And you must deal with slavery in the same way, too—where an Israelite man or woman, one of your fellow-citizens, is sold to you as a slave. What must happen is this: he works for you for six years; in the seventh year you must set him free. What is more: when you set him free, see that he doesn't go away empty-handed. Treat him generously —give him a present from your flock or threshing-floor or winepress. GOD has been good to you; be good to him. Don't begrudge him his freedom. He has worked hard for you for six whole years—and only cost you half of what you would have had to pay a hired man; and you've got GOD's blessing as well. You know what it feels like to be a slave—you were slaves once in Egypt and GOD set you free. That's why I am talking to you like this.

If your slave doesn't want to leave you—perhaps he has grown fond of you and your family or he enjoys working for you—that's another matter. He must be marked on the ear, and then he stays your slave until he dies. You must treat men and women alike in this matter.

GOD's Way is for king and citizen alike

When you are settled in your homeland, you may want to follow the practice of surrounding peoples and have a monarchy instead of a tribal league. This is a perfectly proper kind of government. But no foreigner must ever be king; GOD will choose one of your fellow-countrymen, and you must make him king. But when he's elected king, he must not try to ape foreign kings—no large cavalry divisions (why, he would have to send fellow-countrymen to Egypt to buy war-horses—Egypt indeed!—hasn't GOD forbidden his people ever to go back along that desert road?)—no harem (that will make him forget GOD all right), no vast personal wealth.

When he becomes king, he must make a copy in a scroll of all I am now telling you (he can write it out from the priests' copy), keep it by him and make a habit of studying it. He will learn there what worshipping GOD really means—obeying him and living in his Way. That will keep him from ever lording it over his fellow-countrymen, and help him to make his rule like GOD's rule. That will make his reign long and his dynasty secure.

Treat people as persons

You must always help your fellow-countrymen.

For example: if you come across his ox or sheep or goat straying, you mustn't just pass by and do nothing about it. Take it back to him. If he lives a long way off—or you don't know whose it is—take the animal home with you and keep it until it is claimed; then let him have it back. It doesn't matter what it is that he has lost—his donkey, his overcoat, anything. You mustn't just pass by. If you ever find his donkey or ox lying in the road, don't go on as if it didn't concern you; give him a hand to get it on its feet again.

If you come across a bird's nest—either in a tree or on the ground—when you're out walking, and you notice eggs or young in the nest and the mother-bird sitting on them, you must leave the mother-bird alone. You can take the young birds, if you like; you must let the mother-bird go free. This, too, is something you must do, if you want to live long in your homeland.

Again, when you build a house, build a parapet round the flat roof. Somebody may one day go up on to the roof; if he falls over into the street to his death, that will then be his carelessness and not your fault. Your family cannot then be held responsible.

Generosity and justice for everybody

You must not take a man's mill or even his mill-stone as security for debt. That is to take his very livelihood away from him.

When you lend anything to one of your fellow-countrymen, you must not force your way into his house to take something as security. Stand outside, and let the man himself bring his security out to you. If he belongs to the poorly-paid 'lower classes', you must not keep the cloak he gives you as security all night; give it back to him before sunset so that he may sleep in it—and feel grateful to you. That's what GOD thinks is the 'right' thing to do.

You are not to treat a poor hired servant brutally (though he may belong to the 'lower classes'); and it doesn't matter whether he is a fellow-countryman or a resident-alien in your town. Pay him his wages promptly at the end of the day—and before sunset. Remember that he has little money and the day's wages mean everything to him. If you treat him wrongly, he will appeal to GOD and that will mark you down for what you are—a wicked man.

Capital punishment can be inflicted on a man only for a crime he himself has committed. You must execute the man himself—not his father or his son in his stead.

Don't exploit a resident-alien or a fatherless child and rob him of his legal rights; and you must never take the cloak of a widow as security for debt. You know what it feels like to be a slave—somebody who has no one to stand up for him. Don't forget Egypt and the way GOD rescued you. This lies behind all I am telling you to do.

And let your generosity be real down-to-earth generosity. For example: sometimes at harvest you overlook a sheaf of corn and leave it in the field. When you find out what you've done, don't go back for it. Some resident-alien or orphan or widow will find it a god-send. This is what GOD wants and he will bless you for it. Or again: when you shake the fruit off your olive-trees, don't shake the branches a second time. Let the resident-aliens, the orphans, the widows have the fruit that remains. And do the same when you clip the grapes off your vines; don't pick the branches twice—let the resident-aliens, the orphans, the widows have the grapes that remain. Remember what it was like to be an Egyptian slave.

Limits of citizenship

Nobody whose mother is a foreigner can be admitted to GOD's assembly—nor any of his descendants for ten generations.

No Ammonites or Moabites can be admitted to GOD's assembly—nor any of their descendants for ten generations. The reason is this: on the march across the desert to Jordan River, you were in need of food and water; but these peoples, instead of helping you, hired a foreign prophet to bring a curse upon you. GOD, indeed, didn't listen to him but turned his curse into a blessing, because he cared for you. So you are never at any time to help them or do them good.

But you are not to despise the Edomites (they are your kinsmen) or the Egyptians (you once lived as resident-aliens in their country). The great-grandchildren of Edomites and Egyptians and their descendants can be admitted to GOD's assembly.

Thanking GOD

Three times each year you must meet—not anywhere but in the one place GOD has chosen—to thank him for his kindness to you: at the Pilgrim Festival of Cakes-made-without-yeast, at the Pilgrim Festival of Weeks, and at the Pilgrim Festival of Tents. You must not come to these festivals empty-handed; every man must give what he can, remembering how GOD has helped him. Treat April as a special month by celebrating Passover at the Pilgrim Festival of Cakes-made-without-yeast. For it was in April that GOD rescued you from Egypt. Offer as your 'Passover' sacrifice a lamb or a kid or a calf, and eat cakes made without yeast—iron rations that will remind you of the panic of that night of escape and will keep it in your mind as long as you live.

Count seven weeks from the time you began reaping the standing corn; that will give you the date for the Pilgrim Festival of Weeks to begin. Make your gift match GOD's kindness to you, and enjoy your worship of him. You must not come alone, but bring your children, slaves, the priests, foreigners, fatherless children and the widows of your town.

At harvest time, when you are cleaning your threshing-floors and wine-presses, meet again for a whole week to celebrate the Pilgrim Festival of Tents and thank GOD for blessing your farming and your business. Again, do not come alone, but bring your children, your slaves, the priests, foreigners, fatherless children and widows. You are to have a thoroughly happy time.

The Harvest Festival

When you've settled down in your homeland, take some of the produce of the first harvest of the year and carry it in a basket to the place GOD has chosen for his worship.

At the harvest festival you shall always make this statement of your faith: 'My ancestors were a small company of homeless nomads who entered Egypt and lived there as resident-aliens. We became a strong and large tribe. The Egyptians gave us a hard time and treated us brutally and forced us to work as slave labourers. We appealed to GOD, our ancestral God. He took note of us and saw what a brutal life we were forced to live as slaves. He rescued us with terrifying deeds of violent strength—with many signs and wonders—and led us here to this rich and fertile homeland of ours. Look! I bring the harvest of the soil which you O GOD, have given me.'

Put down your basket in GOD's presence, and bow in reverence before him.

And then—because GOD has given you all these good things—enjoy yourselves, not alone by yourselves but with all your family and the priests and the resident-aliens who live in your neighbourhood.

A final word

All these things I have told you to do are not beyond your powers or out of your reach. They are not, as it were, 'high up in the sky'; you can't say 'Who can get up so high and tell us what they are all about and make them plain to us so that we can do something about them?' Nor are they, as it were, foreign laws from some country far beyond the sea; you can't say 'Who can sail across the seas for us and translate them into our language and make them plain to us so that we can do something about them?' GOD's Way is right within your reach—you can talk about it, understand it and walk in it.

Not the End but the Beginning

9 July 586 was the Black Day of Israelite history. The historians describe what happened on that day and tell us a little about the twenty years that followed. Then silence. We do not come again on any contemporary historical records for more than 140 years. What was there to write down?

Many thought that the end had come—there was nothing left to live for. But there were others whose trust in God was deeper and for whom the words of men like Amos and Jeremiah (now written down in scrolls) began to take on a new meaning. For them the terrifying disaster of political extinction was not the end; it was rather a strange and unexpected beginning. They recovered their sense of God's presence, and began to look forward to new life in the old homeland.

Historians reckon that about 250,000 people were living in Palestine at the time of the fall of the city. Many escaped to Egypt and elsewhere; this was the beginning of the dispersion of the Jewish people throughout the world. Several thousands were deported to Babylon—probably much less than 10,000, a figure given in one of their later accounts. But it was among these few thousand that life was reborn.

The deportees in Babylon were allowed considerable freedom to live their own lives in their own community, to meet for worship and to carry on trade; and they kept in touch with their fellow-countrymen in Palestine.

Life for those who still lived in Jerusalem and its surrounding villages was pitiful. The city itself was in ruins; temple, buildings, city wall were a mass of rubble. A contemporary poem (from *Lamentations*) paints a vivid picture—

> City gates gone,
>   only rubble and broken bars;
> king and government in exile,
>   everyone for himself;
> no prophets any more,
>   no visions of GOD!

There were no priests and no temple. All the hopes of the Israelite people in GOD's purpose—that Palestine should be the land of his people—were destroyed.

People had no heart—and no resources—to start building again; the ruins were to lie there, little changed, for more than sixty years. They were merely a neglected part of the Babylonian empire, at the mercy of a hostile governor in Samaria.

In 538, a great upheaval took place in international affairs. The Babylonian empire collapsed; the Persian empire, under its remarkable leader, Cyrus, took its place. The rise of Cyrus to power brought new hope: was not GOD at work in this imperial upheaval? Was not this the signal for their return home?

This lively hope was the theme of the poems of 'The Prophet of the Exile' (see p. 285). So it happened, and a few thousand began the long trek home.

Those who returned home in 538, full of high hopes, soon faced disillusion. The immensity of the task that faced them—the sheer work of rebuilding houses and temple—overwhelmed them. Some twenty years went by before, fired by two prophets, they had vigour enough to rebuild the temple, but even this was a 'poverty-stricken affair'. They had, of course, already rebuilt many houses; but much of the city and its surrounding wall lay still in ruins.

It was some fifty years later—in 444—that their first outstanding leader arose—Nehemiah, a high official at the Persian court. He spent two terms as governor (444 and 432). Some forty years later—in 398—another Persian official, Ezra, was made 'Commissioner for Jewish Religious Affairs', and came, with royal authority, to complete Nehemiah's work. Nehemiah rebuilt the city; Ezra re-established the religious life of the people. Both kept diaries. Here is what they had to say.

Nehemiah (444–432 B.C.E.)

News from Jerusalem

I was a royal cupbearer and in December of the year 445 I was in the fortress in the city of Susa, the winter residence of the Persian emperor, when Hanani my brother and some of my fellow-countrymen arrived with news from Palestine. I asked them how people were faring there and what Jerusalem City was like.

'There's been a great disaster,' they told me, 'and the survivors are in trouble. The walls of the city have been levelled to the ground and the city gates burnt.'

I broke down and cried. I spent several days mourning and praying.

Emperor's Commissioner

It was now April. One day I took wine to the emperor (the empress was with him) and was offering it to him. I was feeling very unhappy. It was forbidden to show grief in the royal presence; but the emperor noticed something in my looks.

'You aren't ill, are you?' he asked. 'Why are you looking so depressed? You seem very upset these days.'

I felt afraid to tell him. But I spoke up.

'Long live your Majesty!' I said, 'I can't help feeling upset. My family graves are in disrepair and my city's gates have been burned down.'

'Well, what do you want me to do for you?' he asked.

'If it pleases your Majesty and your Majesty thinks well of me,' I said, 'send me back to my own city where my ancestors are buried. Give me authority to rebuild it.'

Jerusalem in flames ▶

'How long will you be away?' he asked. 'When will you get back?'

I told him and he was gracious enough to send me as governor of Jerusalem City.

'If your Majesty pleases,' I said to him, 'give me your written authority to present to the governor of Beyond-Euphrates for any help I may need. And I shall need written authority to present to the Warden of the Royal Forest to bring timber for the rebuilding of the gates of the Temple Fortress and for my own Residence.'

The emperor gave me an escort of army officers and cavalry. My coming displeased Sanballat the governor of Samaria (he was in temporary charge of Jerusalem City) and a Persian official, an Ammonite called Tobiah. They didn't want anybody to come and take over the cause of the Israelites.

Inspection of the city

So I came to the city.

For three days I stared at the devastation.

On the third night, I got up. I told nobody about my plans. I ordered two or three men from my escort to come with me and I rode out on the only animal there was—my own. In the darkness I went out by the Valley Gate in the west to the Dragon Spring and the Dung Gate in the south which led out to the refuse dump where once human sacrifices had been made. I inspected the ruins of the city walls and the burned gates from the outside, but at the Dung Gate I had to follow the eastern walls inside the city—the cliffs fell steeply into the Kidron Valley. I went on to the Fountain Gate and the King's Pool. Beyond this my animal could not get through. In the darkness I went down into the valley and looked up at the ruined walls. I went back by the way I'd come and entered the city again by the Valley Gate. And so home. The city officials had no idea what I'd been up to. I had said nothing to them or to the workmen who were to help me in rebuilding the city.

I now called them together.

'You see the devastation of the city,' I told them. 'Let us start the rebuilding of the walls.'

I made it quite clear to them that God had given me this work to do. They all agreed and began with a good heart.

Three men opposed us—the two I've mentioned and Geshem the Arab, the governor of Idumea, the old land of Edom to the east.

They spread vicious rumours about us.

'What do you think you're up to?' they said. 'Starting a rebellion?'

'You've got nothing to do with this,' I told them. 'This is God's work; we are his servants. We're going on with the rebuilding.'

◄ The Ishtar Gate, Babylon

From an old labour register

A record was kept of the men who worked on the rebuilding and the work each did.

Everybody took part from the High Priest himself to farmers from neighbouring villages—and girls, the daughters of one of the city magistrates. Men from Jericho and Tekoa (though the gentry here at first resented taking orders as common workmen) and Mizpah and Gibeon came along. Magistrates worked alongside caretakers. Goldsmiths, perfumers and merchants gave a hand.

Most of the men were organized in gangs to rebuild the city gates or particular stretches of the city wall. But some men preferred to rebuild that part of the wall opposite their own houses.

Here is a list of the city gates that were rebuilt, beginning from the north and going round the city anti-clockwise: Sheep Gate, Fish Gate, Old Gate, Valley Gate, Dung Gate, Fountain Gate, The Angle, Water Gate, Horse Gate, East Gate, Muster Gate.

Trouble from outside

So we went on rebuilding the wall. We built the whole length of it but only to half its proper height. The people worked with a will.

The governor of Samaria, Sanballat, and Tobiah the Ammonite and representatives from Ammon and the Philistine city of Ashdod were in conference when news reached them that the city walls were actually being rebuilt and the great gaps in the wall closed. This made them bitterly angry. They put their heads together to plot a military attack on the city and throw us into confusion. But we prayed to God and posted a twenty four hour guard on the walls.

We had trouble with some of the workers. They went on strike. They were actually singing a strike song—

> We can never, never
> build the wall—
> mountains, mountains of rubble,
> no strength left to shift it.

Our enemies were talking too.

'We'll steal secretly into the city,' they were saying, 'and catch them unawares. We'll have them dead and the work stopped in no time.'

Our countrymen living in enemy territory came to us again and again.

'They're calling up their men from all over the country,' they warned us.

So we doubled our guard. We stationed spearmen in the exposed open places behind the wall and called out the citizens with their swords, spears and bows.

'No panicking,' I said. 'Remember God's terrible power and fight for your fellow-citizens, your families and your homes!'

Our enemies soon discovered that their secret plot was public news and that their plans were now useless. Each of us could take up his work on the wall again.

But we didn't relax our guard. We worked in shifts, half of us working on the wall, half of us armed and standing guard. The leaders stood behind the countrymen who had come in to work on the wall. We saw to it as well that all the men carrying loads were armed—they worked with one hand and carried a sword in the other—and that the builders wore their swords like soldiers. The bugler stood beside me.

These were the orders of the day: 'We are scattered over the whole city, and we are far from one another on the wall. Rally at the sound of the bugle—it will be blown where fighting has broken out. Our God will fight for us.'

So we went on with the rebuilding. Half of us were armed from dawn till the stars came out.

The men from the villages used to come into the city each day and go home at night. This was becoming dangerous. So I issued further orders: men from the villages—and their servants—must spend the night in the city; they can carry on their work as usual in the daytime, but through the night they must help in guarding the walls.

None of us ever took our clothes off; we kept our weapons at the ready all the time.

Trouble in the city

Then we had trouble between rich and poor—between wealthy citizens who had made their money in Babylon and brought it back with them and the peasants who had been left to carry on when the city fell. The poor peasants were full of angry protests.

'We are reduced to giving our children in pledge as slaves,' some said, 'just to buy corn to keep alive.'

'And we,' said others, 'we've got to mortgage our fields and vineyards and houses to get corn. There isn't enough food—that's the trouble.'

'And we've had to borrow money to pay the royal taxes,' said others.

The burden of their complaint was that there was no real sharing.

'We're as hungry as they are,' they said. 'Our children are no different from theirs! Yet we have to sell our children as slaves—some of our girls are slaves already. And we can't do anything about it—these tycoons have taken our land.'

This made me very angry.

I thought the matter over, and then charged them, at a public meeting, with taking interest from their fellow-citizens.

'We've done what we could to bring you back from foreign slavery,' I told them, 'and now we're going into the slave trade ourselves!'

There was dead silence. They hadn't anything to say.

'It's a dreadful thing you're doing,' I went on. 'Doesn't our religion mean anything to you? Are you going to make us the laughing-stock of the world? I myself have been lending money and corn to these needy people. Drop this business of taking persons as pledges for debt. Give them back their land you've taken, and pay them back the interest you've been charging.'

'We'll give them back whatever we've taken from them,' they said at last. 'We'll do what you say—we'll charge no interest.'

I called the priests and made the men swear an oath to do what they had promised. I shook my cloak as though I had been carrying something in it and was emptying it on the ground.

'May God throw you away—just like that,' I said, 'if you go back on any of your promises!'

They did as I ordered.

My own practice

I have just mentioned my own practice. Let me say something about it.

There had been governors before me. All of them had taxed the people heavily in money and kind. Minor officials had been petty tyrants. My religion meant something to me and I never did that sort of thing. I bought no land while I was governor—I had enough to do with the building of the wall. I actually used my own servants only for work on the wall.

Besides this, a hundred and fifty people shared my table—common people and officials as well as refugees from abroad. Every day we had to find oxen, sheep, fowls, skins of wine—and I could afford to do this. But I refused to take the official allowance—my people were suffering too much.

Remember, O my God, what I've tried to do for these people!

Trouble again

The wall was now finished. All the places where it had been breached had been dealt with. Only the doors of the gateways had not been set up.

News of all this reached our enemies.

Sanballat and Geshem tried to draw me into a trap.

'Meet us for peace talks,' was their first message. 'We suggest

Kephirah village in the Ono plain on the road to Joppa.'

I saw through their cunning.

'I have important work to do,' I replied. 'I can't go down to the plain. Why should the work stop just to meet you?'

Four times they pressed me to meet them there; four times I said No. They tried another trick.

Sanballat sent one of his officers with an open letter: 'There are rumours in the surrounding countries (Geshem confirms this) that you and the citizens of Jerusalem are plotting rebellion. That's why you are rebuilding the city walls. Rumour has it that you intend to proclaim yourself king, and that prophets are proclaiming it openly on your streets. You know rumours like this get round to the emperor. Be sensible and let us talk it all over.'

'There are no such rumours,' I replied. 'You've invented them.'

They were only trying to scare me.

I just worked all the harder.

Sanballat tried to trap me again.

We had a man called Shemaiah, a false prophet with contacts abroad, detained in house-arrest. I went to his house one day.

'Let us meet in the temple,' he said, 'and have the doors shut. Men have been sent to assassinate you, and they'll do it under cover of darkness.'

'Should such a man as I run away?' I said. 'Would any man in my place go into the temple just to save his life? I stay where I am.'

It was clear he had been bribed by Tobiah and Sanballat; God had not sent him to me. They had hired him to try to frighten me and bring me into bad odour with the people and hold me up to ridicule.

Remember Tobiah and Sanballat, O my God, and all their deeds—and Noadiah the prophetess and the other prophets who wanted to frighten me from doing my duty.

So in October 444—in fifty two days—the city wall was finished. It was reported to our enemies in Samaria. News about what we had done spread, too, throughout the surrounding countries. There, people didn't think much of the citizens of Samaria—they had lost much of the reputation they once had—but they respected our religious convictions.

Quite a number of the Jewish nobles in the city were bound in loyalty to Tobiah the Ammonite who had married into the family of one of the 'Founding Fathers', those who had come back to Palestine a hundred years before. (His son also had married the daughter of one of the builders of the wall.) Letters passed between these nobles and Tobiah. All I did was reported to him and the nobles spoke well of him to me. He wrote to me, but all he was concerned with was scaring me off the work I was doing.

Excavated walls of old Jerusalem. The wall built by Nehemiah is on the earthen bank at the top left of the picture

Dedication of the walls

The walls had now been built, the city gates finished and regular gatekeepers appointed.

I now handed over the control of the city to my brother Hanani and to Captain Hananiah, the governor of the Fortress—a man whose loyalty to God could be trusted more than that of many others.

The city covered a large area and the citizens were too few to defend it properly; houses for the people had yet to be built. So I gave special instructions about the city's safety: the city gates were not to be left open during the heat of the day when the guards were taking their siesta; they must be kept shut and barred. Each citizen was to be held responsible for sentry-duty or for guarding that part of the wall opposite his own house.

I called a full conference of officials and people. They decided that for the present only one in ten of the citizens should come to live in the city; the rest must still stay in the villages round about. All the leaders, of course, had to live in the city. The others to live in the city were chosen by lots or were volunteers. The volunteers were cheered by the people.

Then we held a great procession to dedicate the city walls. We divided ourselves into two great companies—one went southwards round the walls and the other northward. We started and finished in the temple. We sang and offered sacrifices—a very happy company, men and women and boys and girls. The joy of the city was public news in the surrounding countries.

Religious reform (432)

Twelve years went by.

Eliashib, the High Priest, was now a very old man. He was related by marriage to Tobiah the Ammonite and let him live in the disused tithe-room in the temple.

I was not in the city at the time. In the year 434 I went back to report to the emperor. I stayed there some time and then asked the emperor's permission to visit Jerusalem again.

I discovered Tobiah living in the tithe-room. I was very angry and pitched all his furniture out in the street. I re-established the tithe-system and rededicated the tithe-room to its proper use.

The whole organization of the temple had collapsed. The temple care-takers (whose wages were payed from tithes) had had to earn their own living by farm work. I put all this right.

Remember me, O my God, and this work I did—don't let my work for you be forgotten.

I next tackled the question of the Sabbath. I found that the Sabbath was not being kept. Farmers were treading wine-presses; loading grain on donkeys and driving them into the city; and the markets were open—all on the Sabbath. Tyrian merchants were bringing fish and all kinds of wares into the city and selling them—all on the Sabbath. I warned the people and argued with the leaders.

I put this right. The city gates were to be closed at sunset on Friday night, the beginning of the Sabbath; they were to remain shut until the Sabbath was over. I stationed my own officers at the gates to see that there was no traffic through them while the Sabbath lasted. The merchants started lodging just under the walls outside the city. I threatened to arrest them if they stayed there. That settled that.

Remember this work of mine, O my God, and have mercy on me according to the greatness of your steadfast love.

There was a third matter to put right.

I noticed how many mixed marriages there were. When the exiles first came back, there were very few Jewish girls; so even Jewish priests had married girls from Ashdod, the Philistine city, and from Ammon and Moab. The children spoke the Ashdod or Ammonite or Moabite language—they hadn't even learned to speak Hebrew. I condemned all this—and even lost my temper with them, man-handling some of them.

'No more mixed marriages,' I ordered. 'It doesn't matter what you have to say—marrying foreign women is disloyalty to God.'

I was having no more quislings in the city. I deported the grandson of Eliashib the High Priest—he had married Sanballat's daughter.

Remember them, O my God, to their shame.

So I got rid of every foreign influence in the city.

Remember this, O my God, to my credit.

Ezra (398 B.C.E.)

Royal Commissioner

Artaxerxes II, the Persian emperor, appointed Ezra the priest Commissioner for Religious Affairs for all the Jewish people.

In the year 397, Ezra with other leading Jews, paid a visit to Jerusalem City—the journey took him five months. On the way, he stayed in Ctesiphon, on the Tigris River, and met the Jewish community there.

Renewing the Covenant

We reached Jerusalem, and three days after I arrived I inspected the temple. I was given an account of the enormous wealth the returned exiles had brought back and handed over.

The people gathered in a packed crowd in the Water Gate Square. They asked me to get the scroll of the Law from the temple to read it to them.

I stood on a wooden pulpit (made specially for this occasion) well above the crowd, and when I began to read the whole crowd stood. I read from the scroll, facing the Water Gate Square, from early morning till noon. The crowd listened quietly.

Officials, who stood by me on my right and on my left, helped the people to follow what I was reading, summarizing and explaining it, passage by passage.

The people wept when they understood what the Law said.

'No weeping or mourning,' I said. 'This is a day holy to GOD. Go home and have a good meal—don't forget to share it with those who are starving. Remember, GOD's joy is your strength.'

The people went home in great happiness.

Next day, the heads of families and temple officials met with me to study the scroll in detail. We found the regulations about the Festival of Tents which ought to be celebrated just at this time of the year. We decided to hold the Festival together. The people went out into the countryside and cut down leafy branches to make tents. These they set up on their flat roofs, in their courtyards, in the temple courts and in the Water Gate Square and the Ephraim Gate Square.

Each day of the Festival—it lasted a week—I read to them the scroll of the Law. On the eighth day we held a great religious service, just as the scroll set it out.

Mixed marriages

It was then reported to me that mixed marriages were still taking place. I was appalled at this news and spent the day in confession and prayer.

A great crowd gathered outside the temple.

Then Shecaniah—who himself had married a foreign girl—spoke to me.

'We have broken faith with God,' he said. 'But we can put it right. Let us make a covenant with God to divorce our foreign wives. This is your task, and we will stand by you in this.'

So they all took an oath.

A proclamation was issued calling a great assembly in the city; anyone not coming within three days would have his property forfeited and himself excommunicated.

The crowd gathered in the open square before the temple. They were rather nervous, both because of the reason for the meeting and because it was raining heavily.

I addressed the crowd and told them what we had decided about mixed marriages.

'We agree with you!' the crowd shouted. 'We must do as you say. But we can't go on standing here in the open. We are a large crowd and it's raining heavily. Nor can we settle this matter in a day or two. Let it be dealt with, on our behalf, by our officials.'

It took three months to clear it all up.

The Story in Worship

The story has now been told. What did it mean to the Israelite people?

The very stories we have been reading tell us something; they were selected by their historians, as we have said, to bring home to those who heard them read in the synagogue the truths they had learned. But a people's deepest convictions are seen most clearly in their songs and poetry and hymns; here we can 'read their hearts'. The hymns of the Israelite people are gathered together in *The Psalms*.

The Book of Psalms, as we find it now in the Old Testament, is 'The Hymn-book of the Second Temple', the temple that was rebuilt when the exiles returned to their homeland. But like all church hymnbooks, it had a long history behind it and it contained hymns both old and new.

The building of the great temple in Jerusalem in King Solomon's time made a great difference to the people's worship. Village worship went on in the old hill-top shrines. But in the temple, king and religious leaders made their influence felt, and poet and musician developed a deeper and richer form of worship. Here the great national religious festivals were held; here the king was crowned at the New Year Festival; here were sung their joys and sorrows, their fears and hopes, their praise and penitence as 'GOD's People'. The heart of their worship was what GOD had done for them, and through them, for the world.

The hymns sung in the first temple were gathered together in what might be called 'The Prayer Book of Solomon's Temple'. As time went on, before and after the Exile, other collections of hymns were made. At last, all these were gathered together in 'The Hymnbook of the Second Temple', *The Psalms*.

There were different kinds of hymns.[1] Most of them were hymns for Congregation and Choir—praise to God as Lord of History and Lord of Nature, New Year hymns and hymns for the king's coronation, national laments (for dark days of national danger) and national thanksgiving (for times of deliverance). Some of the hymns were for individuals—hymns of lament for those who were sick and in trouble, hymns expressing individual joy and thanksgiving. At their most important festival, the New Year Festival ('the Festival of Tents'), held in late September or early October, they celebrated their national story—how GOD rescued them from Egypt and made them his People.

Some of the hymns that follow here were sung in Solomon's temple; others were written and sung after the Exile in the rebuilt temple. They all celebrate the story we have been reading—a story not just to be recited but a story to be sung. Here are real hymns. Here are real convictions, with their greatness and their littleness, their high vision (which has inspired all later generations) and their inhibiting bitterness (when their suffering robbed them of their generosity and dimmed their sense of humanity). They hide little.

---

[1] In indicating the different types of psalms and the way some of them have been sung in worship, I have followed Elmer A. Leslie, *The Psalms*.

GOD—Lord of History

Psalm 105

Thank GOD and call upon him,
    tell the whole world what he has done;
sing to GOD, sing his praise,
    remember his wonderful deeds!

When our ancestors were but a handful of men,
    mere strangers in the land,
trekking from country to country,
    from people to people,
he guarded them from tyrants,
    rebuking kings.

When famine broke out in the land
    and their livelihood was lost,
he sent a man ahead of them,
    Joseph, sold as a slave.

His feet were hurt by fetters,
    his neck clamped with an iron collar—
until GOD's word came true,
    GOD's promise was made good!

Pharaoh ordered his release,
    the people's ruler set him free,
made him master of the palace,
    governor of his dominions,
giving courtiers their orders,
    teaching royal advisers wisdom!

GOD made his people grow
    in numbers and in strength;
the Egyptians hated them
    and deceived them.

He sent Moses and Aaron,
    his chosen servants;
showing his signs and wonders
    in the land of Egypt.

He turned day into deep darkness
    but they ignored his commands;
he turned their rivers to blood
    and killed their fish.

Frogs swarmed over the country,
    even into the royal palace;
at his word, flies and gnats
    covered the countryside.

He turned their rain to hail,
    lightning flashed
blighting vine and fig-tree,
    splintering the trees.

He sent locusts,
    innumerable locusts,
eating the greenness,
    the fruit of the fields.

He struck their eldest sons,
    the flower of their youth.

He led his people out
    laden with silver and gold,
    marching, not stumbling;
the panic-stricken Egyptians
    were glad to see them go.
He screened them with a cloud
    and lit the night with fire.

When they were hungry
    he gave them quails and manna;
water gushed out of the struck rock,
    a river in the desert.

He remembered his promise
    to his servant Abraham—
he led his people out
    singing victory songs.

He gave them a homeland
    aliens had worked for—
that they might obey him
    and live in his Way.

Psalm 114

O praise GOD!

When GOD's People escaped from Egypt
  and its barbarous speech,
the South became GOD's home,
  the North his country.

The sea stared and fled,
  Jordan River flowed back,
the mountains skipped like rams,
  the hills like lambs.

What made you flee, O Sea?
  What turned you back, O Jordan?
Why skip like rams, you mountains?
  and like lambs, you hills?

Dance, O Earth, in GOD's presence,
  in the presence of our God—
he turned rocks into clear water,
  granite into living spring!

Songs of the New Year

Psalm 2 (A Coronation Hymn)

Choir

Why is the world in a welter,
  foreigners in futile ferment?
Kings stand on guard,
  rulers are rebels
    against GOD and his King?—
'Shake off their shackles!' they shout.
  'Throw away their chains!'

GOD laughs from the sky,
  holds them in scorn,
speaks in anger,
  terrifying them with his fury.

King

'I have crowned my King
   on my Holy Mountain!'
     GOD said to me.
'You are my son,
   I have made you my son today!
Ask, and I will give you the world
   as your inheritance,
the whole world
   as your empire—
you shall smash them with iron clubs,
   shatter them like a clay pot!'

Choir

Take care, you kings!
   Learn your lesson, you governors!
Submit to GOD as loyal subjects,
   reverence the king's authority—
or you will lose your way
   in GOD's sudden anger!

Happy are they
   who find GOD their fortress!

Psalm 72 (A Coronation Hymn)

Help the king, O GOD, to rule as you do
   and to live in your Way,
dealing with your people as you deal with them,
   seeing the poor get justice.
So shall the mountains be dressed with peace
   and the hills with justice
    as with the greenness of spring.

May he stand by the helpless,
   rescue the poor,
    crush their oppressors!

May he live for ever
   like the sun and the moon!
May he be like rain falling on fields,
   like showers watering the earth!
May enduring justice and lasting peace
   flourish under him
    till the moon is no more!

May he rule from sea to sea
  from the Euphrates to the world's end.
May his enemies pay him homage,
  his foes meet defeat.
From the western lands of the Great Sea
  to Arabia and Egypt,
kings shall pay him tribute-money
  and bring him gifts.
All kings shall do him homage,
  all nations be his servants!

For he shall rescue the poor from the rich,
  sufferers who have none to help,
looking on them with pity
  and saving their lives,
    guarding them from violence.
The lives of common people
  are precious to him.

So the poor man shall share his country's wealth,
  praying for the king,
    blessing him every day.

There will be abundant harvests
  waving on even the hill-tops,
corn like Lebanon Forest,
  sheaves as common as grass!

May his fame last for ever—
  as long as the sun in the sky!
May the whole world
  speak his name as a blessing!

Psalm 124

If GOD had not been on our side—
  let GOD's People say—
If GOD had not been on our side
  when armies attacked us,
they would have swallowed us alive
  in the flood of their fury:
waters would have swept us away,
  torrents overwhelmed us,
    raging rivers drowned us!

Praise GOD
who never gave us up
to their wild hunger.
We have escaped
like a bird from a farmer's trap.
The trap is broken!
We have escaped!

Our help is in GOD
who made earth and sky!

Psalm 132 (A Coronation Hymn)

Congregation   Remember King David, O GOD,
and the hard times he went through,
his vow to you,
the God of his people:
'I will not go home
or go to bed,
I will not sleep
or take my rest,
until I find a home for GOD,
a home for his people's God.'

Choir   We heard of the Ark in Bethlehem,
we found it in Kiriath-jearim.
Let us bring it to its true home,
let us worship GOD!

Congregation   O GOD, come home,
you and your Ark!
Let the priests live in your Way,
let your people shout for joy!
For your servant David's sake
do not reject your anointed king!

The official   GOD made a vow to David
Prophets   and he will faithfully keep it:
addressing   'From your descendants I will raise
the King   kings on your throne.

If they keep my Covenant
  and walk in my Way,
their descendants, too, for ever
  shall sit on your throne.'

GOD has chosen this mountain
  for his home:
'This is my home for ever,
  my desire is to live here.

'I will bless her destitute people,
  I will satisfy her hungry with bread,
I will clothe her priests with true religion—
  her citizens shout for joy.

'I will give David's dynasty new strength,
  giving my anointed king a burning lamp,
humiliating his enemies,
  making his crown sparkle on his head!'

National Lament

Psalm 74

Why have you abandoned us, O God?
  Is it for ever?
Why does your anger smoke
  over the flock in your fields?
Remember your people—
  the people you established long ago!
Remember your Holy Mountain,
  your home!
Come—rebuild the untouched ruins,
  the temple wrecked by the enemy!
It's your enemies who have stampeded
  and run riot in your temple,
hacking wood and swinging axes
  like timbermen in the forests,
ripping the panels out,
  smashing them
    with hatchets and hammers,

firing the buildings,
  desecrating your home—
'We'll smash it all!
  We'll burn all God's temples down!'

No sign! No prophet!
  Nobody to tell us how long!

How long, O God, will the enemy scoff?
  Will he curse your name for ever?
Why do you hold back,
  why hide your hand?

Yet you are our king from of old,
  conqueror of the earth.
Your power split the sea-monster
  and broke the heads of the sea-serpent;
you crushed the sea-dragon
  fed him as food for sharks!

You struck open springs and torrents,
  dried up the unfailing waters
    to make dry land appear!

Yours is the day, yours the night,
  you made the moon and the sun,
you fixed the regions of the earth,
  you planned winter and summer!

Remember this, O GOD!—
  it's you the enemy slanders,
  your name pagan soldiers insult!
Do not surrender us who acknowledge you,
  do not for ever forget your suffering people!
Look at the men you have made—
  they have corrupted the earth,
  turned it into fields of violence!

Don't let the oppressed be humiliated!
  Let the poor and needy praise you!
Arise, O God, and take your stand,
  remember the insults of brutal men!
Don't forget your enemies' threats—
  their rage rising to a roar!

Psalm 77

I shout to God for help,
  I shout to God to listen to me.
I seek him in the day of my distress,
  stretching out my hands to him.
Through the night I cannot stop weeping,
  I can find no peace of mind.

I groan at the very thought of God,
  my mind dark with questions.
I shut my eyes
  lying dazed and speechless.

I remember the story of my people,
  the years of long ago,
thinking—thinking—in the darkness,
  questioning and searching:
Will GOD ignore us for ever,
  forever be against us?
Has his love utterly gone?
  Do his promises no longer stand?
Has he forgotten what kindness means?
  Has his sternness silenced his compassion?
'Has his hand lost its grip,' I say to myself,
  'hanging limp at his side?'

I will recall what GOD has done,
  his great deeds of long ago;
I will think quietly and deeply
  about what he has really done.
Your Way, O God, is the good Way—
  what other god is like you?
You act—you do not just talk—
  everybody can see your strength;
you rescue your people
  with your power.

The waters saw you, O God,
  the waters saw you and writhed,
    the deeps were in storm.

Clouds poured the rain down,
  thunder rolled across the sky,
    the lightning flashed everywhere.

The crash of your thunder was like chariot wheels,
  your lightning lit the world,
    the earth quaked.

The sea was your highway,
  the oceans your pathway,
    your footprints unseen.

You led your people like a shepherd
  by the hand of Moses and Aaron.

Psalm 83

This is no time for peace, O God,
  for 'silence' and 'stillness'.
Look—your enemies are crowding in,
  those who hate you are on the march,
with crafty plots like conspirators,
  against your people, your treasure—
'Come, let us wipe them out as a nation
  from the memory of man!'
They come as one man,
  sworn enemies of yours—
Arab tribes from the east,
  Tyrians and Philistines from the west.

Treat them as you treated Sisera
  at the Kishon River;
destroy them as you destroyed the Midianites
  at Harod Well.
Scatter them like a dust-storm,
  like chaff in the wind,
like a forest fire
  in the blazing mountains!
Hunt them with your whirlwind,
  terrify them with your hurricane!
Fill their faces with shame,
  till they confess your greatness, O GOD.
May they for ever be shamed and dismayed,
  destroyed and disgraced!

Let them know that you alone
  rule as GOD
  over the whole world!

Psalm 129

'All my life I have been bitterly persecuted,'—
    let GOD's people say—
'All my life I have been bitterly persecuted,
    but never beaten.
They have driven me like a beast of burden,
    ploughing their own long furrows;
but GOD cut the pagan harness off
    and set us free!'

May all who hate GOD's people
    be shamed and defeated!
May they be like grass growing on the roofs
    scorched by the hot east wind,
grass no harvester bothers with,
    no binder can use,
like people nobody greets
    as they pass in the streets!

Pablo Picasso: *Woman Weeping*

Psalm 137

By Babylonian rivers
    we sat down in tears
remembering Jerusalem,
    hanging our harps on the poplars.

Our captors called for a song,
 our plunderers for a tune!—
 'Sing us one of your Jerusalem songs!'
How can we sing GOD's song
 on alien soil?

If I forget you, O Jerusalem,
 let my right hand hang helpless!
Let my tongue stick in my mouth
 if I stop remembering you,
if I don't think more of you
 than anything else in the world!

Don't forget the Edomites, O GOD,
 their 'Day of Jerusalem',
the attack and the shouting—'Down with it,
 Down with it to the ground!'

And you, O Babylon, Babylon the Destroyer!—
 he'll be a happy man who treats you
 as you have treated us!
Happy if he seizes your children
 and dashes their heads on the rock!

Individual Thanksgiving

Psalm 66

Choir

O wide, wide world
 Raise a shout of joy to God,
 sing the honour of his name,
 speak the glory of his praise!
Make this your theme—
 'How awe-inspiring your deeds, O God!
 Your enemies cringe
 before your greatness and your strength!
Let the whole earth worship you,
 sing to you,
 praise your name!'

Come and see what God has done,
  his awe-inspiring deeds to men!
He turned the sea into dry land,
  his people crossed the sea on foot!

Listen! Let us rejoice in him
  who rules in strength for ever,
keeping watch over the world—
  no rebel can rise against him.

O peoples, bless our God,
  make his praise heard near and far—
he has given us life,
  kept us from slipping.

You tested us, O God,
  you refined us as silver is refined;
you led us into the siege—
  our backs broken with their burdens,
  men riding rough-shod over us.
We went through fire and water,
  but you led us into freedom.

Individual   I offer my sacrifice in your temple
worshipper   to honour my vows,
vows my lips uttered,
  my mouth spoke, when I was hard-pressed.

Come, listen, all you who worship God,
  I will tell you what he has done for me!
I cried out to him for help,
  sang his high praise.

I had said to myself
  'God won't bother with me!'
But that's just what he did do,
  he listened to my voice!

Blessed be God—
  who didn't ignore my prayer,
  who didn't stop loving me!

Psalm 107

Priest	Thank GOD for his goodness!
Congregation	His steadfast love endures for ever!

Priest Let those GOD rescued make it plain—
those he rescued from oppression
and brought back from foreign lands,
from the east and from the west,
from the north and from the south!

Pilgrims come forward

Choir Some got lost in the desert wastes,
looking in vain for a city home.
Hungry and thirsty
they lost all hope.
They shouted to GOD for help
and he rescued them,
leading them along the right road
to their city home.
Let them thank GOD for his steadfast love
and the wonderful help he gives men,
quenching their thirst,
satisfying their hunger with good food!

Former prisoners come forward

Choir Some were living fettered
in the pitch-darkness of a prison cell.
They had not listened to what God had to say
and they had refused to walk his Way.
They were utterly miserable,
there was no lifting hand when they stumbled.
Then they shouted to GOD for help,
and he rescued them,
leading them out of their prison darkness
and breaking their fetters.
Let them thank GOD for his steadfast love
and the wonderful help he gives men.
He shattered prison gates, though made of bronze
and prison bars, though made of iron!

Sailors come forward

Choir   Some went down to the sea in ships,
            trafficking on the great oceans.
          They watched what GOD can do,
            the wonder of his way in great waters.
          At his word, the storm broke,
            whipping up the waves.
          Lifted to the sky,
            plunged to the deeps,
          they staggered like drunken men,
            sailors though they were.
          They shouted to GOD for help
            and he rescued them.
          The storm died down
            and the sea was still;
          they were glad to be on calm water again,
            sailing safely into port.
                Let them thank GOD for his steadfast love
                  and the wonderful help he gives men.
                Let them speak GOD's praise
                  in the public assemblies of the people
                  where the elders sit.

Making Sense of the Story

Introduction

The story of this small highland people has now been told: we have listened to what they have had to say, in their own records, about their rise and fall; and we have seen something of the vision that helped them to survive the loss of their political independence.

We come now to the inescapable questions—as inescapable for us as for them: 'How can anybody make sense of such a brutal story?' 'What kind of world is it in which this sort of thing can happen?' 'Was the vision of Moses and David merely an idle dream?' We have now to see what kind of answers they gave to questions like these.

The Israelite people took what we call 'politics' and 'economics' and 'social questions' quite seriously. But the answers to the questions they were asking were not to be found there; they went deeper. Rightly or wrongly, they found them in their 'religious' experience.

But what is 'religion' about? And what do you mean by 'religious experience'?

Read these words carefully:

When a man thinks where deep speaks to deep, he thinks religiously. When he ponders the things that really matter, that give meaning to life itself, upon which his own life, in fact, depends, he is wrestling with things religious. Religion is facing reality. Religious thinking is deciding what reality is all about and how to deal with it.[1]

If religion is 'facing reality', it cannot be just one specialized activity among a lot of other specialized activities; it can only be the way we live the whole of our lives.

This is the truth that the Israelite people—or the best minds among them—had been slowly learning from the day when they escaped from Egypt to the time when, their cities in ruins and their political independence destroyed, they faced their darkest hour and lived through it. That is why, in the long run, the popular religions they encountered in Palestine held no enduring meaning for them. They had outgrown them.

The men who saw this clearly were the 'great prophets', of whom Amos was the first to appear. So we come now to listen to three of them: Amos himself who spoke as the storm clouds were gathering on the northern horizon; Jeremiah who was caught up in the siege and fall of Jerusalem itself; and the unknown prophet who was one of the exiles in Babylon.

These men stood above the panic of their contemporaries. They looked the real world in the face and refused to be intimidated by what

[1] Nels N. F. Ferré, *Making Religion Real*, p. 12.

Dietrich Bonhoeffer,
a modern prophet

must have seemed to others overwhelming human disaster. But they did not come suddenly 'out of the blue'. There was a long story behind them.

For a thousand years at least there had been men in the Middle East who were known as 'prophets'. The word 'prophet' itself probably means 'spokesman'. 'Prophets' were 'spokesmen' of the god—or gods —their people worshipped; they announced the god's will. We have, for example, an account of a prophet who spoke to his king in the name of his god as far back as 1700 B.C.E. in the city of Mari on the river Euphrates. From the time of the Philistine attack on the highlands, we meet them in the story of the Israelites themselves.

Earlier prophets were very different from men like Amos. Most of them lived in groups and were associated with local shrines and temples as officials. They spoke in excited speech, and they stimulated this frenzy and excitement with music. There were groups of 'royal prophets' who advised the kings and announced God's will to them (see the stories on pp. 27, 230).

There were, however, others who belonged to no such group but lived independent lives. These 'independent prophets' were the real predecessors of men like Amos. We shall begin this part of our book with the stories of two of them, Elijah and Micaiah, to show what kind of men these earlier 'prophets' were.

The great prophets themselves were not eager to be called 'prophets'; and they would have nothing to do with the 'official prophets'. They were new and original men; they looked beyond their own nation to the world of nations, and they spoke out of their own intimate experience of God with a freshness and directness which we have not met before—and which moves us still.

As we read their poems we must note and remember three things.

First, they begin with their own personal experience of God: 'GOD spoke to me'. They believed they were 'called' by God to speak to his people in his name; some of them have left accounts of their 'call'. This experience had a compelling quality—they dared not say No. They chose to face death itself rather than keep quiet. This compelling experience came out of their every-day life as farmers or villagers or city men. The convictions to which it led did not come easily; they had to think hard and live dangerously to get them clear. They claimed no authority for their experience except the reality of the experience itself; they believed what they had to say ought to be clear to all men's consciences.

Secondly, when they spoke about events in their own country or in neighbouring countries, they knew what they were talking about. They took the trouble to find out what was happening, probably through the merchants and travellers they met in market or temple. As far as they could, they 'got their facts right'. They were dealing with the real world.

Thirdly, they found their clue to the meaning of their total experience (their experience of God and their experience of the world as they knew it) in the religious traditions of their people—the story of the escape from Egypt and the Covenant on the Holy Mountain—about which they had thought long and deeply. They worked out the convictions of Moses afresh in the light of the new world in which they and their countrymen found themselves.

They had no use for mere 'nationalism' or the 'national religions' either of their own people or of other countries. Their eyes were on the whole world. They judged their own countrymen and foreign peoples by the same standards. The God in whose presence they stood was the God of the whole universe. They had no interest in religion as 'social custom'; they wanted to know the truth about the human situation in which they and all men stood. They spoke to men face to face—on the street, in the Temple court. They took their lives in their hands.

There is one other thing to remember. The great prophets were poets; what they had to say must be read as poetry. They were seeing the whole world in the light of their experience of God and in the light of the religious traditions of their people. They were making their 'vision' clear—what they had heard and what they had seen; they were calling their people to 'listen' and 'look'. Poetry was their natural language; they wanted to change men's hearts as well as their minds, get them to feel and think and live in a new way, God's Way. Their charge against their people—and the world—was that they would not 'look' and they would not 'listen'.

As we read, we must put ourselves in their place to listen with their ears and look with their eyes, and try to see the world we live in as they saw the world they lived in.

Two Ninth Century Prophets

Elijah (850 B.C.E.)

Elijah comes suddenly into the story, like a thunderbolt, out of the eastern desert—a bold and unforgettable figure. He was an independent prophet, though he had some connections with the prophetic groups of his time. His name came, in later centuries, to represent the whole prophetic movement.

We see him, in gaunt outline, through the mists of the popular stories told about him, with their love of miracle and marvel. But his greatness shines through the stories—his passionate loyalty to GOD alone and his fearlessness in denouncing a king's crime to his face.

He was concerned with a very vital issue: there could be no toleration of any worship other than the worship of GOD among his own people. A treaty had been made between Tyre and the North, and in this alliance the North was very much the weaker partner. Under its provisions King Ahab had married a Phoenician princess; she was a dominating woman as well as a princess of a great and famous country, and she was determined to introduce the worship of her own god, Baal, into the country of her adoption.

King Ahab himself seems to have been a sincere worshipper of GOD; he gave his son the name 'Ahaziah', 'GOD holds me'. His marriage treaty with Jezebel would include, however, her right to have a temple of her own in the capital city; she wanted more than this.

Elijah was concerned to see that no Baal worship was established in the North where GOD alone should be worshipped. The stories of the great drought and of the incident on Carmel Mountain make this issue clear. He was also concerned with the laws of his people, which were laws for king and commoner alike. Kings, thought Jezebel, could do what they liked, as they did in her own country. 'Not so,' said Elijah, 'GOD's law rules here—for everybody.' This is the issue in the story of Naboth's vineyard. That Elijah was concerned to see that the traditions of Moses were maintained is shown in the story of his visit to 'GOD's Mountain'.

The Drought

Elijah, whose home was in the wild country of Gilead, east of Jordan River, sought an audience with King Ahab.

'As GOD lives, whose servant I am,' he told him, 'there will be drought here for two whole years—no rainy season in the winter, no dew in the summer—unless I say so.'

And he went out of the presence of the king.

GOD spoke to him again.

'Go east,' he said. 'Hide in the Cherith Valley, east of Jordan River. You'll find water in the stream to drink; ravens will bring you food.'

He went to the Cherith Valley. Ravens brought him bread in the

The island city of Tyre ▶

morning and meat in the evening; and he drank from the stream. After some time, the stream in the valley dried up; the great drought had come.

GOD spoke to Elijah again.

'Get up and go north to Sidonian territory. A widow there will look after you.'

He got up and went north.

Nearly two years passed by. One day, GOD spoke to Elijah.

'Go and seek an audience with King Ahab,' he told him. 'I am going to end this drought with a storm.'

Elijah set off to meet the king.

'You Trouble-maker!'

Now the drought was very severe in Samaria, the capital city.

Ahab's Chief Minister was a good man called Obadiah, loyal to the true worship of GOD. In the persecution of GOD's prophets which Queen Jezebel had ruthlessly carried out, he had hidden two hundred of them, in groups of five, in the hilly limestone country where there were many caves, and sent them bread and water.

The king summoned Obadiah.

'Let us survey the land,' he said, 'and examine all the streams and valleys to see if there is any green grass still growing. We don't want to lose our war-horses and mules if there is any chance of saving them; and we don't want to lose the cattle either.'

They divided the country between them, the king going in one direction, Obadiah in the other.

Obadiah was out in the open country when, suddenly, he found himself face to face with Elijah. He knew at once who he was and fell on the ground in reverence before him.

'Is it you, my lord Elijah?' he said.

'Yes, it is,' said Elijah. 'Go to your master the king. Tell him I am here.'

'What wrong have I done?' asked Obadiah. 'Why do you want me to risk my life like this? The king's been looking for you everywhere. When anyone tells him "Elijah's not here" he makes him swear an oath on pain of death that he is telling the truth. And now you command me to tell the king you're here—just like that! I know what will happen. When I'm gone, GOD's spirit will whisk you away. I shall tell the king you're here; he'll come—and you'll have gone! He'll have me executed on the spot. I've worshipped GOD all my life—you know that. Haven't you heard what I did for the prophets when Queen Jezebel was

◀ A plague of locusts (p. 233)

murdering any she could find? And you say "Tell him I'm here"—and send me to my death!'

'I speak in GOD's name,' said Elijah. 'I swear to you I will meet the king here, where we are now standing, today.'

Obadiah went off to tell the king and the king came quickly.

'It's you, is it, you trouble-maker!' said the king to Elijah as soon as he saw him.

'I'm no trouble-maker,' said Elijah. 'You and your family are the trouble-makers. You've abandoned the true worship of GOD for all these pagan cults. Call an assembly of the people on Carmel Mountain. And make sure the dervishes of the pagan god Baal and the pagan goddess Asherah—the dervishes the Queen's so fond of—are all there.'

The king called an assembly of people and dervishes on Carmel Mountain.

Carmel Mountain

Elijah faced the crowd.

'How long are you going to stand shilly-shallying at the cross-roads?' he asked them. 'If our GOD is God, follow him. If Baal is God, follow him.'

There was dead silence.

'I am the only prophet of GOD left,' he went on. 'There are more than four hundred prophets of Baal here; I stand alone. Let us be put to the test. Bring two bulls. Let them choose one, prepare it for a burnt-offering, and put it on the wood—but no fire, if you please. I'll dress the other bull and put it on the wood—and I'll have no fire either.'

He paused and turned to the pagan prophets.

'You pray to your god and I will pray to mine,' he told them. 'The God who answers by fire will be God!'

'It's a fair test!' shouted the crowd.

'You begin,' said Elijah to the prophets. 'There are more of you.'

They prepared the bull and the wood.

'O Baal, answer us!' they prayed. They went on praying like this from morning to noon, dancing a ritual dance round the altar. But there wasn't a sound or a word in answer.

Elijah could keep quiet no longer.

'You'll have to shout louder!' he taunted them. 'He's a god, isn't he? Perhaps he's just thinking—or somebody's called him away—or he's on a journey—or he's dozed off—you'll have to see if you can wake him up!'

They shouted out at the top of their voices, and cut themselves with knives and lances till blood flowed (this is a custom of pagan worship). This went on till early evening—but no voice, no answer, nothing.

Elijah spoke to the watching crowd.

'Come nearer to me,' he said.

There was an old ruined altar to GOD on that part of the mountain. Elijah chose twelve stones from it (representing the twelve tribes of the old tribal league), and made a new altar. He dug a trench round it, deep enough to take about twelve gallons of water. He stacked wood on it and put the bull on the wood.

He told the crowd to pour water over it.

'Do it a second and a third time,' he said.

The water drenched the altar and filled the trench as well.

He went up to the altar.

'O GOD,' he prayed, 'God of our ancestors, let nobody here today doubt that you are God in this country and that I am your servant, carrying out your orders. Answer me, O GOD, answer me! Let everybody here know that you are God and that you are bringing them back to your true worship!'

Lightning suddenly fell out of the cloudless sky and burned up bull and wood and stones and dust—and all the water in the trench.

The crowd fell down on their faces in reverence.

'GOD is really God!' they shouted. 'GOD is really God!'

'Arrest the pagan prophets!' Elijah told the crowd. 'Don't let any escape!'

They arrested them and marched them down the mountainside to the Kishon River in the valley below and butchered them there.

Everybody had been fasting all day.

'You can eat and drink now,' Elijah told the king. 'There's the sound of beating rain!'

The king went up to the altar to eat and drink; Elijah climbed almost to the top of the mountain and squatted on the ground with his face between his knees. He called to the lad, his servant.

'Go up to the very top, and look out to sea,' he told him.

'I can't see anything,' the lad called back.

This happened six times. But the seventh time there was something to see.

'I can see a cloud coming in from the sea!' he shouted down. 'It isn't a very big one—it's about the size of a man's fist.'

'Up!' said Elijah, 'run back to the king. Tell him to harness his horses if he doesn't want to be held up by the rain!'

The sky grew black with clouds and wind and there was a great storm of rain.

King Ahab mounted his chariot and made for the royal city of Jezreel. Elijah tied his cloak round his waist and ran in front of the royal chariot all the seventeen miles to the city—GOD gave him superhuman strength to do it.

Panic and rebuke

The king told the queen what had happened, and especially about the butchery of the pagan prophets. She immediately sent a message to Elijah:

'You're not Elijah and I'm not Jezebel—if you're not as dead as my prophets before tomorrow's out!'

Elijah was in a panic, and fled for his life to the south. He reached Beersheba and left his lad there. He himself went on for twenty miles into the desert. He found a broom-bush and rested in its shade.

'Let me die,' he prayed to GOD. 'I can't stand any more, O GOD! Kill me—I'm not the leader that I thought I was.'

He lay down and went to sleep.

Suddenly an angel was waking him.

'Get up and eat something,' he said.

Elijah looked round and saw a round flat cake of bread and a flask of water. He got up, ate the cake and drank the water; and then lay down again.

The angel came back a second time and wakened him.

'Get up and eat something,' he said. 'You've a long journey in front of you and you'll need all your strength.'

Again Elijah got up and ate and drank. He felt a new man now and went on and on until he reached the Holy Mountain where Moses had met GOD. He found a cave and spent the night there.

Then GOD passed by.

A storm of wind swept over the mountain, pulling up great rocks and smashing them to pieces. But the storm wind wasn't GOD's presence.

An earthquake shook the mountain. But the earthquake wasn't GOD's presence either.

Then a forest fire swept the mountainside. But that wasn't GOD's presence.

After all this, there was a silence so deep that it was almost like a sound itself.

Elijah left the cave, hiding his face in his cloak, and stood at the cave's mouth.

He heard a voice:

'What are you doing here, Elijah?'

'Because I've been utterly loyal to you,' said Elijah. 'The people of the North have abandoned you. The Covenant means nothing to them, your altars are deserted ruins, your prophets butchered. I'm the only one left—and I'm a wanted man!'

'Go back!' said GOD. 'Sow the seed of revolution. Anoint Hazael King of Damascus, Jehu King of the North—and Elisha to carry on your work. Refugees from King Hazael will be killed by King Jehu, and anybody escaping from King Jehu will be killed by Elisha. You are not the only one loyal to me—there are many men who have never worshipped a pagan god, and never kissed Baal's image.'

Elijah went back.

On the way he came upon twelve men ploughing, each driving a pair of oxen in harness. Elisha was the last of the ploughmen. Elijah walked over the ploughed land and threw his cloak over him. Elisha dropped the reins of the oxen and ran after him.

'Let me say goodbye to my parents,' he asked. 'I'll come with you then.'

'Go home,' said Elijah. 'But don't forget what I've just done.'

Elisha went home. He sacrificed his two oxen, using the wooden plough as firewood, and he and his companions had a religious meal together. In this way he dedicated himself to the service of GOD with Elijah, and swore in his companions to help in his new work. He then left home and became Elijah's follower and friend.

A Farmer's murder

Naboth was a farmer. His vineyard had belonged to his family for many generations and lay next to the palace grounds in Jezreel City.

King Ahab asked Naboth one day about it.

'I'm wanting a vegetable garden,' he told him. 'Your vineyard is just what I want—it's next-door to my palace. Will you let me have it? I'll give you a better vineyard for it; or I'll pay you a fair price, just as you like.'

'No,' said Naboth. 'The vineyard was my father's and my grandfather's. I should be an irreligious man if I sold my ancestral lands.'

The king went back to his palace a vexed and sullen man; he'd set his heart on that vineyard. He went to bed and sulked and wouldn't have anything to eat.

'Why are you sulking?' asked the queen. He told her what had happened.

'You're a fine king,' she said (she was a foreign princess, and was thinking of what her father, the king of Tyre, would have done). 'Get up and eat your food and stop worrying. I'll see you get the vineyard.'

She sent a royal letter, sealed with the royal seal, to the aldermen and freemen of the city, all Naboth's fellow-councillors:

'Proclaim a religious fast, and put Naboth where everybody can see him. Get two witnesses—you know what kind of men to get—to sit facing him and to charge him with cursing GOD and the king. You know what the sentence is—death by stoning.'

The city council carried out the royal orders to the letter. They held the fast, suborned the witnesses and had Naboth executed outside the city.

They sent a brief report: 'Naboth has been executed.'

The queen received the report and went straight to the king.

'Get up and go down to the vineyard,' she told him. 'It's yours now. Naboth wouldn't sell it to you would he? Well—he's dead!'

The king got up and went down to the vineyard to take possession of it. (By law the property of rebels and criminals became the king's.)

GOD spoke to Elijah.

'Get up,' he said, 'and go and meet King Ahab face to face. He's in Naboth's vineyard; he's gone to take possession of it. Give him this message from me: "You've committed murder to get hold of a vineyard. Where the street-dogs are licking up Naboth's blood, they'll one day lick up yours!"'

'Have you caught up with me, my enemy?' the king said to Elijah.

'I've caught up with you, all right!' said Elijah. 'You've sold your soul in this foul deed; you've signed your own death-warrant—and that of your family. "I'll get rid of you all!" says GOD.'

When King Ahab heard these words, he tore his robes and wore sackcloth. He accepted Elijah's rebuke.

Micaiah (850 B.C.E.)

King Ahab of the North and King Jehoshaphat of the South were together in Samaria, the Northern capital. They were discussing with their ministers the attack on Ramoth-Gilead, east of Jordan River. King Jehoshaphat asked that GOD's will should be sought, and the professional court prophets told the two kings that GOD's will was that they should attack the city. At this point in the story later editors inserted the following prophetic story (see p. 161).

'Isn't there another prophet here?' asked King Jehoshaphat, 'to tell us what GOD's will is?'

'There is,' said King Ahab, 'there's Micaiah. But I've no use for him— he's always against me!'

'You mustn't say that,' said King Jehoshaphat.

King Ahab sent for Micaiah.

The Council of War was, of course, a state occasion. The whole court was there; the kings were sitting on their thrones, in full regalia, in the open square by the City Gate. All the professional prophets were shouting 'GOD's word': 'Go up and conquer—GOD will put the town at your Majesty's mercy!' They were in a wild frenzy. One of them,

Zedekiah, had made some iron horns and was wearing them and shouting: ' "You will gore the Syrians like a bull," says GOD, "and destroy them!" '

Meanwhile, the officer sent to fetch Micaiah had found him and was talking to him.

'Now remember,' he was saying, 'all the prophets are for the king and his plans. Take the same line yourself.'

'As GOD lives,' said Micaiah 'I will say only what GOD tells me to say.'

He came into the presence of King Ahab.

'Micaiah,' said the king, 'shall we attack Ramoth-Gilead or shall we not?'

'Go up and conquer!' said Micaiah (mimicking the professional prophets). 'GOD will put the town at your Majesty's mercy.'

'How often have I to command you to tell me what GOD really says,' said the king, 'the truth and nothing but the truth?'

'I saw the Northern soldiers scattered on the mountains like sheep without their shepherd,' said Micaiah. ' "They have no king," GOD told me. "Let them disband and go peacefully home".'

'Didn't I tell you he would talk like this?' said King Ahab to King Jehoshaphat. 'Didn't I tell you he would be against me and not for me?'

'You asked me to tell you what GOD had to say,' Micaiah went on. 'I saw GOD sitting on his throne, surounded by his heavenly court.

' "Who knows how to mislead King Ahab," GOD asked them, "so that he may die in battle at Ramoth-Gilead?"

'There was a debate among his counsellors.

'Then one of them stepped out before him.

' "I know how to mislead him," he said.

' "How?" asked GOD.

' "I will go down and fill the minds of the professional prophets with lies," he said.

' "Do just that," said GOD. "You've got your orders: go!"

'GOD is surely against you; the court prophets are all lying.'

Zedekiah stepped up to Micaiah and struck him on the face.

'How did GOD's spirit go from me to you?' he shouted.

'You'll know the answer to that question,' said Micaiah, 'when you find yourself hiding as a refugee in a house!'

'Arrest the fellow!' ordered King Ahab, 'and hand him over to Governor Amon and Prince Joash. Tell them to lock him up, and feed him on bread and water till I come for my victory parade!'

'If you come home as victor,' said Micaiah, 'then GOD hasn't spoken through me!'

Voice of a Farmer: Amos
(760 B.C.E.)

We know little about Amos. All we know comes from the brief account of the 'Incident in the North' which follows and the impressions his poetry gives us. He was a shepherd.

The times he lived in were times of great prosperity for the North and the South; both kingdoms were ruled over by able kings— Jeroboam II in the North and Ahaziah (Uzziah) in the South. There is little about these kings in Israelite historical records. Jeroboam is dismissed as a bad king; though we are told he was 'the Saviour of the North' and ruled an empire 'like Solomon's'; what is told of Azariah is found on p. 173. Prosperity for both kingdoms was possible because Assyria and Egypt were preoccupied with their own internal affairs. Within a few years, however, Assyria was to resume her march to the west.

So, for the moment, the North was revelling in her wealth and in the expansion of her trade. But the wealth brought with it corruption in the courts of justice, contempt for the rights of ordinary citizens, the growth of large estates (with their summer houses) at the expense of small landowners, the neglect of the poor. The worship at GOD's Temple was a 'contemptible side-show, its religious tradition merely a cloak for pride and complacency'. Everybody seemed so engrossed in 'getting on' and 'keeping up with the Joneses' that nobody bothered about what was happening in the world outside or noticed the storm clouds blowing up beyond their northern borders.

Amos was a Southerner; but he spoke in the North, where perhaps his business took him to the market at Bethel.

Incident in the North

Amos was a farmer, dealing in sheep and cattle and sycamore figs in the Southern village of Tekoa. He spoke openly in GOD's name in the famous royal city of Bethel in the North.

Amaziah, the temple priest there, sent a report to the king:

'Here, in the heart of the country, Amos is plotting revolution; he is a danger to the state. The theme of his harangues is—"King Jeroboam shall die in the war that's coming and the people will be deported!" '

Amaziah faced Amos himself.

'Get back to the South, you visionary!' he told him. 'Earn your living by preaching there! And don't you ever come back here to Bethel with your wild talk. This is a royal city with a royal temple and a royal palace!'

Amos was not slow to defend himself:

'I was no professional prophet—I'd no official standing!
I was a cattleman, growing the fruit the poor eat!
GOD seized me when I was out with the sheep,
and told me to give his message to the North.

Now listen to what GOD has got to say to you!

You tell me to keep my mouth shut,
stop dribbling prophecies over you Northerners!
    You yourself will know what war means—
        your wife driven to live on the streets,
        your children dead in the fighting,
        your estate shared out as booty,
        yourself dying in a foreign land.
        The Northerners shall be deported!'

Amos's Call

These four 'visions' probably represent Amos's account of his call by GOD to be his 'spokesman'. They are set in the form of brief conversations. Amos had been thinking deeply about the story of his people in the light of what he knew of his time and what life was like in his own country and in the North. Incidents from his own village experience (as with Jesus) gave him the imagery with which to express his sense of GOD's presence: a plague of locusts, a forest fire, building the wall of a village house, carrying the fruit for the autumn festival at the end of the agricultural year. He was aware of the terrible threat of Assyrian invasion, to which both North and South seemed blind. The experiences he describes seem to have taken some time: in the first two he thinks that the people may change their ways; in the last two there is no hope at all. These, then, were his marching orders.

Brief though the 'visions' are, they are crowded with meaning. The words echo not only his farming experience but the language of temple worship and the religious traditions of his people. For example, the forest fire blotting out the hillside calls to mind the Great Deep that, in the ancient story, covered the world. These are the words of a poet and carry more meaning than a first reading reveals. They are the clue to all that he later had to say.

The Vision of Locusts
GOD opened my eyes and I saw him at work:
the spring crops were beginning to grow when a plague of locusts

blotted out the countryside. When they had eaten up everything that
was green, I prayed to GOD:

> 'O GOD, forgive us,
> how can the North face this?
> It's a very small country!'

GOD changed his plans.
'Very well, it won't happen,' he said.

The Vision of the Forest Fire

GOD opened my eyes and I saw him at work:
a great fire was raging, devouring the Great Deep[1] and threatening
the whole countryside. I prayed to GOD:

> 'Stop the fire, O GOD, stop the fire!
> How can the North face this?
> It's a very small country!'

GOD changed his plans.
'Very well, this won't happen, either,' he said.

The Vision of the Plumb-line

GOD opened my eyes and I saw him at work:
a man had taken up his stand by the wall of a house and was holding
a plumb-line to test it.
'What are you looking at, Amos?' GOD asked me.
'A plumb-line,' I said.
'I am testing my people of the North,' he said, 'as the man is testing
this wall—I cannot keep on overlooking things!

> Northern hill-shrines shall be deserted;
> Northern temples tumble into ruin;
> the Northern royal house perish in war!'

The Vision of Autumn Fruit

GOD opened my eyes and I saw him at work:
there was a basket of autumn fruit in the street, ready for the autumn
festival at the end of the year.
'What are you looking at, Amos?' he asked me.
'A basket of autumn fruit,' I said.

---

[1] A reference to the watery chaos mentioned in this story of creation (see p. 307); it is to be found
under the earth and from it flow springs and rivers.

'A great fire was raging . . . threatening the whole countryside' ▶

'It's autumn for the North, too,' he said. 'Autumn—and the end. I
cannot go on overlooking things!

> Temple songs will turn to temple laments—
> war and many deaths,
> streets choked with dead soldiers
> and silence!'

GOD's Way: the Common Law of the World

Damascus in the North-East

These are GOD's words:

> Crime upon crime upon crime—
>   that is the rebellious story of Damascus.
> I will not come
>   to save them from their fate!

> They beat up Gilead villagers
>   like a threshing sledge
>   threshing grain.

> Therefore
> the royal family shall know what war means:
>   palaces and fortresses
>   in flames;
>   peasants driven from their fields,
>   the king from his throne;
>   people deported
>   back to their ancestral home!

This is GOD's Word!

Philistine Gaza in the South-West

These are GOD's words:

> Crime upon crime upon crime—
>   that is the rebellious story of Gaza City.
> I will not come
>   to save them from their fate!

> They deported a whole people
>   to the slave-markets of Edom.

Therefore
they shall know what war means:
   city walls and fortresses
     shall go up in flames,
   sister cities
     perish with them:
       citizens killed,
       kings dethroned,
       the last Philistine dead!

                This is GOD's word!

Ammon in the East

Crime upon crime upon crime—
   that is the rebellious story of Ammon.
I will not come
   to save them from their fate!

They murdered helpless women
   in their border warfare.

Therefore
kings and nobles shall know what war means:
   the royal city
     in flames,
   fortresses crashing in ruins
     with battle cries
     like thunder on a stormy day,
     kings and nobles together
       deported as prisoners!

                This is GOD's Word!

Moab in the South-East

Crime upon crime upon crime—
   that is the rebellious story of Moab.
I will not come
   to save them from their fate!

They burned to lime
   the bones of Edom's king—
     a shameful outrage![1]

[1] Such treatment was reserved for the worst of criminals

Therefore
Moab shall fall in flames,
    its fortresses in fire.
They shall die
    with stormy shouting
    and bugles blowing,
sheik and his captains
    perishing in battle!

This is GOD's Word

The North

Crime upon crime upon crime—
    that is the rebellious story of the North.
I will not come
    to save them from their fate!

They sell innocent men for money,
    destitute men for land,
trampling on poor men's heads,
    robbing them of their rights.
A man and his father
    sleep with the same slave-girl,
    holding my true worship in contempt.
They use pledged clothes to sleep on
    by every altar,
drink wine taken in fines
    in every village temple.

Yet it was I who gave them their homeland,
    destroying the Amorites who lived there—
        men tall as cedars,
        strong as oaks—
    destroying them root and branch.
It was I who rescued them from Egypt,
    and led them across the desert
    to occupy Amorite territory.

I gave you prophets
    and dedicated men;
you corrupted the dedicated men
    and told the prophets to shut their mouths.
Is not this the plain truth,
    you Northerners?
I will shake you

to the depth of your being,
like a loaded harvest waggon
   creaking over rough ground!

Swift runner
   shall fall with fatigue,
strong man
   become a weakling,
soldier die in battle,
   bowman be beaten back.
In that day
army-runner and horseman
   will be captured,
bravest hero
   will run naked away!

                              This is GOD's Word!

Is this the Way GOD's People should live?

Your wealth won't save you!

A PROCLAMATION TO BE MADE IN PHILISTINE AND EGYPTIAN PALACES:

Gather in the central highlands,
survey the confusion in Samaria City,
   the oppression in her streets:
      honesty means nothing to her people,
      violence and robbery are their way to wealth!

This is what GOD has to say:

Like the knuckle bone or tip of an ear
   which is all the shepherd grabs from the lion's mouth,
there will barely be a survivor
   from the North and its capital city—
only here a man cowering on the corner of a couch,
   there a man sitting on the cushion of a bed.
Temple altars shall be toppled
   and tumbled to the ground;
winter house and summer house
   be smashed down;
great houses with their ivory and ebony
   be shattered wreckage.

                              This is GOD's Word!

You did not turn back to me!

> Starvation in your cities,
> famine in your villages—
>> yet you did not turn back to me,
>> says GOD.

> No rain in spring,
> no harvest coming in summer—
>> yet you did not turn back to me,
>> says GOD.

> Blight and mildew,
> ravaged gardens and vineyards—
>> yet you did not turn back to me,
>> says GOD.

> Commandos dead on the battlefield,
> stink of corpses—
>> yet you did not turn back to me,
>> says GOD.

> Everywhere devastation,
> only a charred stick snatched from the fire—
>> yet you did not turn back to me,
>> says GOD.

> That is why I deal with you as I do,
> O North!

'GOD's Day' indeed!

> Woe
>> to you who make justice bitter—
>>> trampling on the common rights of men;
>>> hating the honest witness,
>>> bold speaker of the truth;
>>> robbing the peasant of his land,
>>> raping his harvest with your 'fines'!

> Therefore
>> build your stone houses—
>>> they will never be your home!
>> plant your vineyards—
>>> you will never drink their wine!

I know all about your untold crimes,
   your bold rebellion—
      bullying innocent men,
      taking any blood-money you can,
      brow-beating poor people in the courts!

When I pass through your homeland,
   there'll be moaning in the market-place,
   anguish in the streets,
farmers off their farms, away at funerals,
   professional mourners howling in the villages!

Woe
   to you who want 'GOD's Day'—
      what good will that Day do you?
   Day of Darkness,
      no Day of Light!—
   like a man running from a lion
      and meeting a bear!
   like a man leaning on a house-wall
      and being bitten by a snake!

I hate and loathe your harvest festivals—
   your religious services mean nothing to me!
Make your offerings—
   I won't accept them!
Give your richest gifts—
   I won't bother to look at them!
Stop singing your noisy hymns—
   your harps are no music to me!
Let justice roll down
   like the winter rains,
and righteousness
   like an unfailing river!

Woe
   to those who fancy themselves safe
      on Samaria Mountain!
   who can't be bothered about 'the evil day',
      forcing frightening disaster nearer—
      lounging on ivory beds,
      sprawling on couches,
      fetching from their farms
      fresh lamb and fatted veal,
      bawling their 'new songs'

to the music of the harp,
swilling bowlfuls of wine,
painted with costly cosmetics!
For the break-up of their country
they don't care a damn!

Therefore
they'll be the first to be marched away—
no sprawling revellers then,
just silence!

I despise this Northern insolence
and hate their proud palaces.
I will surrender the city
and everybody in it!

Do horses gallop up a cliff?
Can you drive an ox-plough on the sea?
Can you get justice in your corrupt courts?
An honest man might as well poison himself!
Yet you boast about the Gilead war—
'Oh, the capture of Karnaim was a walk-over!'

I am calling out an empire against you,
O men of the North!
They will be your masters
from your farthest north
to your farthest south!

You'll pay for your sharp practice!

Listen—
you who trample down the common people
and tyrannize the needy—
moaning and groaning
all day Sunday:
'Will Sunday never be over?
Why doesn't Monday morning come?—
selling the corn,
giving short measure,
tampering with the weights,

tilting the scales,
slipping in the sweepings!'
I swear by all your accursed insolence:
'I won't forget!'

Is this the Way GOD's People should worship him?

Hold to me!

'Hold to me
if you want to be really alive!
No pilgrimages to Bethel or Gilgal!
No travelling to Beersheba!'

Hold to GOD
if you want to be really alive—
lest he leap like a forest fire
over the North:
there'll be no putting
that fire out!

Listen!

With you alone I have been intimate
among all the peoples of the world, have I?
It is you, then, I will punish
for all your crimes.

Do two men walk together along a country road
without having planned it together?
Does a lion roar in the forest
without having caught its prey?

Does a bird drop to the earth
without being lured down?
Does a ground-trap snap
without being triggered off?
If the bugle blows in the city
aren't the people terrified?
Does a town meet disaster
without GOD having something to do with it?

The lion has roared—
  who can help shuddering?
GOD has spoken—
  who can help announcing what he has said?

You do have a good time!

Worship at Bethel—
  and be a rebel!
Worship at Gilgal—
  and be a traitor!
Bring your sacrifices
  every morning!
Take three days
  to offer your tithes!
Burn your thank-offering—
  make sure there's no leaven in it!
Shout out your subscriptions—
  let everybody hear!
You do have a good time,
  you Northerners!

This is GOD's Word!

You are my favourites, are you?

Don't you know that African negroes
  matter to me,
  matter as much as you Northerners?
Wasn't it you I led
  out of Egypt?
I know it was!
I also led the Philistines
  from Crete,
and the Syrians
  from beyond Damascus!

This is GOD'S Word!

A Hymn

When Amos's friends gathered his poems together (he may have written some down himself), they put with them verses from a hymn which seemed to them to make clear how Amos thought about GOD. GOD, for him, was the God of men and nature, Lord of the universe. This is the theme of these verses. They probably come from a temple hymn. Their style is very different from Amos's style, but they match the thought of God which shines through his 'visions' and his poetry.

Look!—
    he who shapes the thunder clouds,
      makes the storm,
      showers the soil with rain,
      makes early morning dark with cloud,
      walks on earth's high hills—
        GOD is his name!

He who makes 'The Bull'
    rise after 'The Goat'
    and set after 'The Grape-gatherer',
      made the Pleiades and Orion,
turned pitch darkness into the morning,
    darkened day into night,
summoned the ocean
    and poured it over the earth—
      GOD is his name!

He at whose touch the earth heaves—
    rising like the Nile,
    sinking like the Nile—
who builds his terraces in the sky,
    his dome over the earth—
      GOD is his name!

Voice of a Villager: Jeremiah (626–585 B.C.E.)

Jeremiah's story is a tragic story set in tragic times. Over a hundred years had passed since Amos spoke in Bethel; the whole situation of the Israelite people had dramatically changed. What Amos foresaw had happened: Assyrian armies had marched westward, trampling into subjection the little countries between them and the Mediterranean coast. The North had fallen in 721 and had become an Assyrian province. The South was an Assyrian province in all but name, and now the sky was darkening for it too. For a moment in the last years there had seemed a chance of escape: Assyria collapsed. But Babylon took its place and carried on its policy of westward expansion. Jeremiah lived through it all—the fall of Assyria, the march of Egyptian armies north to save it (when King Josiah died in the fight at Megiddo Pass), the decisive battle of Carchemish (605) when Egyptian power was smashed, the march west of the Babylonian armies, the first capture of Jerusalem in 597 (when the king and some of his high officers were deported), and the final fall of the city in 586 and the end of Israelite political independence.

Jeremiah was a poet to his finger-tips; sensitive, shy and retiring, he was driven into the very heart of the storm that overwhelmed his people—

'desperate tides of a whole world's anguish
forced through the channels of a single heart.'[1]

Some of his private poems have survived, poems he made for himself and never intended for anybody else; we owe their preservation probably to his friend and secretary, Baruch. We call them his 'Confessions'; we have to wait for a thousand years before any writing like them appears again. They tell the story of his heart.

We know so much about Jeremiah because Baruch wrote down an account of the last thirty years. He was rather a prosy writer (unlike his master), but in the stories he gives us we can see what Jeremiah had to face. The background of the story we have already read on pp. 171–183; read it again before you begin this account of Jeremiah.

We give first Baruch's stories; then the poems of Jeremiah in this order: 1. his call; 2. his 'Confessions'; 3. poems about contemporary events; 4. then, as with Amos's poems, what he had to say about everyday life and about religion.

---

[1] Dr A. S. Peake prefaced these lines from F. W. H. Myers *S. Paul* to his great commentary on *Jeremiah*.

Baruch's Stories of Jeremiah

In the Stocks

Jeremiah was speaking to the people in the valley outside Jerusalem City. He had a potter's earthen jar in his hand. He smashed it on the ground.

'These are GOD's words,' he said. ' "When you smash a jar like this, nobody can mend it again. That's what I mean to do with this city and its inhabitants—smash it and make it like this burial ground. House and palace alike shall be as cursed as this valley; on their flat roofs you have made sacrifices to the sun and the moon and the stars, and worshipped the foreign gods of the country".'

He left the burial ground and went to the temple court.

'These are GOD's words,' he told the crowd there. ' "You have been obstinate. You would not listen to what I have to say. I am about to bring on this city and the surrounding villages the disaster I have announced".'

The Chief Temple Officer, a priest called Pashhur, was standing by listening. He immediately arrested Jeremiah, and had him flogged and put in the stocks near the Benjamin Gate on the north side of the temple.

Next day, he came back and set him free.

'GOD's changed your name,' Jeremiah said to him. 'You're no longer Pashhur ("Safety"); you're Magor-missabib ("Total Terror"). These are GOD's words: "You and all your friends will know the Terror when it comes. You'll see your friends die in the fighting. The Babylonian emperor will capture the city, loot the houses and the palace, and march the people away to Babylon. You and your family will be among them. You will all die and be buried in a foreign land—you and all your friends who have listened to your lies".'

In the Temple Court

King Jehoiakim, son of the good King Josiah, had just succeeded his father (the Egyptians had put him on the throne in place of his younger brother).

GOD spoke to Jeremiah.

'Go and stand in the temple court,' he told him, 'and speak to all the crowds there. Tell them everything I command you to tell them; keep nothing back. They may listen and change their ways; if they do, I will not send the disaster their present behaviour deserves. Tell them this from me: "If you won't listen to me, live in my Way, take note of what my servants the prophets tell you (which is just what you haven't done), then I will make this temple like burnt-out Shiloh.[1] I will make this city the sort of city the whole world will despise".'

Priests, temple prophets and people listened while Jeremiah was speaking. As soon as he finished, they arrested him.

'You shall die for this!' they shouted. 'Speaking in GOD's name indeed! Talking about the temple being burned to the ground and the city becoming an empty desert! Death's what you deserve!'

The crowd hemmed him in.

The incident was reported to the king's ministers and they immediately left the palace and held court at the New Gate of the temple.

'Lynch him!' the priests and prophets were shouting. 'You've heard how he's attacked this city!'

'GOD sent me to speak against this temple and this city,' said Jeremiah. 'What I've said is what GOD told me to say. What you've got to do is clear—change your ways and listen to GOD's warning; then the disaster GOD speaks of may not happen. You can do what you like with me—I am at your mercy. But don't forget this: if you kill me, an innocent man, you will have to face the consequences of such a brutal act. What I said is what GOD sent me to say; I am sure of this.'

'The man's innocent,' was the judgment of the ministers. 'It's obvious he speaks with GOD's authority.'

Some elder statesmen were present, and they spoke up.

'We'd better remember what happened once before in King Hezekiah's days,' they said. 'Micah told the people just what Jeremiah's told us—he was telling them what GOD had to say:

> Ploughland, tumbled-down walls, sprouting trees—
> that's what this stronghold, this city,
> this temple will be like.

'Did the king—did the people—kill him for talking like that? Didn't they take GOD seriously and ask his forgiveness? And didn't GOD listen to them? The disaster never happened. We're just making it dead certain.'

'Ah, but what happened only a short time ago to Uriah?' the crowd protested. 'King Jehoiakim didn't treat his bitter words about this city like that—he held them to be treason. Uriah escaped to Egypt, but he was brought back to this country and executed and his body thrown into a common graveyard!'

It was at this moment that a man called Ahikam stood by Jeremiah and saved him from being lynched by the crowd.

---

[1] It is now known that the destruction of Shiloh Jeremiah refers to was a recent event and not the Philistine destruction of the town five hundred years before.

The Burning of the Scroll

A little later—King Jehoiakim had been on the throne for three years —GOD spoke again to Jeremiah.

'Write down in a scroll all I have told you to say since I first spoke to you,' he told him, 'all I have told you to say about the North and the South and the surrounding countries. If they'll listen, perhaps the Southerners will take some note of what I have to say about the disaster which threatens them; they may yet change their ways and be forgiven.'

Jeremiah sent for Baruch. He dictated all he had said and Baruch wrote it down. Then he gave Baruch some careful instructions.

'I can't go into the temple,' he told him. 'You can. There are special services being held at the great December Fast; the courts will be crowded with people from the city and the country villages. Go and read this scroll to the crowds there. These are GOD's words. Perhaps the people will change their ways and worship GOD as they should; the disaster which is threatening them is a very real and terrible disaster.'

Baruch did as he was told. He read Jeremiah's words in the room in the upper temple court by the New Gate used by one of the king's ministers, Gemariah.

Micaiah, Gemariah's son, was in the crowd listening. When the reading was over, he went post-haste to the Adjutant-General's room in the palace where a cabinet meeting of the king's ministers was being held. He told them what he had just heard.

The ministers sent an officer to fetch Baruch and his scroll.

'Read it again to us,' they ordered.

Baruch read it to them.

As the reading finished, they turned in panic to one another.

'We must tell the king about this,' they said.

'How did you come to write it down?' they asked Baruch. 'Did Jeremiah dictate it?'

'He did,' he said. 'He went on dictating, and I wrote it all down as accurately as I could in ink in this scroll.'

'You and Jeremiah had better keep out of the way,' they warned him. 'Don't let anybody know where you're hiding.'

The ministers left the scroll in the Adjutant-General's room and went to seek an audience with the king. They reported all they knew about the incident in the temple.

The king ordered one of the secretaries to fetch the scroll.

He was sitting in his winter house with a fire burning brightly in the brazier in front of him. The secretary began to read.

When he had read three or four columns, the king leaned forward and slashed them off with a penknife and threw them into the fire.

So it went on until the whole scroll had been burned.

The king and his court weren't in the least troubled by what they heard; they showed no sign of fear at all. Three of his ministers tried to stop him burning the scroll. But he took no notice. All he did was to order two of his officers to arrest Baruch and Jeremiah. GOD saw to it that they weren't found.

GOD spoke to Jeremiah again.

'Get another scroll,' he told him, 'and write it all down again. Then tell the king in my name: "You have burned the scroll, but no son of yours shall succeed you on the throne. You will die in the fighting and your body will lie in the city streets—burned by the midday heat and frozen by the night frost".'

Jeremiah dictated the words again, and Baruch wrote them down on another scroll. Other words that GOD had spoken were also added, words dealing with the coming disaster.

Two Prophets meet

Jeremiah was wearing a wooden halter on his shoulders as a sign to the people that what had happened to King Jehoiachin would happen to them all. (In 597, King Jehoiachin and leading citizens had been deported to Babylon—they had no more choice than a farm animal which has to go where its driver makes it go.)

One day, that winter, he went into the crowded temple courts. Hananiah, the prophet from Gibeon, accosted him. Everybody could hear what he said.

'This is what GOD says,' Hananiah called out to him, ' "I have broken the harness which the Babylonian emperor has put on you—in two years everything he looted from the temple will be recovered, and King Jehoiachin and all Jewish prisoners will be back home again!" '

Jeremiah faced Hananiah with the crowds standing round.

'Very well!' he said. 'May GOD do just that—as you say. May loot and exiles all come home again. But there's something else to be said. Listen, you and all this crowd: in days gone by, the prophets, our predecessors, spoke only of disaster; a prophet who talks about peace can only be proved a true prophet when peace has come.'

Hananiah got hold of the halter Jeremiah was wearing round his neck, took it off and broke it up.

'These are GOD's words,' he told the crowd. ' "In the same way, within two years, I will break the harness the emperor has put on your necks!" '

Jeremiah went home.

Some days later, GOD spoke again to him.

'Go and tell Hananiah this,' he said. ' ''You have smashed the wooden halter; I will make an iron halter to take its place. Listen to me. It is I who have made all these nations the slaves of the Babylonian emperor —they shall stay his slaves''.'

Jeremiah went to Hananiah.

'Listen to me, Hananiah,' he said. 'GOD never sent you. You have made these people trust a lie. These are GOD's words to you: ''I have finished with you!'' '

Hananiah died in April.

Letters to Babylon (after 597)

This is the letter Jeremiah sent from Jerusalem to Babylon to the leaders of the exiles there (he got King Zedekiah's envoys to Babylon to deliver it for him):

These are GOD's words: 'This is what I have to say to all those I sent as exiles to Babylon:

> Make Babylon your home—
>   build houses,
> grow food in your gardens,
>   marry and rear families;
> you will not die out,
>   you will become a great community.
> Work for the good of the country
>   I have made the place of your exile.
> When you pray to me,
>   remember Babylon in your prayers—
> you and she
>   stand or fall together.
>
> This is what I have to say to you:
>
> Remember my plans for you,
>   plans of peace, not plans of disaster,
>   a future to hope for.
> Pray to me and I will listen;
>   seek me and find me;
> when you seek me with all your hearts,
>   you shall find me.'

Jeremiah received an answer to this letter. This is his reply to it:

'You answer me by saying ''GOD has given us prophets here in Babylon. We don't need any words from you.'' Then hear what GOD has to say about your prophets, Ahab and Zedekiah: ''I will deliver them into the emperor's power; he will execute them in your sight.

Their names will become by-words among you—all this because of their infamous conduct and their false prophecies. I never gave them the right to speak, but I noticed what they did. These are my words".'

Shemaiah sent a letter from Babylon to Zephaniah the supervisor in Jerusalem:

'GOD appointed you to take the place of the priest Jehoiada to keep order in the temple—to arrest any madman who plays the prophet and put him in irons. Why, then, haven't you arrested the self-styled prophet Jeremiah? He sent a letter to us here in Babylon telling us that we are here to stay for a very long time and that we must settle down and make Babylon our home.'

Zephaniah read the letter to Jeremiah.

GOD spoke to him:

'Send a message in my name to the exiles in Babylon. "What Shemaiah has told you is a lie. This is what I have to say: I will punish Shemaiah and his descendants; they will not live to see the good I mean to do to you".'

The Scroll and the River

Seraiah, the Quartermaster, brother of Baruch, had business in Babylon.

Jeremiah had written in a scroll what GOD had told him about the Babylonian empire: that it would not last for ever, doom would one day overtake it.

Jeremiah went to Seraiah.

'When you get to Babylon,' he said, 'make sure that you read all the words of this scroll to the exiles there. Then pray this prayer: "O GOD, you have spoken against this great empire. You will bring it to an end; the city will become desolate ruins, abandoned by man and animal."

'This done, tie the scroll to a stone and throw it into the Euphrates River.

'Then repeat GOD's words: "So shall Babylon sink, to rise no more; I am bringing her doom upon her!" '

Slaves—Pawns in the Political Game (between 597 and 586)

King Zedekiah made a solemn agreement with the citizens of Jerusalem to free all Israelite slaves—men and women; no citizen was to hold a fellow-citizen as a slave. So all slaves were set free.

After a time, the citizens went back on their word; they forced the freed slaves into slavery again.

GOD spoke to Jeremiah:

'This is what I have to say to them: You did a fine thing when you

The Euphrates River near Babylon

set the slaves free and made a solemn agreement to do so in my presence. But you have gone back on your word. You have put me to shame by forcing men and women back into slavery.

'This is what I now have to say to you: You have flouted me in this matter of a Declaration of Freedom. I will therefore set you free—to become yourselves the slaves of a new master: war and hunger and the disease they breed. The whole world shall hold you in horror. As for the men who broke my Covenant by disowning their solemn Declaration of Freedom, I will hand them over to their enemies, and they will know what war means. The Babylonian army has raised the siege—for the moment. But king and ministers shall become its victims—I order it back to the city. Jerusalem shall be attacked, captured and burnt to the ground. Its villages shall be left desolate and deserted.'

In the Besieged City (587–6)

King Zedekiah—son of the good King Josiah—was now on the throne, put there by the Babylonian authorities. But neither he nor his ministers nor the common people took Jeremiah seriously. They did not believe that GOD was speaking to them through him.

But one day King Zedekiah sent two men to Jeremiah with a message. 'Pray to GOD for us,' he asked.

Jeremiah was still a free man; he had not yet been put into prison.

The Babylonian armies had been besieging Jerusalem; but news that the Egyptians were marching north had forced them to withdraw their troops to the coast.

GOD spoke to Jeremiah.

'This is what I have to say,' he told him. 'The king sent to you to pray for him. Tell him: "The Egyptian armies have retreated: the Babylonian armies will come back to carry out their attack on the city. They will capture it and burn it down. Don't fool yourself and think that they will abandon their attack; they won't. Even if you had troops enough to defeat their entire army and the soldiers in their camp were all wounded men, they would still march and burn the city down!" '

There was a lull in the siege while the Babylonian armies were back on the plain facing the advancing Egyptian troops. Jeremiah set off through the Benjamin Gate of the city to go to his native village of Anathoth to deal with some property there. A sentry challenged him.

'Running away, are you?' he said.

'That's a lie!' said Jeremiah. 'I'm no deserter.'

The sentry wouldn't listen. He arrested him and marched him to the city authorities. The officials were so angry with Jeremiah that they had him flogged and kept him in the secretary's house which was being used as a prison. And there he stayed, shut up in an underground pit, for a long time.

The king, at last, heard about his arrest, and had him brought secretly to the palace.

'Has GOD said anything to you?' he asked.

'He has,' said Jeremiah. ' "You will become a prisoner of the Babylonian emperor."

'What wrong have I done to your Majesty or your ministers or my fellow-countrymen?' he went on. 'What have I done to deserve prison? And what's happened to all the prophets who said the Babylonian armies would never come back to attack you or the city? Your Majesty, I beg you to listen to me. Grant me this petition: don't send me back to that pit or I shall die there.'

The king gave orders for Jeremiah to be detained in the Guards' Barracks; and he was to have a loaf from the Bakers' Bazaar until bread rations gave out.

So that's where Jeremiah stayed.

Four of the king's ministers were noting down the kind of message Jeremiah was still giving to the people about the Babylonian attack on the city. Here are two they seized on:

'The man who stays in the city will face death; war or starvation or disease will see to that. The man who surrenders to the Babylonians will at least save his life, if only by the skin of his teeth. At any rate he will stay alive.'

'The city will certainly fall to the attack of the Babylonian armies.'

The four men asked for an audience with the king.

'Order this man's execution,' they advised him. 'This kind of talk is undermining the resistance of both troops and civilians. This fellow isn't trying to help his country; he is merely making sure of its defeat.'

'Well,' said the king, 'he's at your mercy'—by this time, he was a mere figure-head.

The men arrested Jeremiah and threw him into a pit in the Guards' Barracks. The pit was empty but muddy, and Jeremiah sank in the mud.

One of the palace chamberlains, an African called Ebed-melech, was on duty at the palace and heard about what had happened to Jeremiah. He left the palace and found the king at the Benjamin Gate.

'Your Majesty,' he said, 'your ministers have done a dreadful thing in throwing Jeremiah into the pit. If he's left there, he'll die.'

'Take three men,' said the king, 'and get him out. I don't want him to die.'

Ebed-melech and the men got some rags and old clothes from a wardrobe. They lowered them by ropes, so that Jeremiah could put them under his armpits to stop the ropes chafing his skin. Then they pulled him up and got him out of the pit. But he stayed on in the Guards' Barracks.

One day, King Zedekiah again summoned Jeremiah to a secret interview. They met at the gate where the king's bodyguard entered the temple.

'I've a question to ask you,' said the king. 'Tell me the truth.'

'If I tell you the truth,' said Jeremiah, 'you'll only order my execution. You never listen to what I have to say.'

The king swore an oath:

'As GOD lives who made us,' he said, 'I won't execute you and I won't hand you over to the men who want to get rid of you.'

'Well,' said Jeremiah, 'this is what GOD has to say: "If you surrender to the Babylonians, you will escape with your life and the city will escape being burned down—and your family will escape with you. If you don't surrender, the city will be captured and burned to the ground; you yourself certainly won't escape".'

'I am afraid of the Jews who have already deserted to the Babylonians,' said the king. 'I don't want to be handed over to them and beaten up.'

'You won't,' said Jeremiah. 'Do what GOD tells you through me;

you will be safe, your life spared. If you don't surrender, this is what GOD has shown me: I have seen in a vision the women abandoned in the royal harem being led out by the Babylonian officers and chanting this lament about their country as they walked along—

> Even your friends have let you down,
>   they've had their way with you,
> they've pushed you into the deep mud
>   and left you there!'

'If you want to escape death,' said the king, 'don't breathe a word about this conversation. If the officials hear about it and question you, tell them you were presenting a petition to me not to be sent back to certain death in Jonathan's house.'

News about this secret interview with the king did leak out; the officials came and questioned Jeremiah about it. He answered them as the king had told him to. They let him be; the conversation with the king had not been overheard.

Jeremiah stayed in the Guards' Barracks until the fall of the city.

Freedom again

The city was captured in the summer of 586. The Babylonians entered it and set up their headquarters at the Middle Gate. They sent for Jeremiah who was still in the Guards' Barracks and put him into the custody of Gedaliah to be taken out to his Residence. (Gedaliah, son of his old friend Ahikam, was soon to be made governor of the Jerusalem area by the Babylonian authorities.)

Before Jeremiah left the Guards' Barracks, GOD spoke to him.

'Send this message to the African Ebed-melech,' said GOD. ' "I am about to carry out all I have threatened against this city—words of disaster, not words of victory—and you will see it happen. But I will rescue you and see that you do not fall into the hands of the men you fear. I guarantee your escape—you will not be killed in the fighting. Your life will be saved because you trusted me. These are my words".'

Some months later, Jeremiah was rounded up with the crowd of prisoners being taken on the long journey to Babylon. The assembly-point was Ramah, some five miles north of the city. Here he was found in chains by Captain Nebuzaradan, the commander of the Babylonian Guards. He ordered him to be unchained.

'You are a free man,' he told Jeremiah. 'If you want to come with me to Babylon, I will see that you are in no danger. But do what you like. Stay here if you want to.'

Jeremiah chose to join Governor Gedaliah in Mizpah, a town some

Into exile ▶

few miles to the west, where he had set up his headquarters, and those who had rallied round him.

Murder of the Governor

Jewish soldiers who had escaped from the city were fighting as guerillas in the hills. News reached them of Gedaliah's appointment as governor of the remaining population (mostly poor peasants). The guerilla captains—Ishmael, Johanan and Jonathan, Seraiah, Ephai's sons, Jezaniah—marched their men to Mizpah to serve under him.

'Don't worry about the Babylonian officers here,' the governor told them. 'Settle down in the country, accept our new masters loyally and everything will be all right. My work's clear: I will deal directly with the Babylonian authorities from my headquarters here. You can get on with your farming wherever you want to.'

He swore an oath of loyalty to all his countrymen.

Many Jews had fled as refugees across the eastern frontiers. When they heard of the new government in Mizpah, they came back and took up their farming again. There were splendid harvests that summer.

Captain Johanan and the guerilla leaders came in to Gedaliah to report a plot against his life; it was being hatched, they said, in a neighbouring state.

'Haven't you heard what King Baalis of Ammon is up to?' they asked him. 'He's sent Prince Ishmael to assassinate you.'

Gedaliah thought it was only a rumour—there was nothing in it.

But Captain Johanan saw him privately about it.

'Let me deal with Prince Ishmael,' he said. 'Let me get rid of him; I can do it without any public fuss. Why should we take any risk? Your death would be a disaster for the whole country. We should have to take to the hills again.'

'I forbid you to do any such thing,' said Gedaliah. 'There's nothing in this rumour, I tell you.'

In the spring, Prince Ishmael and ten conspirators arrived in Mizpah and were entertained by the governor. In the middle of the meal, the eleven men carried out their plot, murdering the governor and the Jewish advisers and Babylonian officials who were with him. They sealed off the Governor's Residence; nobody in the town suspected anything.

Next day, eighty pilgrims from three northern towns arrived; they were going to Jerusalem to share in a service in the ruined temple there. Prince Ishmael went out to meet them as they walked along singing hymns of lament, and lured them into the town.

'Come and meet the governor,' he said.

When they reached the town centre, he and his men butchered them

◀ Peasants ploughing

and threw their bodies into a well. Ten of them begged for mercy.

'Don't kill us, don't kill us!' they pleaded. 'We've lots of wheat and barley and oil and honey hidden out in the open countryside.'

He spared their lives.

But he rounded up the Mizpah townspeople and some royal princesses Captain Nebuzaradan had put in the care of the governor, and at dawn next day marched them off as prisoners toward the eastern frontier and Ammonite territory.

News of the governor's murder quickly reached Captain Johanan and his friends. They called out their men and caught Prince Ishmael at the Pool of Gibeon. The crowd of prisoners were filled with joy when they recognized the soldiers and soon showed whose side they were on. Prince Ishmael and eight of his men made good their escape across the frontier.

Captain Johanan gathered together the people he and his men had rescued. But instead of going back north, they marched south and stopped at Kimham's Sheepfolds near Bethlehem with the idea of going on to Egypt. They were terrified at the thought of the reprisals the Babylonians would take.

Panic

Captain Johanan and Captain Azariah and the crowd of survivors consulted Jeremiah (he had been marched away with the others).

'Do what we ask you,' they said. 'You have often told us what GOD has to say to us. Ask him to guide us now and tell us what to do. There are not many of us left.'

'Very well,' said Jeremiah. 'I will do what you ask and tell you what GOD has to say. I won't hide anything from you.'

'GOD knows that we mean what we say,' they said. 'We will do whatever he tells us to do. We will obey him—whether we like it or not. That's why we're asking you to pray for us. We want to do the right thing, and we know we can only do the right thing if we obey what GOD says.'

Jeremiah waited ten days before GOD spoke to him. He called the captains and the people together.

'This is what GOD has to say to you,' he told them, ' "Stay here in this country and I will build you up as a strong people—you need not fear ruin or death. I will not deal with you as I have done in the past. I know you are terrified of the Babylonian emperor and what he may do. Don't be frightened. I am with you and I will deal with him. I will show my kindness to you by making him treat you kindly and let you settle in your own country. But if you refuse to listen to me, if you say 'No, it's Egypt for us—we've finished with fighting and hunger —we're going to live where there's peace and plenty. We're going to Egypt'—if you talk like this, then listen, I have something to say to you. You're only a handful of refugees; you'll find in Egypt only what you're trying to escape from here—fighting and famine and death. And there'll be no escaping from Egypt; you'll never see your native land again. I have warned you. You go to Egypt at your own risk. You asked for my guidance and you promised to do whatever I told you. I have now told you. But in your hearts, I fear, you are not keeping your promises''.'

Jeremiah finished.

'You're lying,' the captains had the insolence to say to him. 'GOD never said that. Baruch's been putting you up to talking like this. All he wants is for the Babylonians to capture us—and we know what that means: death or deportation.'

They refused to stay in Palestine. The captains led the whole crowd of refugees south across the Egyptian border and made Jeremiah and Baruch go with them. They settled in the Egyptian town of Daphne.

In Egypt

GOD spoke to Jeremiah in Daphne.

'Take some large stones,' he told him, 'and bury them in the pavement in front of the Government House in Daphne—let the Jewish refugees see you do it. Then tell them: This is what GOD has to say to you—"I will bring my servant, the Babylonian emperor to this place. He will set up his throne on these very stones and raise his pavilion over them. He will conquer Egypt with all the horrors of war —the very things you are trying to escape—and rob and burn the Egyptian temples, even the obelisks of the great temple of Heliopolis. He will deal with Egypt as a shepherd deals with his coat—picking lice out of it. Nobody will stop him''.'

Jewish refugees in Egypt were now living at Migdol, Daphne, Memphis (the old Egyptian capital) and even in the south in Upper Egypt. GOD told Jeremiah to speak to them when they met together for an act of worship.

'This is what GOD has to say to you,' Jeremiah told them, ' "You have yourselves seen the disaster which has overtaken your native land and its capital city. It all lies desolate. You know the reason: you were not loyal to me; you worshipped the pagan gods of the country. I told you plainly that this was wrong; I sent my servants the prophets to tell you. But nobody took any notice. That's why disaster over-whelmed you. Why are you following the same suicidal path here in Egypt? Why are you worshipping in Egyptian temples? You are only courting disaster again—the same disaster which has overtaken your country and your capital city. You will meet the same fate: there will be no survivors!" '

The women and their husbands screamed at Jeremiah.

'We won't listen to you!' they shouted. 'We've made up our minds. We'll worship Ishtar, the Queen of Heaven. That's what our fathers did and we were happy and well-fed and safe then. We've had nothing but trouble since we listened to men like you and stopped worshipping her.

'We made cakes stamped with her image,' the screaming women went on, 'and we poured libations out to her—and our husbands knew all about it!'

'All right, you've made up your minds,' said Jeremiah. 'Go on with your Egyptian worship. But remember what GOD is saying to you: "I have sworn by my name that you will never use my name in worship again, and you will suffer the disaster you deserve—the very things you came here to escape. The refugees from that disaster will be few indeed. You will discover then whose word is the truth—mine or yours. And this will be the sign of disaster: the Egyptian Pharaoh will be defeated by his enemies as surely as King Zedekiah was captured by the Babylonian emperor!" '

A Word to Baruch

'That is what GOD has to say to you, Baruch,' said Jeremiah one day when Baruch had finished writing down his poems in the scroll:

' "I know what you have been saying, that all I've meant to you is trouble and sorrow, that you're tired of complaining and that you can't settle down. Listen to me.

> I am about to pull down what I built up,
>   root up what I planted.
> You're a very ambitious man—
>   this is no time for ambition.
> I am about to bring disaster
>   on the whole world of men.
> You'll have to live dangerously;
>   all you'll get will be strength to see it through!" '

Jeremiah's Call

Jeremiah was quite a young man when he became aware of GOD's call to be his 'spokesman'. When this happened is not quite clear but it was a time of international turmoil and uncertainty. The date given in the records is 626. Whatever the truth about this, most of Jeremiah's poems and Baruch's stories come from the years after the death of King Josiah (609).

He described his Call (as Amos had done) in symbolic language. The sight of almond blossoms in spring, the first flowers to appear, stirred his mind; the word for 'almond blossom' (shaqed) and the word for 'wakeful' (shoqed) sound very much alike; one word recalled the other. The open oven he passed by was facing north and being fanned by a northern wind; this reminded him of the danger from the north—where all real danger—Scythian horde or Assyrian army—came from. It was his people's danger that brought Jeremiah from the seclusion of his little village of Anathoth (where his father was village priest) into the public life of the nation.

GOD's Spokesman

GOD spoke to me:

> 'Before you were born
>   I chose you,
>   and set you apart,
>   appointed you
>   to speak in my name to the whole world!'

'But GOD,' I said, 'I am too young. I don't know how to speak to people at all!'

GOD's answer came clear:

> 'Don't talk like that!
>   You shall go
>   to whomever I send you!
>   You shall speak
>   whatever I tell you!
>   Don't be afraid of anybody—
>   I am with you,
>   I am looking after you!'

GOD touched my mouth with his hand and told me:

> 'Look, I have given you the power
>   to speak my words,
> power over the whole world
>   to pluck up and plant,
>   to break down and build up.'

Almond Blossom
>God spoke to me:
>'What are you looking at, Jeremiah?' he asked.
>'Almond blossom,' I said.
>'Just so,' he said,
>
>>'I stand wakeful over my word
>>   to make it my deed!'

A Boiling Pot
>GOD spoke to me again.
>'What are you looking at, Jeremiah?' he asked.
>'A boiling pot,' I said, 'and a fierce north wind is fanning the fire!'
>GOD's words came clear:
>
>>'A north wind wildly blowing
>>   on the people of this land!
>>I will pass sentence on them
>>   for deserting me so falsely,
>>sacrificing to village gods
>>   carved with their own hands.
>>
>>'These are your marching orders:
>>   up and tell them what I tell you.
>>Don't let them frighten you—
>>   or I will really make you frightened
>>   when you meet them!'
>>
>>>This is GOD's Word.

Jeremiah's 'Confessions'

These poems are prayers in which Jeremiah lays bare his heart to God. Here we can see what questions and conflicts went on in his mind, and how he had to fight his way through to his faith in God.

Alone against the world

>Alas, my mother,
>I wish you had never given me birth—
>   a man at odds with the whole world!
>I stand in no man's debt—
>   yet all men curse me!

You know all about me, O GOD—
    remember me and come to me!
Set me right with those who are against me—
    and set me right quickly.
It's men who care nothing for you
    who have heaped insults on me.

My joy and my happiness
    is to listen to your words.
I am wholly yours,
    O GOD of the whole world!
I never joined the village merry-making—
    that gave me no pleasure at all.
I sat alone—
    you were urging me on,
    your anger was my anger.

Why does my pain go on and on,
    my wounds incurable?
You are to me like a waterless gorge,
    and a dried-up spring!

GOD answered me:

I will heal you, if you stay loyal,
    and you will indeed be my servant;
call right right and wrong wrong,
    and you will be my ambassador.

It's for others to take your side,
    and not for you to take theirs.
Against the assault of this people
    I will make you like bronze battlements!

They will attack you
    they will not conquer you.
I am with you,
    I will rescue you
        from the power of vicious men,
        from the grip of ruthless men.

The human heart

GOD once said to me:

> How deep is the human heart—
>> deep as an unfathomable sea!
>
> Its sickness defies cure—
>> who knows its secret?

> I, GOD,
>> plumb the secret mind
>> and test the secret heart.

'Let's dig a pit to catch him!'

> 'Come!' they said, 'let's put him in his place,
>> frame charges against him
>> and take no notice of what he says!'

> Watch them, O GOD,
>> listen to my accusers!
>> Is evil all I get for doing good?

> Remember: I stood before you
>> to plead for them,
>> to stave off your anger!

> And all they could do
>> was to dig a pit to catch me,
>> set a trap for me to walk into!

Out of the depths

> You have deceived me, O GOD,
>> and I let myself be deceived!
>
> You were too strong for me,
>> you did with me what you wanted.
>
> I'm everybody's laughing-stock,
>> a daily joke!

> I've only to speak to be laughed at
>> with my 'Violence!' and 'Wrong!'—

'GOD's Word' I talk about
    is no joke!

'I'll give it all up,
    I'll be no ambassador of his!'—
my protest dies
    for his word within me
sets my heart ablaze,
    scorches my very soul.
I can stand no more of this,
    I can't go on!

I know what they're all whispering,
    my old friends whispering:
'He and his "Terror is coming!"—
    let us denounce him!
He'll slip up somewhere
    and we'll get our own back!'

But GOD is with me,
    giving me a hero's courage.
It's they who'll slip up,
    they'll not get the better of me!
It's they who will fall
    and fail.
Their shameful behaviour
    shall not be forgotten!

Why was I born?

I hate the day
    when I was born,
I don't want
    any birthday greetings!

I hate the man
    who told my father the happy news—
'You've a son now!'
    'Happy' indeed!

May his fate be like the fate of the towns
    that died in the Sodom earthquake—
its morning disaster,
    its noon black with battle!

Why didn't he kill me
    there and then—
        making my mother my grave
        big with my dead body?

Why was I born
    for trouble and hard labour,
    a lifetime of shame?

The Tragedy of GOD's People

Why go to Egypt?

Was the North a slave bought in the slave-market
    or born in bondage?
Why, then, is he at the mercy of invaders,
    his towns smoking ruins?

Egyptian legionaries
    are shaving you bald—
and your abandonment of GOD
    is the cause of it all!

Why go off to Egypt
    to quench your thirst in the Nile?
Why go off to Assyria
    to quench your thirst in the Euphrates?

Disaster will teach you
    the error of your ways—
how bitter a thing it is
    to abandon your GOD,
    to scorn my help!

Danger from the north

It used to be thought that this danger was the raiding of the Scythians from the north. But it is now doubted whether there were any such raids. However, whether Jeremiah is referring to Scythians or Assyrians, his argument is clear—the danger to the Israelite people was what was happening over their northern borders, and to this they were strangely blind.

Watchman's Shout

Blow the bugle,
  shout across the hills—
'Fly from the villages!
  Gather in the walled towns!'

Hoist the signal in Jerusalem city!
  Escape while you can!
Danger and disaster
  march down from the north!

The lion has leapt from his lair!
  Destroyer of Nations is marching,
  marching south,
harrying your homeland,
  murdering your people
  in town and village!

Put on mourning,
  lament and wail!
GOD's fierce anger
  pursues us still!

Gathering Storm

Look!

Soldiers like thunderclouds!
  Chariots like storm-winds!
Cavalry like vultures!
  All is lost!

Look!

Runner from the frontier,
  herald from the highlands:
'Enemy troops are marching,
  marching on Jerusalem!'

Invaders pour over the border,
  threatening our Southern towns,
sleepless pickets
  ring them round!

The Pity of it All!

> My heart! My heart! The pain of it!
>   The wild beating of my heart!
>   The tumult of my mind!

> Bugles blowing,
>   soldiers shouting,
> crash upon cruel crash
>   in the deserted towns!

> Tent and curtains
>   of my beloved city
>   torn in tatters!

Pablo Picasso: Guernica (1937 C.E.)

How long must I watch
    the signal on the hills?
How long listen
    to the blare of bugles?

'Roads crowded with fugitives'

Vision of Chaos

> I looked at the earth beneath me—
>   Chaos again!
> stared at the sky above me—
>   starless dark!
>
> I looked at the mountains—
>   they were quaking!
> at the highlands—
>   they were shaking!

I looked and looked again—
    empty roads,
    empty skies!
I looked and looked again—
    everywhere
    deserted and smoking cities
        before GOD's anger!

Invasion

Thud of galloping cavalry!
    Swish of archers' arrows!
Roads crowded with fugitives,
    crawling into caves,
    hiding in thickets,
    climbing crags!
Towns
    empty and deserted!

Dreadful City

Dressing in scarlet still?
    Flaunting your trinkets?
Painting your face?
    You are wasting your time!
Your lovers don't want your beauty,
    they want your blood!

Scream like a woman's scream
    in her first child-birth!—
Scream of the city
    clenching her fists:
'Woe! Woe! Woe!
    I faint at my murderers' feet!'

Death of King Josiah (609)

No dirge for the dead king,
    no lament!
Keep your tears
    for the king in exile—
no home-coming for him,
    no sight of his native land!

Megiddo (*609*)

My grief knows no relief,
  my heart sinks!
Far and wide
  my people shout for help:

'Is GOD no longer
  on the Temple Hill?
Has her king
  deserted her?
Harvest's over, summer's gone
  and we're not rescued!'

My people's wounds
  have broken my heart;
sorrow and dismay
  overpower me.

Is there no healing oil in Gilead,
  no doctor there?
Why, then, is my people's wound
  raw and bleeding?

Would to GOD my head were a sea,
  my eyes a river—
I would weep for ever
  over the dead of my people!

Jehoiakim's Palace

Woe to him who builds his palace
  on injustice,
its upper rooms
  on fraud!
conscripts labourers
  and robs them of their pay!
with only one thought in his head—
  'A spacious palace!
  airy rooms!
  wide windows!
  cedar panels!
  scarlet paint!'

What kind of king do you think you are?
  Is cedar all you can think about?
Your father was a different king—
  eating and drinking indeed,
  but caring for justice and right,
  defending the humble and poor.
He was a king indeed
  his was honest religion!

                       This is GOD's Word!

Lament for King and Queen Mother (after 597)

Tell the king and queen mother:
  'No throne now—only a peasant's chair!
Your splendid crown
  fallen on the palace floor!

'Towns of the steppes blockaded!
  Guards at the gates gone!
The South swept away,
  swept away into exile!'

King Jehoiachin's Surrender (597)

King Jehoiachin!—a broken pot
  nobody wants any more!
Why—why was he flung headlong
  into an unknown land?

O Earth—Earth—Earth!
  Listen to what GOD has to say:

'Write this man down as an outlaw,
  a stumbler all his life.
No descendant shall succeed him
  sitting on David's throne,
  king of the South!'

Is this the Way GOD's People should live?

No Covenant for them!

'Explore the city's streets,
　　search the market-places;
find, if you can, anybody who acts justly
　　or values honesty,
　　　that I may forgive the city,'
　　　　says GOD.

Its people use your name
　　but it doesn't mean anything.
Yet it's honesty
　　that matters to you, O GOD.
You have punished them
　　but they didn't even wince!
They won't learn—
　　they've set their faces like flint,
　　no repentance for them!

They're only peasants (said I),
　　they know no better,
they haven't really understood,
　　their 'worship' is all mixed-up.
I'll try the 'important people',
　　I'll talk with them,
they understand what you want,
　　their worship is real worship.

But even they just please themselves
　　like a runaway horse—
　　no Covenant for them!

Violence everywhere

False city,
　　full of oppression!
Like cool water in a well
　　your heart is cool with evil!

Everywhere victims shouting
　　'Violence!' 'Robbery!'
I can see nothing
　　but a sick and wounded city!

Hard hearts

These are GOD's words:

> If a man falls down
>   he gets up again;
> if he loses his way
>   he finds the track again.
> My people have wandered from the road—
>   why don't they find their way back?

> They cling to deceit,
>   they won't repent.
> I've been listening hard—
>   I can't hear a whisper.
> Nobody stops and says
>   'What have I done?'
> They are as headstrong
>   as a horse galloping into battle!

> Stork flying in the sky
>   knows how to find her way;
> dove and swallow
>   keep their appointed time.
> My people have no sense
>   of my time or way!

Nobody trusts anybody

> O for a traveller's hut
>   in the desert,
> to be quit of my folk
>   and far away!

> Adulterers all!
>   Gang of traitors!
> They use words as men use a bow,
>   loyalty means nothing to them!
> They heap crime on crime,
>   they've no use for religion!

This is GOD's Word!

Guard against your friend!
  Don't trust even your brother!
Brother cheats brother like Jacob,
  neighbour slanders neighbour!

Cheating is a common game,
  truth doesn't matter,
lies are a habit,
  nobody says 'I'm sorry'!
Violence is their easy answer,
  cheating their trade!
Nobody wants to know about me,
  says GOD.

A word to the Government

Listen to what GOD has to say,
  O dynasty of David!

Make justice your concern,
  rescue the robbed from the robber—
lest my anger blaze like a fire—
  and no fitful fire!—
  lit by your foul play.

Is this the Way GOD's People should worship him?

'I remember!'

GOD said this to my people through me:

I remember
  your youthful affection,
    the love of our honeymoon—
  the love with which you followed me
    on the desert march!

Strange ingratitude

Listen to what GOD has to say to you:

> What fault did your fathers find in me
>   to leave me,
> becoming as false
>   as the false gods they followed?
>
> They never asked
>   'Where is GOD
>   who rescued us from Egypt,
>   marched us across the desert
>   with its wild and shifting sands,
>   its drought and desolation,
>   where nobody travels
>   and nobody lives.'
>
> It was I who
>   brought you to the arable lands
>   with their happy harvests!
> And all you could do when you got there
>   was to become pagan as the pagans,
> no priest asking 'Where is GOD?'
>   no judge aware of my Way.
>
> This is what I have to say:
>   I will stand up to you,
> I will stand up
>   to all your descendants!
>
> Search—and search again—
>   in the west, in the east:
> can you find anywhere
>   a people changing its religion?
>
> Yet my people have changed me, their glory,
>   for a helpless idol—
> the very heavens stare aghast,
>   scared and shocked!

This is GOD's Word!

Springs and wells

> My people have done
>   two evil things:
> They have abandoned me,
>   a mountain spring of running water;
> they have hewed out for themselves
>   cracked and leaking wells!

'Can't you hear the bugles blowing?'

> Stand by the cross-roads and look,
>   ask where the old paths are—
> then use them
>   and learn what quietness of heart means.
> 'Not likely!'
>   is all they said.
>
> I gave you watchmen—
>   can't you hear the bugles blowing?
> 'No, we can't!'
>   is all they said.
>
> I call the nations to witness,
>   the earth to listen:
> the disaster I bring upon them
>   is of their own evil making!
> They would not listen,
>   they flouted my Way.
>
> What good's Arabian incense,
>   sweet spices from overseas?
> I can't stand your 'Sabbath services'!
>   I hate your temple 'worship'!

Snow on Hermon Mountain

These are GOD's words:

> Ask anybody:
>   have you heard anything like this?—
> my unravaged people
>   are guilty of shameful wrong.

Does the white snow
   melt from Hermon Mountain?
Do the waters
   fail from the Great Sea?

Yet my people have forgotten me,
   given their heart to idols,
stumbling on the road,
   walking along rough by-paths.

They've made their homeland a desert,
   a thing of scorn for all time;
passers-by are shocked
   and shake their heads.

I will scatter them before their enemies
   like the east wind blowing.
I will turn my back on them and not my face
   in the day of their disaster!

GOD and our Conscience

These are GOD's words:

Don't listen to the professional prophets
   who talk—talk—talk,
filling you with false hopes
   dreaming their own dreams:
   not a word is mine!

They talk—talk—talk
   to men who care nothing for me:
     'You're all right!'
   to men who are stubbornly selfish:
     'You've nothing to worry about!'

He who has really stood in GOD's presence
   must listen with awe;
is there any other way
   to hear and understand?

Look—a great storm
   is sweeping down,
a great wind whirling round
   shattering injustice!

There'll be no calm weather
   till GOD's will is done;
in the years ahead
   you will face this plain truth.

I never sent these professional prophets—
   but what a time they've had!
I never spoke a word to them—
   but they talked as if I had!

If they had really stood in my presence
    they would have told my people the truth—
and persuaded them to repent
    of their dishonesty and injustice!

Am I not GOD—
    God of the near and the far?
Can anybody escape
    my all-seeing eye?
Do I not fill
    heaven and earth?
                              This is GOD's very Word!

Recognizing a Prophet

Let the prophet who's just dreaming
    go on dreaming!
Let him I have really spoken to
    say honestly what I have said!

Can't you tell chaff from wheat?
    (asks GOD)
Isn't my word like fire?
    (asks GOD)
like a hammer smashing rock?

But there's still hope

Learn from Experience

Set up signals on the hills,
    signposts along the road,
the long, long road
    you've walked along!

Come home, my people,
    come home!
Are you in two minds still?
    Has your disloyalty taught you nothing?

GOD's New Covenant

>In the days that are to be,
>   GOD says,
>I will make a new covenant
>   with both North and South.

>It won't be like the old covenant
>   I made on the desert march
>when I led your ancestors
>   out of Egypt.
>That covenant was broken long ago—
>   that's why I said No to them.

>This is the new covenant
>   I will make with the whole people:
>My Way shall be clear to everybody's conscience,
>   something every man can recognise;
>I will really be their God,
>   they shall really be my people.

>There'll be no need for teachers,
>   for anybody to say
>'Live in GOD's Way'
>   to neighbour or brother.
>Each shall know for himself
>   what my Way is—
>humble peasant
>   and king on his throne alike,
>   says GOD.

>I'll forgive them
>   the wrong they've done—
>their disloyalty
>   shall be a thing of the past.

Voice From Babylon: The Prophet of the Exile

We know little about what happened during the fifty years of the exile in Babylon. The exiles there were not imprisoned; they were allowed to lead normal lives in their own community, trading and worshipping as they wished.

About 540, there was a great international upheaval. The Babylonian empire fell, two years later, to the Persian leader, Cyrus; and the Middle East became the Persian empire.

It was in the years when Cyrus was rising to power that the unknown Prophet of the Exile gave his message to the Jews in Babylon.

His message was one of liberation and deliverance: God, the creator of the world, is also he who will now rescue his people from the nations who have oppressed them. This is the Good News: God will lead them out of Babylon as long ago he led his people out of Egypt.

The most remarkable poems of the prophet deal with GOD's 'Suffering Servant'. In his portrait of the Servant we can recognise features drawn from the story of Jeremiah; but the Servant represents the Israelite people, GOD's People who have suffered at the hands of the nations but through whom GOD's love and power are to be made clear to the whole world. 'Supreme power is in love rather than in coercion.'

The Road Home

Our slavery is over!

> 'Comfort, comfort my people,'
>   says your God.
> 'Speak to the heart of Jerusalem,
>   tell her
> her slavery is over,
>   her penalty paid,
>   she has suffered, under GOD,
>   full measure for her sins.'

The Voice

> Listen! Someone is calling!—

> 'Build GOD's road
>   across the wastelands—
> clear a highway for our God
>   across the desert!

Valleys shall be raised,
  mountain and hill levelled out,
rough ground and rugged heights
  smoothed to a plain.
GOD's glory will dawn
    and the whole world stand in its light.
      GOD himself has spoken!'

Listen!

'Shout!' someone is calling.
  'What shall I shout?'
'Men are like grass,
    their devotion like a fading flower.
Grass dies,
    flower fades
      when great winds blow!
Grass dies,
    flower fades:
      GOD's Word stands for ever!'

Good News

Climb the Olive Hill,
  herald of good news to Zion!
Shout with all your strength,
  herald of good news to Jerusalem!
Shout aloud—
    there's nothing to fear!—
      shout to all the Southern cities:
'Look!—your God!'

He comes
  with vigour
    and victory!
His reward and his wages are with him:
  his people marching ahead of him!
He feeds his flock like a shepherd,
    carrying the lambs in his arms,
      holding them to his breast,
and gently leading
    the ewes heavy with young!

A word to the world

> Who has measured the oceans
>   in the palm of his hand?
> marked off the skies
>   with the span of his fingers?
> picked up the earth's dust
>   in a pan?
> weighed the mountains with scales
>   or the hills with a balance?
>
> Who grasped GOD's intention
>   or stood by him as his Counsellor?[1]
> Whom did he consult
>   for guidance?
> Who taught him
>   how to order the world
>   or how to use his skill?

[1] The reference here seems to be to GOD's Heavenly Court (see also pp. 360, 376 where this Court is mentioned) which acted as his Advisory Council; GOD needed, they thought, his advisers and ministers as kings do. The poet here suggests that GOD created the world without any such help.

Open your eyes!

The very nations
  are like a drop of water
    dripping from a bucket!
  like damp
    on the pan of the scales!
He picks up the coasts and islands
  like specks of dust!

To whom, then, can you liken God?
  What image can show you what he is really like?
Don't you know?
  Haven't you heard?
Isn't it old news?
  Haven't you ever learned anything?

He sits on the dome of the earth,
  people like grasshoppers below him!
He stretches out the skies
  like fine gauze,
spreading them out like a tent
  as his home!

He puts emperors and governors
  in their place,
treating them
  as though they didn't even exist!
They are only just planted,
  only just sown,
    their roots only just gripping the earth—
when he blows on them
  and they shrivel up,
    the storm sweeps them away like straw!

'To whom, then, can you liken me
  that he should be my equal?'
    asks the Holy One.
Look up at the sky—look up!—
  who made the stars?
GOD marshals them like a mighty army
  and numbers their ranks!
He is the Great Commander—
  none dares desert!

A word to GOD's People

Why do you talk and grumble,
  you who are my people?—
'GOD can't see what's happening to us,
  he isn't bothered about us and our rights!'

Don't you know?
  haven't you heard?
GOD is always God,
  creator of the whole universe!

He does not faint or fail,
  he knows what we can never know.
He gives new life
  to those who are worn out;
he revives
  those who are ready to drop!
Commandos get tired and faint,
  seasoned veterans fall out with fatigue;
But those who trust GOD
  grow stronger and stronger—
    soaring like eagles,
    running without tiring,
    marching without flagging!

GOD's new Deed

GOD's Servant—first song

Look—my servant whom I steady,
  my chosen one, in whom I delight!
I have given him my spirit,
  showing the whole world
  what religion really means.

His is no clarion voice,
  no demagogue he
    haranguing at street corners!
He is too gentle to break a bruised stalk,
  to snuff a flickering wick!

But his is no flickering wick,
   his no timid heart;
honest and plain-spoken
   he makes the heart of religion clear.
And he'll go on
   till he has made religion real
      throughout the world—
      the world that longs for what he has to say.

The Servant's Commission

These are GOD's words—
the God who made and stretched out the skies,
   created the richness of the earth,
the source of all human life,
   the source of all living things:

I, GOD, have called you—really called you—
   I have grasped you by the hand
to help men everywhere to see,
   to rescue the prisoner from his prison,
   from the darkness of the dungeon cell.

I am GOD—that is my name—
   I come myself,
      sharing my presence with no one,
      least of all with man-made idols.

Emperor Cyrus has gone from victory to victory—
   this is nothing to the new triumphs I now proclaim;
and before they happen
   I announce them to you!

New Song

Sing a new song to GOD,
   sing in far-off lands!
Let the sea and its vast waters thunder,
   and the island people of the west!
Let desert villages and bedouin tribes
   shout aloud!

A fortified city ▶

Let the Rock Dwellers sing,
    shouting from the mountain tops.
Let them give GOD glory
    till all the islands ring!

GOD shall march out like a soldier
    in the excitement of battle
with war-cry and shouting,
    a hero facing his foes!

GOD is coming!

Far too long have I held my peace,
    saying nothing, holding myself back!
I will groan like a woman in child-birth,
    gasping and panting!

I will demolish the mountains,
    scorching the mountain grass!
I will turn rivers into deserts,
    drying up their pools—

that I may lead blind people along unknown roads,
    guiding them along strange paths,
turning the darkness ahead of them into light,
    making rough country level plain!

These are the things I will do—
    I will not leave them undone!

GOD's Servant—second song

Listen to me, you islands!
    Listen, you far-off peoples!

GOD called me from my birth,
    the day I was born he gave me my name.
He made my tongue a sharp sword,
    holding me in the grip of his hand;
he made me a polished arrow,
    ready in his quiver.

◀ The road home

'You are my servant,' he told me,
  'my people through whom I shall be known
    as I really am.'

'All I've done has come to nothing,' I answered,
  'I have wasted my strength on an empty dream.
Yet my cause is safe in GOD's keeping,
  he will make all I do worthwhile.'

GOD took me to task—
  GOD who made me his servant at my birth
    to bring his people back home:

'Is being my servant
  and bringing my people home
    too little a thing for you?

'I will make you
  the light of the whole world,
through you deliver
  the remotest people on earth!'

'*I will lead them home!*'

These are GOD's words:

I have answered and helped you
  in this day of good fortune and deliverance,
rescued your homeland,
  replanning its desolated countryside,
calling to prisoners 'You're free!'
  to men in darkness 'Stand in the light!'

They shall go home like a flock
  finding pasture on sand-dune and desert;
they shall not be hungry or thirsty,
  at the mercy of the scorching sun.

I who love them will lead them,
  showing them where the springs are;
I will make mountains into good roads,
  build my highways for them.

Shout for joy, O Skies!
  Triumph, O Earth!
    Break into singing, O Mountains!
GOD has comforted his people,
  showing mercy to his suffering folk!

'Your devastated land . . .'

New city

'GOD has abandoned me,' says GOD's People,
  'GOD has forgotten me!'

Can a mother forget her baby,
  neglect her own son?
Yes, she can—
  but I will not forget you!
Look! I have branded your name on my hands,
  your city walls are never out of my sight!
Your builders outnumber your destroyers,
  your overlords are marching away!

Look up and look around—
  my scattered people are coming home!
As I live (says GOD),
  you will wear them like pearls
  like a bride putting her finery on!

Look! They are coming from far away,
  from the north and from the west,
  from the cataracts of the Nile!
Your empty and deserted villages,
  your devastated land,
will be too narrow for all your people
  when your conquerors have marched away!

Those who were deported in your dark days
    will tell you plainly—
'The land isn't big enough for us;
    find us room to live!'
'Where have all these children come from?'
    you will say to yourself.
'I was bereaved and childless—
    who looked after them all?
I was left all alone—
    where have they all come from?'

The world GOD's People

These are GOD's words—
the God who made the sky
    and the firm and solid earth,
an earth which is no waste-land
    but a home for men to live in:

I am God—
    there is no other.
My word is clear
    making plain what is true and right—
no secret muttering
    in murky darkness.
I have never told my people
    to seek me in any waste-land.

O wide, wide world
    turn to me for rescue.
I am God—
    there is no other.
I have sworn by myself,
    I have given my unbreakable word
that everybody everywhere
    shall find themselves
        in my worship and service—
only in GOD (shall they say)
    can we find victory and strength.

GOD's Servant—third song

GOD has given me
    the tongue of a teacher,
to cheer with a word
    men who are tired out.

Morning by morning
   he wakens me,
wakens me
   to listen as his disciple.

GOD helped me really to listen;
   I wanted to learn,
   I've always walked with him.

I let my accusers whip my back,
   pluck my beard;
I stood facing
   the insult and the spitting.

GOD stands by me to help me—
   that's why I stand my ground;
I've set my face like flint—
   nobody can put me to shame.
My Defender stands by my side—
   who can take me to court?
Let us stand together
   at GOD's judgment bar!
Who is my accuser?
   Let him approach me!

See! GOD helps me—
   who can win his case against me?
They'll all be worn out
   like a moth-eaten coat!

GOD's Servant—fourth song

GOD   See! My servant shall win through;
            he shall be exalted and lifted up,
            lifted up high!
        The world was shocked,
            kings were sneering—
        looking at an unknown man,
            listening to an unheard-of story.

The World   Who could have believed what we've heard?
     Who has ever seen GOD at work?
This man grew up like a young plant
    with its roots in arid soil.
He was nothing to look at,
    with neither beauty nor charm.
He seemed inhuman,
    not like an ordinary man.
We despised and ignored him
    in his sickness and sorrow—
    a figure you don't like to look at.
We held him in contempt,
    took no notice of him.

Yet it was our sickness he was suffering,
    our pains that hurt him.
We thought that it was he who was doomed,
    his suffering a punishment by GOD.
But he was the victim of our violence,
    crushed by our wrong-doing;
his punishment was for our good,
    his whipping brought health to us.
We had all wandered where we pleased
    like silly sheep;
GOD laid on him
    the guilt of us all.

He was brutally treated,
    humble and quiet though he was.
Like a sheep on the way to the butcher,
    like a ewe in the hands of the shearer,
      he was dumb.
He was marched off to execution—
    who gave a thought to his fate?
He was cut off from the living world of men,
    beaten to death for our rebellions.
He was buried in a criminal's grave—
    buried with vicious men—
he who was never guilty of any violence,
    never pretended to be other than himself!

Yet GOD remembered and healed
   his suffering servant
who had given himself
   that the world might be forgiven.
Others will follow him
   to make life worth living—
GOD's work shall go on
   because of him.

GOD   After his terrible torture,
   after his disgrace
      my servant shall step into the light.
He shall be the world's saviour,
   bearing its evil-doing himself.
I will give him the world for his inheritance,
   his 'spoil' will be too vast to be counted.
He faced death in the depth of his being,
   standing alongside the rebels themselves.
He took the whole world's sin
   on his own shoulders!
He stood between them
   and their deserved fate!

Come!

GOD   Hi! You who are thirsty
   come and drink!
You who are starving
   come—buy and eat!
Come and buy!
   You don't need money—
   everything is free!

Why waste money
   buying what isn't bread?
Why work so hard
   for what gives you no joy?
If you listened to me
   you could enjoy a real feast!
Come here to me
   and hear what I have to say
and learn the secret
   of being really alive:

I will make an unbreakable covenant with you,
　　give you my steadfast love
　　　as I gave it to King David!
I made him a witness to the world,
　　a leader and commander;
so shall you hail nations you never heard of,
　　they shall come running to you—
for GOD, the Holy One of his people,
　　has shone in glory upon you!

Delay will be fatal!

Seek GOD while he is here,
　　pray to him while he is close at hand!
Let the bad man have done with his bad deeds,
　　and change the way he thinks!
Let him come home to GOD,
　　home to our God—
his mercy and his pardon
　　are for everybody.

These are GOD's words:

'I don't think as you think,
　　I don't live as you live.
The sky towers over the earth—
　　my Way towers over your way,
　　my thoughts over your thoughts!
Rain and snow fall from the sky,
　　watering the earth,
　　refreshing everything,
　　giving the sower his seed,
　　the eater his bread;
so is the word I speak—
　　it does not come back to me empty:
it does what I mean it to do,
　　carrying out my purpose.

You shall go out in joy,
   be led out in peace.
Mountains and hills
   shall break into singing before you,
wild trees
   clap their hands,
pine trees grow
   where there were only thorns,
myrtles
   where there were only briars!

All this is the sure sign
   of GOD's presence!

Enduring Convictions

Introduction

We can now look back on the long stormy story of this highland people —what happened to them (Parts I–III) and what their greatest men had to say about it (Part IV). What did they learn from it all? What convictions about God and man and the world did they find they were driven to hold to be able to live through it?

We can summarize them as three: 'God is with us'; 'We must live as God's people'; and 'God has the last word'.[1]

These three convictions underlie their deepest thought and their daily life. They prompt their poets and psalmists and inspire their historians. They explain their power to survive.

God is with us. The temptation to interpret this as meaning simply 'We are God's favourites' or 'God is on our side' was—and is—always very strong; for many Israelites it meant no more than this. But its real meaning is very different. We may put it in this way: God loves and cares for all men everywhere, and comes to us in our day-to-day experience in village and town. We have to learn how to be aware of his presence; we can never take him for granted. He gives us no easy answers—and sometimes seems to give us no answers at all (see *The Book of Job*, pp. 359–370). What he does, however, is to be 'with us' all the time, stand by us and call us to be his 'fellow-workers'. It is not an accident that it was in their dark days that the profoundest Old Testament thinkers came to be most sure of God's presence with them—just when conventional religion broke down in despair. This conviction finds its supreme statement in the Twenty-third Psalm (p. 406).

We must live as God's People. From the very beginning, religion was never for Israelite or Jewish thinkers a solitary adventure of individuals; it was an adventure for individuals living together in community. God's world is always in the making; religion is taking our part with God, as his 'fellow-workers', in the making of his family. The Old Testament knows nothing of 'solitary religion'; we must live as 'God's People' and help the whole world to live as his people. What this means finds one of its greatest expressions in the 'Servants Songs' of the unknown prophet of the exile (pp. 289–297).

God has the last word. The story which the Old Testament records might well be read as a story of a people's defeat—their political independence is lost, their homeland becomes a foreign province, most of their people are scattered as exiles in distant lands. Powerful empires, with their military might and economic wealth, dominate the story and do what they will—or so it seems to the outside observer. But Egypt,

[1] So Martin-Achard, *An Introduction to the Old Testament*, pp. 52ff.

Assyria, Babylon, Persia, Greece pass away. The world is not in their hands—it is in God's. Ultimately, they are his 'servants', for the world itself is not theirs but God's, and men can live in it with joy and confidence only in so far as they live in 'God's Way'. God is always Lord—Lord of history and Lord of nature.

These three convictions are found in the Old Testament in many different forms and with a great variety of interpretation. They undergird it all—prophetic poetry, temple hymn, historical narrative and law. They are the theme of the great preface to the Old Testament—*Genesis* —with which we begin this final part.

But there is a remarkable fact to keep in mind. These convictions were held (in Old Testament times) without any awareness of a real life beyond this. The Israelite people present us with 'the only example of a specifically religious civilization and yet they do so without any belief in life after death'. They thought their convictions out in terms of this world only; they held that, after death, men entered a subterranean land of gloom where they lived a shadowy existence that could hardly be called 'living' at all. Only in the centuries just before the Common Era—after the story we have told in this book was over—did they develop any belief in a real life after death.

The centuries that followed the exile—when they had little but their faith to sustain them—were a great 'testing-out ground' for their central convictions. The Jews were but a handful of people in a vast empire, strangers in a hostile world. Their convictions must sometimes have seemed to them as grandiose and unreal as they did to outsiders.

Many just accepted the new situation and ceased to care. Others held on to their faith and believed that GOD who had revealed himself to their ancestors was indeed the Lord of history and could bring triumph out of overwhelming disaster. For some this triumph would be a military triumph over his enemies, for others (in whom the spirit of the prophets still lived) the conversion of the world to his Way.

A violent change in their life occurred in the second century when the powerful king, Antioches Epiphanes, tried to exterminate their religion. This provoked a violent reaction and the Jewish Resistance Movement was born—with a hardening of all hearts. The temptation to keep themselves to themselves in so hostile a world had been there since the exile; now, for many, it hardened into hatred of the foreigner and the practice of apartheid.

So we give, after the great preface of *Genesis*, a selection of passages to show the very varied responses found among the Jewish people.

The three convictions, however, survived and became the heritage of the world.

What Kind of World Do We Live In?

Genesis is, as it were, the great preface to the story which follows it. It is world-wide in its sweep, dealing with the character of human society and the world which is its home (chapters 1–11), and with the question of how men ought to live, God being what he is (chapters 12–49). Much in it was written down in King Solomon's reign (about 950), but it was added to, commented on and expanded throughout the next six hundred years. In reading it, we are listening to people of many generations asking fundamental questions about the world they lived in, and working out their answers.

How do we deal with fundamental questions like 'What kind of world is it?' or 'What is the meaning of human existence?' These are not scientific or historical questions like 'How was the earth made?' or 'How did civilization arise?' Such questions can only be answered by scientific and historical methods. We are asking religious questions, and religious question about the fundamental meaning of things can only take the form of stories or pictures—of poetry in fact. The scientist and historian tackle the question 'How?'; the poet asks the question 'Why?' That is why the Old Testament contains so much poetry.[1]

The early peoples of the Middle East accounted for the world they lived in by stories (historians call them 'myths') which often seem to us crude and sometimes even repulsive. But these old stories can embody profound insights, and we must distinguish between the form and the insight the form embodies.

The Israelites drew their stories about the world they lived in from the common stories of their time and culture.[2] But they told them in their own way and in the light of their new experience of God. They made great changes in them, for they were using them to express their new convictions. As they went on using these stories over the thousand years of their history, they constantly revised their 'science' (compare the two accounts of creation) but enlarged their faith.

When they came to consider what kind of persons God wants us to be, the Israelites used old tribal stories of their famous ancestors, and added comments and notes as the years passed. They were, of course, deeply interested in their own remote past (as all peoples are); these old stories were their only source of information. But they were more concerned with the future—what sort of people God wanted them to be and how they could live in God's Way; they used these stories to make this clear.

The opening words of *Genesis* are a prose statement based, so some scholars believe, on an old poem. Hence the verse form in which we give them.

---

[1] Even modern scientists, when they are concerned with fundamental questions, use myths as a tool of explanation or exploration—what Plato called 'a likely story'. Note, too, the use of myth and folk tale in modern literature, especially in countries where freedom of speech is limited (e.g., Ferenc Juhász, *The Boy turned into a Stag*, Penguin Modern European Poets, pp. 97ff).
[2] See, e.g., *The Epic of Gilgamesh*, version by N.K. Sanders, Penguin Classics.

God's Intention

The later Account (450 B.C.E.)

This is the story of the making
of earth and sky:
in the very beginning,
God made them both.

Earth was formless chaos
   lost in darkness
with stormy winds
   sweeping over the vast waters.
'Let there be light!' said God —
   and everywhere there was light,
   splendid in his eyes.
He marked off light from darkness,
   calling light 'day'
   and darkness 'night':
so came the evening and the morning
   of the first day.

'Let there be a vault,' said God ,
   'separating the waters above the vault
     from the waters on the earth below!'
The great vault was made;
   he called it 'sky':
so came the evening and the morning
   of the second day.

'Let all the earth's waters
   be gathered together!' said God.
     'Let dry land appear!'
He called the dry land 'earth'
   and the gathered waters 'sea'—
     splendid in his eyes.
'Let the earth grow plants and trees!' said God,
   'seed-bearing plants and fruit trees!'
Plants and trees appeared—
   splendid in his eyes:
so came the evening and the morning
   of the third day.

'Let there be lights in the sky,' said God,
   'marking off day from night,
signs for festivals,
   for seasons and years!
Let the lights of the sky
   shine down on the earth!'
He made the sun,
   dominating the day,
the moon and the stars
   dominating the night—

' " Let all the earth's waters
   be gathered together!" said God' ▶

he set them in the sky
  to shine on the earth,
    day and night,
    light and darkness—
      splendid in his eyes:
so came the evening and the morning
  of the fourth day.

'Let there be fish in the waters!' said God,
  'and birds flying in the sky!'
And there they were—
  great sea-monsters,
    shoals of fish,
      flocks of birds—
        splendid in his eyes.
God blessed them all—
  'Be fertile,' he said,
    'swarms of fish in the sea,
      flocks and flocks of birds in the sky':
so came the evening and the morning
  of the fifth day.

'Now for the animals!' said God.
  'Let there be living creatures on the earth,
    domestic animals,
    reptiles and wild animals!'
He made all the animals—
  splendid in his eyes!

'Let us now make man in our image,' said God,
  'like ourselves,
  to be master
    of fish and wild birds,
    of domestic animals,
    of reptiles and wild animals!'
He created man in his own image—
  in his image both sexes were created.
He blessed them too—
  'Be fertile,' he said, 'and increase!
    Fill the earth and conquer it,
  be master of all living creatures.

Plants and trees
   shall be your food;
green plants
   food for all living creatures—
   animals, birds, reptiles,
   everything alive.'

It was all splendid in God's eyes:
so came the evening and the morning
   of the sixth day.

Earth and sky were made,
   crowded with life.
On the sixth day
   God finished his work;
on the seventh day
   he stopped working.

He blessed the seventh day—
   the day he stopped work.
He had brought into being
   everything he had set himself to make.

The earlier Account (950 B.C.E.)

In the very beginning no prairie bush was yet to be found anywhere; no wild grain had started to sprout. No rain had fallen on the ground; there was nobody to till the ground if it had—there was only the water rising up from beneath the ground and covering the land.

Then GOD moulded Man[1] from the ground[2] itself and breathed into him the breath that made him a living creature.

He then planted a park away in the east, in Eden, and gave it to Man as his home, planting all sorts of lovely and useful trees. In the heart of the park he planted two special trees—the Tree of Life (the fruit of this tree made those who ate it immortal) and the Tree of Knowledge.

GOD put Man in the park to work in it and guard it.

'You can eat the fruit of any tree you like,' GOD told him. 'But the fruit of one tree you must never eat—if you do, it will mean certain death. That tree is the Tree of Knowledge.

'It is bad for Man to live here all alone,' GOD went on. 'I must make a mate for him!'

---

[1] Hebrew 'adam'.   [2] Hebrew 'adamah'.

So GOD moulded all the wild animals and the wild birds—again, out of the ground itself. He led Man to them to see what names he would give them—these would be the names they would always be called by. Man gave names to all the domestic animals, the wild birds and the wild animals. But none of the animals could be a mate for him.

So GOD put him into a deep sleep. While he slept, he took one of his ribs, healing his body afterwards. He then built the rib into Woman, and led her to Man. As soon as he saw her, Man exclaimed—

> This one at last
>   is from my very bone,
>   from my very flesh.
> She shall be called 'Woman',[1]
>   from Man[2] was she taken.

Man and Woman were naked. This was quite natural—there was nothing to be ashamed of.

(This story explains why a man leaves his parents to marry his wife —he is united with her and the two of them become one flesh again.)

Man's Tragedy

'Can't I do what I like?'

The cleverest of the wild animals was the snake.

'So, you can't eat the fruit of any of the trees in the park?' the snake said to Woman.

'Oh yes, we can,' she answered. 'We can eat the fruit of all the trees —except one, the tree in the heart of the park. GOD told us we would die if we ate it.'

'He did, did he?' said the snake. 'You wouldn't die! GOD knows, of course, what would happen if you were to eat its fruit: you'd become clever and know what things are really like, as gods themselves do.'

When Woman saw that the fruit of the tree was good to eat and lovely to look at—and moreover, found it more tempting the more she

---

[1] Hebrew 'Ishshah'.   [2] Hebrew 'Ish'.

thought about it—she plucked some and tasted it. She took some to her husband, and he tasted it, too.

Suddenly their innocence was over—they became aware that they were naked. They made loin-cloths for themselves out of fig-leaves.

It was now evening—the breezy time of the day. They both heard the rustle of GOD walking in the park. They hid themselves among the trees.

'Where are you?' GOD called out.

'I heard you coming,' said Man. 'I was frightened—you see, I am naked. That's why I hid myself.'

'How did you know you were naked?' asked GOD. 'Have you been eating from the forbidden tree?'

'It was Woman's fault—Woman you gave me for a mate,' he said. 'She gave it to me to eat.'

'What's this you've done?' GOD asked Woman.

'The snake tricked me,' she said. 'That's why I ate it.'

GOD said to the snake:

> 'Because of what you have done
> you shall be banished
> from all the animals of the earth.
> You shall crawl on your stomach,
> eating dirt,
> as long as you live.
> You and Woman,
> your brood and hers,
> shall be deadly enemies.
> They shall strike at your head,
> you shall strike at their heels.'

GOD said to Woman:

> 'I will make child-birth
> very painful for you—
> in pain you shall bear children.
> You will love your husband
> but he shall be your master.'

GOD said to Man:

> 'You listened to your wife
> and ate from the forbidden tree.
> The ground is cursed now
> because of you:

you will labour all your life
to make a living.
The soil will only grow
thorns and thistles,
and wild plants for you to eat.
You will have to sweat
to get your food—
until you are buried
in the ground you come from.
You are dust—
and to dust you shall go back!'

Man gave the name 'Eve' to his wife ('Eve' means 'Life').

GOD made clothes from skins for the two of them.

'Look!' said GOD. 'Man has become like one of us—he's become clever. What would happen if he plucked the fruit of the other tree— the Tree of Life—and started to eat it? He'd live for ever!'

So GOD banished him from Eden to work for his living farming the soil he came from. He drove him out. He posted angelic sentries, with fiery, ever-turning swords, to guard the way to the Tree of Life.

'Am I my brother's shepherd?'

Two sons were born to Man and his wife Eve—Abel the shepherd and Cain the farmer.

Cain brought some of his farm produce as a gift to GOD, Abel some of the finest firstlings of his flock. GOD honoured Abel and his gift; he took no notice of Cain and his gift. Cain was angry and sullen.

'Why so angry and sullen?' GOD asked him.

> 'If you've been doing what is right,
>   you can hold your head up.
> If you haven't,
>   sin crouches like a wild beast
>   at your farm-door,
>   savage to get at you,
>   too strong for you to kill.'

'Let's go out into the fields,' said Cain to his brother one day.
Out in the fields, Cain attacked him and murdered him.

'Where's your brother Abel?' GOD asked him.

'How do I know?' said Cain. 'Am I supposed to shepherd my brother the shepherd?'

'What have you done?' asked GOD. 'Listen—your brother's blood is calling for justice from the ground where he's buried. You murdered him. You shall be banished, with a curse on your head, from the ground which drank your brother's blood. Your farming days are over—the soil will serve you no more. Fugitive and vagabond you shall be where-ever you go.'

'I can't face it!' cried Cain in horror. 'You've banished me today from the soil. I must keep away from you and wander aimlessly through the world; I shall be an outlaw at the mercy of everybody I meet!'

'No,' said GOD. 'If anybody murders you, he will be punished seven times more severely than you have been punished.'

GOD put a protective mark on Cain's body.

So Cain left GOD's presence and made his home east of Eden, a fugitive all his life.

'Why should we care?'

GOD saw the sort of thing that men and women were doing on the earth—just downright evil, giving all his plans an evil twist. He was deeply hurt; he was sorry he had ever made the human race.

'I will end the whole dreadful business—men, animals, reptiles, wild birds—everything,' he said. 'I am sorry I ever began it.'

One man, however, was different from the others—Noah. GOD

thought well of him; he was trying to live in GOD's Way.

'Build a ship on dry land,' GOD commanded him.

Noah did what GOD told him to do.

'Now go on board,' GOD said. 'Take your family with you. You're the only good man I can find. And take some animals and birds with you—seven pairs (each with its mate) of the "clean" kind; only a pair each of the "unclean" kind. In a week's time, I'm going to send torrential rain. It will rain for a long, long time—long enough to drown all living things everywhere.'

Noah again obeyed.

At the end of the week, down came the floods of rain. GOD shut him in the ship.

The water rose and lifted the ship off the ground.

All life on land—men, animals, reptiles, birds—died. Only Noah and those who were with him were left alive.

At last the rain stopped, and the level of the waters began to fall.

After a very long time, Noah opened the hatch and let a raven fly away to see if there was any dry land. But it kept flying to and fro until the water was gone and the land was dry.

A week went by. Then Noah let a dove fly off, to see if there was any land free of water. The dove could find no resting place; it just came back to the ship. The water still covered everything; Noah put out his hand and caught her and took her into the ship again.

A week later, he let her fly off again. She came back as darkness fell —and there, in her beak, was a fresh olive leaf! Noah knew now that the water was really going down and the land appearing. He waited another week, and let the dove fly away again. She never came back.

So Noah took the covering off the ship. All around him the land was dry. He disembarked and built an altar to GOD and sacrificed some of the 'clean' animals on it. GOD smelled the pleasant odour.

'I will never again drown the world because of what man has done,' he said to himself. 'His very nature has an evil twist in it; but I will never again do what I have just done.

> As long as the earth lasts,
>   seedtime and harvest,
>   cold and heat,
>   summer and winter,
>   day and night
>   shall never cease.'

'Let us build a mighty city and a tall tower'

'Isn't "getting on" the most important thing?'

Once upon a time, all the people of the world spoke the same language and used the same words.

Now there was once a great migration of people; they settled at last in the Babylonian plain where the Euphrates and Tigris rivers near the sea.

'Let us make bricks,' they said, 'and bake them hard. And let us build a mighty city and a tall tower—tall enough to touch the sky. We must be somebody—or else we shall be nobody.'

GOD came down to look at the city and the tall tower, rising higher and higher.

'If this is the sort of thing they start to do,' said GOD, 'when they are a single people speaking a common language, there's no limit to what they may plan and carry out. Let us go down and turn their common speech into a babble of languages. They won't know what they are talking about, then.'

So GOD broke up the family of mankind into different nations, scattering them over the whole earth. That stopped the building of the city.

What Kind of Persons Should We Be?

Abraham: Facing the Unknown

Destination unknown

Once upon a time there were three brothers living with their father in the Balikh Valley away in the north.

The youngest brother died while his father was still alive. The two other brothers married and settled down. Then their father died.

'Abandon your country,' GOD said to Abraham one day. 'Leave your relatives and your ancestral home and go to a land I will show you. I will make a great nation of you and bless you. You will become famous —men will use your name when they bless one another.

> I will bless those who bless you;
>   I will curse those who curse you.
> By you all the families of the earth
>   will bless one another—
> "May you be as happy as Abraham!"
>   they will say.'

Abraham set out at GOD's command, and travelled south.

He came to the shrine at Shechem in the highlands. Here GOD spoke to him again.

'I am going to give this country to your descendants,' he said.

So Abraham built an altar to GOD there. Then he went on to the highlands east of Bethel and set up camp; he built another altar to GOD and worshipped him there. He then went on by stages to the Negeb in the south.

Egyptian incident

One year, the whole of Palestine was threatened with famine. Abraham moved over the border into Egypt.

'You're a very beautiful woman,' he said to his wife, Sarah, as they were crossing the frontier. 'I know what will happen as soon as people see you. Your beauty will be my undoing; they'll murder me to get hold of you. The only thing to do is for you to say you are my sister. I can get away with it then.'

That is what she did. The Egyptians—even members of the royal court—were struck by her beauty. Her praises were sung to Pharaoh himself. He took her into his harem; and, because he liked her, he lavished gifts upon Abraham—sheep, oxen, servants and camels.

Then everything went wrong in the palace—plague broke out—all because of Sarah, Abraham's wife. Pharaoh found out what had happened.

'Why did you treat me like this?' he asked Abraham. 'Why didn't you tell me she was your wife? Why say she's your sister—and let me take her as one of my wives? Here she is—take her and get out!'

He sent him out of Egypt under military escort; and Abraham, with his nephew Lot, found himself again in the Negeb.

Back in the Highlands

Abraham was now a rich man. He trekked north with his nephew Lot as far as Bethel in the highlands—the very place where he had first set up camp and built an altar to GOD.

Then trouble began. His nephew was also a rich man with many flocks and herds and tents. Fighting broke out between their herdsmen—there were too few good wells and not enough land.

'I don't want trouble between us,' said Abraham. 'We are kinsmen; I can't have this fighting. We must go our separate ways. The country lies before you: if you go to the west, I'll go to the east; if you go to the east, I'll go to the west.'

The Jordan Valley could be seen from the high hills. Lot looked down on the valley with its rich, tropical vegetation, a wonderful garden. (This was before the great disaster in the valley happened.) It reminded him of the wealth of Egypt. He chose the valley and went eastward, as far as the town of Sodom, a notorious city.

When Lot had gone, GOD spoke to Abraham.

'Take a good look from these high hills,' he said, 'survey the land—north, south, east and west. This is the home I am going to give your descendants. They'll be a great people, vast in number. Go through the country and take stock of it. It is my gift to you.'

Abraham struck camp and went south. He settled by the famous Oak of Mamre, in Hebron territory, and built an altar to GOD there.

Time passed. Then GOD spoke to Abraham in a vision.

'Don't be afraid,' he said. 'I am your Shield. You will have a great future.'

'What sort of future can there be for me, O GOD?' said Abraham. 'I've no family; my servant Eliezer will inherit all I have.'

'He shall not be your heir,' said GOD. 'Your own son shall be your heir.'

He led him outside his tent.

'Look up at the sky,' he said, 'and count the stars—if you can. Your descendants shall be as many as the stars.'

Abraham trusted GOD; it was his trust in GOD that made him a truly religious man.

'I am your GOD,' said GOD. 'I brought you here to give you this country as your home.'

'How am I to be sure?' asked Abraham.

'Bring me animals and birds for a sacrifice,' said GOD.

Abraham brought them, prepared them and laid them out. Carrion birds swooped down out of the sky on to the carcases, but he drove them off.

The sun was now setting. He fell into a deep trance—everything was blacked out in a great and fearful darkness.

The sun had now set and it was pitch dark, except for a smoking fire-pot and a blazing torch moving between the carcases.

GOD made a covenant with him.

'I give this land to your descendants,' he said, 'from the Egyptian border in the south to the Euphrates River in the north, with all the tribes living there.'

Trouble at home

Sarah had an Egyptian slave-girl, Hagar.

'I've no children myself,' she said one day to Abraham. 'Make Hagar your secondary wife; her children can count as my children.'

This is what he did.

When Hagar knew she was going to have a baby, she began to sneer at her mistress.

'I've been wronged,' said Sarah to Abraham, 'and it's your business to put it right. My slave-girl treats me with contempt. May GOD see justice done between you and me!'

'You can do what you like,' said Abraham. 'The girl's in your hands. But, remember, she's the mother of my child.'

Sarah began to ill-treat the girl, and she ran away into the southern desert, trying to get home. GOD's angel found her at a desert oasis on the way to the Egyptian border.

'Where have you come from, Hagar,' he asked, 'and where are you going?'

'I'm running away from my mistress,' she said.

'Go back,' said the angel. 'You must go on being her slave.

'Your descendants will be so many that they won't be able to be counted,' he went on. 'You're going to have a baby; you must call him Ishmael. He'll be a wild and roving wanderer—always spoiling for a fight, at odds with all his kinsmen!'

Strange visitors

One day, when it was getting hot, Abraham was sitting at his tent door. He looked up—three men were standing not far away. He got up and hurried to them.

'Sirs,' he said as he greeted them, 'don't go on without staying a while with me, humble as I am. Take a rest under the tree—I will fetch water for your feet and bring you something to eat. That will refresh you. Then you can go on with the journey that brought you this way.'

'Very good,' they said.

He went into the tent.

'Quick!' he said to his wife. 'Get some food ready.'

He hurried off to the herd, chose a tender, choice calf, and gave it to the lad who had run over to help him.

Then he set curds and milk and meat before his visitors, and stood under the tree, waiting on them.

'Where's Sarah, your wife?' they asked.

'She's in the tent,' he said.

'These are GOD's words,' they said. ' "I will certainly come back to you in the spring and Sarah your wife will give birth to a son".'

Sarah was eaves-dropping at the tent door, which was quite near.

She laughed to herself—both she and her husband were growing old.

'At my time of life and my husband an old man!' she said to herself. 'It's absurd!'

'Why did Sarah laugh?' GOD asked Abraham. 'Why did she say it was absurd? Is there anything GOD can't do? I will come back at the appointed time and she shall give birth to a son.'

'I didn't laugh,' said Sarah.

'You did,' said GOD.

The three men got up to go on their way and looked down into the Jordan Valley, towards the town of Sodom. Abraham walked with them along the road to see them off.

An argument with GOD

GOD had told Abraham what he was going to do.

'I have heard a cry for help against the two towns Sodom and Gomorrah,' said GOD. 'I must go down to see what it's all about. I must know if their conduct is what I think it is.'

The men went on down towards the town; Abraham remained standing in GOD's presence. They were on the high hills and the valley lay all below them.

'Would you sweep away the good people with the bad?' Abraham asked GOD. 'Suppose there are fifty good people in the town, would

Rachel (p. 326) ▶

you sweep it away—and not spare it for the sake of those fifty? I don't think you could do such a thing—treat good and bad alike. Must not the Judge of all the earth himself be just?'

'I will spare the whole town,' said GOD, 'if I find fifty good people living there.'

'I am a mere man, and yet I dare to speak to you who are GOD,' Abraham ventured. 'Suppose there aren't fifty; suppose there are five short? Will you sweep away the whole town just because there are five short?'

'If I find forty five good people in the town,' said GOD, 'I won't sweep it away.'

'Suppose there are only forty?' said Abraham.

'For the sake of forty,' said GOD, 'I will not sweep the town away.'

'Don't be angry with me if I go on,' said Abraham. 'Suppose the number is thirty?'

'I will not do it,' said GOD, 'if I find thirty.'

'I am daring to speak again,' said Abraham. 'Suppose there are only twenty?'

'I will not sweep the town away,' said GOD, 'for the sake of those twenty.'

'Don't be angry with me for speaking again,' said Abraham. 'Suppose only ten good people are to be found there?'

'For the sake of those ten,' said GOD, 'I will not sweep it away.'

GOD had no more to say and went on his way; Abraham went home.

A test of loyalty

Isaac was Abraham's only son,[1] and he loved him very deeply.

One day, GOD put Abraham to the test.

'Abraham!' he called.

'Here I am,' said Abraham.

'Take Isaac with you,' he said, 'and go to the distant highlands. I will point out one of the mountains there, and on that mountain you must offer him as a sacrifice.'

At dawn, Abraham saddled his donkey and took two of his men with him—and Isaac. He split the wood for the offering and set off to the mountain GOD had told him about. After two days' march, he looked up and saw the mountain in the distance.

'Stay here with the donkey,' he told his men. 'I and the boy are climbing that mountain to worship. We'll come back to you here.'

He gave Isaac the split wood to carry; he himself picked up the fire and the knife. They both set off.

---

[1] The historian apparently is not counting Ishmael, Abraham's son born to his secondary wife, Hagar, as a full son.

◀ An oasis in the desert

'Dad,' said Isaac.

'Yes,' said Abraham.

'We've got the fire and the wood,' he said, 'but where's the sheep for the sacrifice?'

'GOD will look after that, my boy,' said Abraham.

They went on together and came to the appointed spot.

Abraham built an altar and put the wood on it. He then bound Isaac, laid him on the altar and picked up the knife. Suddenly he heard a voice.

'Abraham! Abraham!' called the voice.

'Here I am,' answered Abraham.

'Don't touch the boy,' said the voice (it was GOD speaking). 'I know now your trust in me is real trust. You didn't say No when I asked for your son, your only son.'

Abraham looked up, and there, behind him, was a ram caught by its horns in the brushwood. He sacrificed the ram instead of his son.

He went back to the men he'd left with the donkey; and they all went back to Beersheba where he made his home.

Jacob: Coming to Terms with Yourself

Brothers' quarrel

After Abraham's death, his son Isaac made his home at Beer-lahai-roi, the oasis which Hagar, the Egyptian slave-girl, reached when she ran away from her mistress.

Isaac had no children. So he prayed to GOD, and GOD answered his prayer. In due time his wife, Rebecca, gave birth to twins. The first to be born was called Esau, and the second Jacob.

Esau grew up into a skilful hunter who loved out-door life; Jacob was a quiet fellow who liked to stay at home in the camp. Isaac made a favourite of Esau—he was very fond of the game he caught. Jacob was his mother's favourite.

One day, when Esau came in hungry from the hunt, Jacob was cooking soup.

'Give me some of that red stuff to swallow,' he said. 'I'm famished!'

'Sell me your rights as the first-born,' said Jacob.

'What do my rights matter?' said Esau. 'I'm dying with hunger.'

'I want your solemn word on that,' said Jacob.

Rembrandt: *Esau making over his birthright to Jacob*

Esau gave him his solemn promise and made his birthright over to him.

Jacob then gave him his bread and lentil soup. Esau ate and drank his fill, and then got up and went off.

That's how much Esau thought of his birthright.

Isaac was now old and blind. One day he called Esau to him.

'I'm an old man and I might die any time,' he said. 'I want to give you my blessing. Take your weapons **and** hunt some game for me. Make my favourite dish and bring it to me.'

Rebecca overheard all this. As soon as Esau had gone hunting, she got hold of Jacob.

'Your father's been talking to Esau,' she said. 'He's sent him out hunting—he's going to give him his blessing. Now listen to me and do as I say. Fetch me two kids from the flock and I'll make him his favourite tasty dish. You shall take it to your father and get his blessing before he dies.'

'It won't work,' said Jacob. 'My brother's a hairy man. My skin's smooth—my father's only got to touch me to find out who I am. It will be obvious I'm playing a trick on him, and I'll get his curse instead of his blessing.'

'Let the curse fall on me,' said his mother. 'You just go and do what you're told.'

The tasty dish was made, and Rebecca made Jacob put on Esau's best clothes which she kept there in the tent. She covered his hands and the smooth skin of his neck with goat skin, and put the tasty dish and bread in his hands.

He went in to his father.

'Hello, Dad!' he said.

'Eh?' said the old man. 'And who are you, my son?'

'I'm Esau,' he said. 'I've got your favourite dish—sit up and eat it. Then you can give me your blessing.'

'However did you find the game so quickly?' asked Isaac.

'GOD gave me happy hunting,' said Jacob.

'Come close to me,' said Isaac. 'I want to feel you. I want to know who you really are.'

Jacob let him feel him.

'Your voice is Jacob's,' he said, 'but your hands are Esau's.'

He didn't tumble to the trick, and he got ready to give him his blessing.

'Are you really Esau?' he asked again.

'Of course I am,' said Jacob.

'Bring me my tasty dish, then,' said the old man. 'I'll eat it and give you my blessing.'

Jacob gave it to him—and wine; and he ate and drank.

'Come near and kiss me, my son,' he said.

Jacob kissed him. When Isaac smelt his clothes, he blessed him:

> 'My son's smell
> is the smell of the open country.
> May God give you
> the sky's dew and the earth's richness,
> corn and wine in plenty.
> People will be your slaves,
> nations acknowledge your lordship.
> Be master of your brothers,
> let them be your subjects.
> A curse on him who curses you!
> A blessing on him who blesses you!'

Jacob had hardly left his father, when in came Esau from hunting. He, too, made a tasty dish for his father and took it in to him.

'Sit up, Dad,' he said, 'and eat some of the game I've caught. Then give me your blessing.

'Who are you?' Isaac asked.

'I'm Esau, your elder son,' he said.

The old man trembled with shock.

'Who was it, then, went hunting,' he asked, 'and brought me a tasty dish to eat? Who was it I blessed? The blessing stands—I can't alter it now.'

Esau broke down in a wild and bitter sobbing.

'Give me a blessing, Father!' he cried. 'Give me a blessing too!'

'Your brother's tricked you,' said the old man.

'He's got the right name!' said Esau. 'He's a Jacob[1] all right! That's twice he's tricked me. He stole my birthright—and now he steals my blessing! Haven't you kept a blessing for me?'

'I've made him your master—and the master of his brothers!' said Isaac. 'I've given him the wealth of fields and vineyards. What can I do for you, my son?'

'Haven't you even one blessing left, Father?' cried Esau. 'Give me a blessing, give me a blessing too!'

Esau broke down sobbing.

So Isaac told him:

> 'Far from earth's richness and sky's dew
> shall be your home.
> You shall live by fighting
> and be your brother's slave.
> You will rebel
> and break his tyranny!'

This last trick of Jacob's made Esau hate him.

'When my father's funeral is over,' he swore, 'I'll murder him!'

He didn't keep quiet about his threat, either, and his mother was told about it.

She immediately sent for Jacob.

'Your brother's threatening to murder you,' she told him. 'Now do what I tell you. Get away from here, and go north to our ancestral home, to your uncle Laban in the Balikh Valley. Stay with him a few months; your brother's anger will die down and he'll forget all about it. Then I'll send for you and fetch you home. I don't want to lose the two of you in one day.'

Night at Bethel

Jacob set off north and reached a lonely spot in the highlands. The sun had set and he stopped there for the night. It was a stony place; he used one of the stones as a pillow and went to sleep.

He had a dream.

---

[1] The popular explanation of 'Jacob' was 'usurper'.

In his dream he saw a great stairway, rising from the ground right up into the sky. God's angels were going up and coming down it.

He woke up—a very shaken man.

'How frightening this place is!' he said. 'This is indeed God's house, this is heaven's gate!'

He got up at dawn, lifted the stone he'd used as a pillow and set it up as a sacred pillar. He poured oil on it and made a vow:

'If God stays with me and guards me on my journey and sees I don't starve to death and brings me safe home again, then GOD shall be my God and this pillar be God's house.'

This was his vow:

'Of all you give me I will give a tenth to you.'

In the Balikh Valley

Jacob set off and came to the country of 'the people of the east'.

He looked round and caught sight of a well in the open countryside, and three flocks of sheep resting beside it. A huge stone lay over the mouth of the well—so huge that it took several shepherds to move it.

Jacob went on to the well.

'Well, my friends,' he said to the shepherds there, 'and where do you come from?'

'The Balikh Valley,' they said.

'Do you know farmer Laban?' he asked.

'We do,' they said.

'And how's he keeping?' he asked.

'Oh, he's all right,' they said. 'Here's his daughter Rachel with his flock.'

'It's still the middle of the day,' said Jacob. 'It isn't time to round the animals up yet. Get on with watering the sheep, and you can take them back to pasture.'

'We can't,' they said. 'We need all the shepherds here to shift that huge stone.'

While all this talk was going on, Rachel came up with her father's flock—she was his shepherdess. Jacob went over to her. He himself shifted the huge stone and watered her flock for her. Then he kissed her in greeting and tears of joy rolled down his cheeks. He told her who he was and she, in her excitement, ran off to tell her father.

Laban ran out to meet him, kissed him and took him home.

'Grand!' he said. 'You belong to my own family!'

Jacob stayed a whole month with him.

'You know,' said Laban to Jacob one day, 'you shouldn't be working for me without pay, just because you're a relative; what sort of wages would you like?'

Now Jacob had fallen in love with Rachel. Her older sister, Leah, had lack-lustre eyes; but Rachel was a lovely girl.

'If you'll let me marry Rachel,' he said, 'I'll put in seven years' work for you.'

'I'd rather give her to you than to anybody else,' said wily Laban. 'Stay with me as a resident-alien.'

Jacob's love for Rachel made the seven years pass like a flash. He went to Laban.

'I've served my time,' he said, 'and I want to marry Rachel. Give her to me.'

Laban held a wedding-feast—everybody was there. But when evening came, he brought his elder daughter, Leah, and gave her to Jacob (she was heavily veiled; Jacob couldn't see who it was) and the marriage ceremony was completed.

Next morning, Jacob found that it was Leah he had married, not Rachel! He tackled Laban.

'What a dirty trick to play!' he said. 'I worked for Rachel. Why have you cheated me like this?'

'Carry through with this wedding,' said Laban, 'and I will give you Rachel in return for a further seven years work.'

That's what Jacob did. He did not repudiate his marriage with Leah, but he married Rachel as well, accepting a new contract for seven years' service. He was very much in love with Rachel.

One day, Jacob went to Laban.

'Let me go back home,' he said.

'Now listen to me, please,' said Laban. 'I can see that GOD is blessing me through you.'

'No doubt,' said Jacob. 'You know how hard I've worked for you and how big your farm's grown since I've been looking after it. You had little enough before. GOD has certainly blessed you since I came here. But what about me? I've got my family to look after.'

'Well,' said Laban, 'what pay do you want?'

'I don't want any pay,' said Jacob. 'I want part of the farm for myself. I'll go on looking after your flock; but give me all the spotted animals for my own—the rest will be yours. You can inspect the two flocks whenever you like. I'll be quite straight with you.'

'That's all right by me,' said Laban. 'Do as you say.'

He moved his encampment three days' journey away and left Jacob in charge of his flock.

Jacob became a wealthy shepherd with large flocks of his own. He grew richer, with slaves and camels and donkeys as well.

Escape south

Jacob now saw that Laban's attitude to him had quite changed.

So one day, when he was out with his flocks in the open country, he sent for Leah and Rachel to meet him there.

'Your father doesn't like me,' he told them. 'I've worked honestly for him, but he has cheated me again and again. God, who met me at Bethel where I set up a pillar and swore a vow to him, has told me to leave this valley and go home.'

'We've nothing here to stay for, either,' they both said. 'Our father treats us like foreigners. He's had our dowry and he's made it pay good interest. What we've got isn't his—it's ours. Do what God has told you to do.'

Jacob mounted his family on camels and drove his cattle away. He crossed the Euphrates River and made for the Gilead highlands.

Meanwhile (Jacob knew nothing of this) Rachel had stolen her father's household gods while he was away shearing.

When, three days later, Laban heard that Jacob had set off home, he went after him and caught up with him after a week's hard riding.

'What do you mean by keeping me in the dark like this,' he asked, 'running off with my daughters like prisoners of war? You didn't even let me kiss my grandchildren goodbye! You've gone mad—I could soon overpower you. I won't, but only because last night your father's God told me to leave you alone. . . . So you're homesick and off back home. But why steal my household gods?'

'I admit I was afraid of you,' said Jacob. 'I thought you'd rob me of your daughters. But if anybody's stolen your gods, he shall die. Call your men in; if you can find anything that's yours, take it.'

Laban searched the camp, but could find nothing. Rachel had hidden the household gods in her camel saddle. She was sitting on the saddle when her father came into her tent.

'I'm sorry I can't get up,' she said. 'I don't feel well. I hope you won't be angry with me.'

He had a good look round, but he didn't find the household gods.

'Now what's my crime?' asked Jacob angrily. 'You come storming after me and rummaging through my goods! Have you found anything? Put what you've found out here for my men and your men to see. They can settle the dispute between us.

'For twenty years,' he went on, 'I've lived with you—worked fourteen years for your daughters' hands, and six years just for you. You cheated me again and again. If God wasn't looking after me, you'd have sent me away with nothing!'

'The girls are my daughters,' said Laban. 'The children are my grand-children. The flocks are mine. Everything's mine! But what can I do about them? Come, let's swear a covenant together.'

So Jacob took a stone and set it up as a sacred pillar; his kinsmen built a cairn.

'May GOD keep watch over us both,' Laban said, 'when we are far away from one another. If you ill-treat my daughters or marry other women, remember God is witness between us.'

Jacob held a religious service on the hill and invited his relations to share the sacred meal beside the cairn. This over, they spent the night there.

Laban got up at dawn. He kissed his daughters and grandchildren goodbye, gave them his blessing and set off home.

Jacob went on south.

Brothers meet again

Jacob was now going home—after twenty years in the north. His mother had long been dead; it was meeting his brother that scared him.

Esau had his camping grounds south of the old home in Beersheba. Jacob sent messengers ahead to get into touch with him.

'Talk to him like this,' he told them. 'Tell him his servant Jacob sends him greeting: "I've been living with Laban in our ancestral country. I've been with him these twenty years. I've become quite rich—I've oxen, donkeys, flocks, slaves. May I hope for your friendship?"'

'We met Esau riding north to meet you,' the messengers brought news back. 'He has four hundred men with him.'

That put Jacob in a panic.

He divided his caravan into two companies—people as well as animals. If Esau attacked one, the other had at least a chance of escaping.

Then he prayed.

'O GOD,' he said, 'God of my grandfather Abraham and God of my father Isaac, you told me to come home. You promised too that you would take care of me. I don't deserve such steadfast love and loyalty as you have shown me. I am only your servant. I had only my staff when I crossed Jordan River twenty years ago on my way north; now I am master of these two encampments. Save me from my brother Esau. I am afraid of him—afraid he may murder us, children and mothers as well. You remember what you promised me—prosperity and many descendants.'

That night Jacob stayed where he was. In the darkness, he got up and sent his two wives and eleven children and all he had across the Jabbok Ford. He stayed behind alone on the hill—and a man wrestled with him till daybreak.[1]

'Let me go,' said the man. 'The day's breaking.'

'Tell me who you are,' said Jacob.

'What do you want to know my name for?' asked the man. But he gave Jacob his blessing.

As Jacob crossed the hill the sun rose.

He looked up—and there, coming to meet him, was his brother Esau and his four hundred men.

He hurriedly rearranged his caravan. He divided his children between the four women, Leah, Rachel and their two maids. He put the maids and their children at the head of the caravan, then Leah and her children, and, last of all, Rachel and her son Joseph.

He himself went on ahead of the caravan, bowing to the ground in greeting until he met his brother.

Esau ran forward, threw his arms round his neck and kissed him. They both wept for joy.

Then the women and the children arrived and greeted him.

'What's all this company mean?' he asked.

'To win your friendship,' said Jacob.

'I've enough, brother, more than enough,' he said. 'You keep it.'

'No, no, no,' said Jacob. 'You must have a present. It's good to see you again. And you've been so friendly. God's been very good to me. I have plenty.'

And he insisted until at last Esau accepted the present.

'Now let's get going,' said Esau. 'I'll ride along with you.'

'I travel slowly as you know,' said Jacob. 'There are the little children, and I daren't over-drive the cattle—I should just lose them if I did. You ride on ahead, my lord, and I'll come along at my own pace. I'll join you again in the south.'

'Well, let me give you an escort, then,' said Esau.

'Oh no!' said Jacob. 'You are too kind!'

So Esau rode south.

Jacob went only a short journey east and camped where the Jabbok Gorge enters the Jordan Valley. Then he went on by stages, through the highlands, as far south as 'The Cattle Tower'.

---

[1] The Jabbok River was the border; Jacob was crossing the threshold of new country. He therefore had to meet the river demon who guards frontiers. But because GOD's blessing was on him, he could meet and conquer it.

Joseph: Learning to be Adult

Joseph was the son of Rachel, Jacob's favourite wife. He had been born in the Balikh Valley. It was after his birth that his father made up his mind to go back to his old home in southern Palestine; Rachel died on the journey south and was buried near Bethlehem. Jacob went on to the Hebron Valley where Joseph's story begins.

Boasting boy

Joseph was now seventeen. His father had been quite an old man when he was born, and he had always openly treated him as his favourite son. He made him a princely coat (a coat with long sleeves) to wear. His brothers resented all this; they hadn't a kind word to say for him.

Now Joseph used to dream, and he couldn't keep his dreams to himself.

'Listen to the dream I had last night,' he would chatter to his brothers. 'It was harvest-time and we were out in the fields binding sheaves. My sheaf stood up; your sheaves gathered round it like a court and kept bowing down to my sheaf!'

'So you're to be our king, are you?' sneered his brothers. 'High and mighty, eh?'

They couldn't stand either his dreams or the way he chattered about them. It made their hate boil over.

'I had another dream last night,' he told his father and his brothers some days later (he had ten older brothers). 'This time the sun, moon and stars were bowing down to me—I was the earth!'

This time even his father told him to be quiet.

'What nonsense!' he said. 'The very idea!—you the earth, and I and your mother and brothers bowing to you!'

But his father didn't forget about these dreams; his brothers were just jealous of him because he was his father's favourite son.

Brothers' revenge

The time came for the brothers to lead the flocks away to the north, to Shechem, to summer pastures. The grass was more abundant there than around Hebron.

His father spoke to Joseph one day.

'Your brothers are away in the highlands,' he said. 'I want you to go and visit them for me.'

'All right,' said Joseph.

'See how they and the sheep are getting on,' he said, 'and bring me any news.'

And off he sent him.

Joseph reached Shechem. His brothers were nowhere to be seen. A man found him wandering about the countryside.

'What are you looking for?' he asked.

'I'm looking for my brothers,' said Joseph. 'Do you know where they've gone?'

'They've left here,' said the man. 'They were talking about going on to Dothan.'

Joseph went after them, and found them near Dothan, an ancient Canaanite city.

They saw him coming. Here was their chance to get their own back. By the time he'd got up to them, they'd made up their minds.

'Here's that dreamer coming!' they said to one another. 'Let's get rid of him and throw his body into one of these rain-pits. We can make up a story about his being eaten by a wild animal. We'll make his dreams come true all right!'

'Let's have no murder,' said Reuben, his eldest brother. 'Throw him into one of these rain-pits, if you want, but keep your hands off him.'

He intended to come back and get him out of the pit and take him home.

They threw him into one of the empty rain-pits.

Quite by chance, some Midianite traders passed by. They pulled the boy out of the pit and took him off to Egypt with them.

Reuben came back to the pit—but there was no Joseph in it. He tore his clothes in grief and ran back to his brothers.

'The lad's gone!' he told them. 'And now what am I to do? How can I go home?'

The brothers had taken Joseph's fine long-sleeved coat off him before they threw him into the pit. They tore it up and took it home with them to their father.

'We found this,' they said. 'Can you recognize it?'

'It's my son's cloak!' said the old man. 'A wild animal's mauled him. He must have been torn to pieces!'

In his grief, Jacob tore his clothes and put sackcloth on. He broke down in tears.

The Midianite traders meanwhile sold Joseph on the Egyptian slave-market. Potiphar, a royal officer, commander of the guard, bought him.

Egyptian slave

So Joseph found himself a slave, but a slave in a good home. He lived in his master's house and he was very industrious. GOD watched over him even there. His master was so impressed with him that he made

WHAT KIND OF PERSONS SHOULD WE BE? 333

him his house-overseer, general manager of all his affairs. From this moment onwards, all his master's affairs prospered, at home and in his official work. He left everything to Joseph. Only in the matter of food did he keep things in his own hands, for here religious taboos had to be observed.

Joseph was a well-built, good-looking fellow. His master's wife fell in love with him.

'Come to bed with me!' she pleaded.

He told her bluntly—No.

'It would be a sin against your husband,' he said, 'and a sin against your husband is a sin against God. My master has left everything in my hands. He doesn't even question me about his business now—I am in sole charge. I can do what I like about anything—except you: you are his wife. How do you think I could bring myself to wrong him so grievously?'

She was so passionately in love with him that not a day passed without her trying to seduce him. Joseph wouldn't listen to her and avoided her company.

But one day she caught him by himself. He'd come into the house to get on with his work, and nobody else was about. She caught hold of his cloak.

'Oh, do come to bed with me!' she pleaded.

But he left her holding his cloak and ran out into the courtyard.

That finished it. He'd run away from her, would he? She shouted to the servants, holding his cloak in her hands.

'Look!' she told them. 'My husband had to bring this outcast to seduce me! He's just tried to rape me! He ran away when I screamed—and left his cloak in my hands!'

She waited for her husband to come home, and then told him the same tale.

'That outcast you've taken up with tried to rape me,' she said. 'He ran off when I screamed out—here's the cloak he left.'

Her husband was furious and had Joseph thrown into the Round Tower (where royal prisoners were kept).

But GOD looked after Joseph even when he was in prison. He got on well with the Tower governor. Before long he was put in charge of the other prisoners and he was soon managing the Tower itself! The governor left the day-to-day work in his hands.

One day, there was trouble in the palace. Two high officials—the Lord High Chamberlain and the Royal Baker—fell from favour and were sent to the Round Tower to await trial. The commander ordered Joseph to look after them, and he waited on them.

Rembrandt: *Joseph interpreting the prisoners' dreams*

Some months went by. One morning, Joseph found them scared and frightened.

'What's the trouble?' he asked. 'Why so glum?'

'We both had dreams last night,' they said. 'We don't know what they mean and there's no means of finding out in this prison. That's what's frightening us.'

'The interpretation of dreams is God's business,' said Joseph. 'Tell me what they were about.'

'I dreamed about a vine tree,' said the Lord High Chamberlain. 'It was growing up right in front of me. It had three branches. It budded, broke into blossom and ripened into grapes. I was back in my old job, standing in Pharaoh's presence with his cup in my hand. I took the grapes, squeezed them into the royal cup and offered the cup to Pharaoh.'

'I can tell you what that means,' said Joseph. 'The three branches mean three days. In three days' time you will be called back to the palace and restored to your old position. You will be Lord High Chamberlain again.

'By the way,' he went on, 'don't forget me when you're back in office. Do me the kindness of mentioning my name to Pharaoh. I was kidnapped in Hebrew country. I've done nothing to deserve prison.'

The Royal Baker had been listening to this happy explanation of his friend's dream.

'I was dreaming, too,' he said. 'I was walking along with three open-work baskets on my head. The top basket was full of cakes and bread for the royal table; but birds kept pecking away at them.'

'I can tell you what your dream means, too,' said Joseph. 'Again, it's a matter of three days—that's the meaning of the three baskets. In three days' time you too will be called back to the palace—but for execution. The birds will peck the flesh from your dead body.'

Three days later was Pharaoh's birthday when he entertained his officers at a feast. The two men in prison were summoned to court—the Royal High Chamberlain back into favour, the Royal Baker to execution, exactly as Joseph had said. But the Lord High Chamberlain never gave a thought to Joseph—he forgot all about him.

Viceroy

One night, two years later, Pharaoh himself had a dream.

He was standing (in his dream) on the banks of the Nile. Seven fine cows waded ashore and began to crop the sedge on the bank. Seven scraggy cows followed them out of the river. The scraggy cows ate up the fat cows—and Pharaoh woke up.

He fell asleep and dreamed again. This time he was looking at a cornfield. Seven good, solid ears of corn were growing on a single stalk. Seven thin shrivelled ears (so thin they seemed to have been blighted by the dry east wind) sprouted after them and swallowed the good ears—and again Pharaoh woke up.

He was so scared by these dreams that next morning he summoned the Egyptian magicians and wise men to the palace. He described his dreams, but not one of them could make head or tail of them.

Then the Lord High Chamberlain suddenly remembered what had happened in the Round Tower two years ago.

He sought an audience with Pharaoh and told him about the dreams he and the Royal Baker had in the Round Tower that night.

'There was a Hebrew lad there,' he went on, 'the commander's slave. He explained our dreams to us. What he told us happened—I was given back my post, the Royal Baker was executed.'

Pharaoh immediately sent for Joseph who was hurriedly brought out of the dungeon, shaved and given a new suit of clothes. He was presented to Pharaoh.

Pharaoh again described his dreams.

'None of these magicians,' he added, 'has any idea what they mean.'

'The dreams are quite clear,' said Joseph. 'God is telling your Majesty what he is about to do. Both dreams are saying the same thing. The number seven in both stands for seven years. There will be seven years of rich harvests; then seven years of severe famine—men will forget what the very word "harvest" means. The reason for two dreams is clear too: God's mind is made up—he will soon do what he says.

'Let your Majesty act at once,' Joseph went on. 'Let an Overseer of the Granaries be appointed for the whole of Egypt with full power to commandeer one fifth of the seven years' good harvests and store them in city granaries against the bad times coming. The famine will not then be a disaster.'

Pharaoh and his court were deeply impressed by Joseph.

'Can we find anybody better than Joseph himself?' exclaimed Pharaoh. 'God's spirit obviously inspires him!'

He turned to Joseph.

'God has clearly told you what he is about to do. You are the shrewd and responsible man we are looking for. I appoint you Viceroy, second in power only to myself, Great Steward of the Lord of the Lands.'

He put his signet-ring on Joseph's finger, had him dressed in the linen robes of a Viceroy and gave him the gold chain of office. He was to ride in the 'Second Chariot' with troops riding ahead and shouting 'To your knees!' and clearing the road.

The Viceroy had to be a full member of the Egyptian Court. So Joseph was given an Egyptian name—Zaphenath-peneah ('the God speaks and he lives')—and was married to Asenath, daughter of the High Priest of Heliopolis ('City of the Sun').

Joseph left the palace and carried out an inspection of the whole country. The harvests of the next seven years were wonderful harvests. He commandeered all the good grain and stored it in central city granaries, each granary dealing with the farms in its neighbourhood.

Two sons were born to him—Manasseh and Ephraim.

Then the harvests failed and famine faced the whole country and neighbouring countries too. People were clamouring for food. Pharaoh issued an edict making Joseph Overseer of the Granaries of Upper and Lower Egypt, and Joseph put the grain on sale to all who needed it.

Joseph and his brothers

There was famine in Palestine as well as in Egypt. Jacob heard about the great Egyptian granaries.

'Why do you stand staring at each other?' he asked his sons. 'There's corn in Egypt, they say. We don't want to starve. Go and buy some.'

So Joseph's ten older brothers set off for Egypt to buy grain. Joseph's younger brother, Benjamin, stayed at home; his father wouldn't let him out of his sight.

Joseph immediately recognized them (they had no idea who he was); he remembered his boyhood dreams.

'You are spies,' he told them. 'You've come here just to see what the situation is and how we can be attacked.'

'That's not true,' they retorted. 'We've come to buy food. We are brothers and honest men. We are not spies.'

'No!' said Joseph. 'You've come to find the weak spots in our defence.'

'Your servants are a family of twelve brothers,' they insisted. 'We live in the land of Canaan, sons of one father. Our youngest brother has stayed at home; our other brother is dead.'

'There you are!' said Joseph. 'You are spies as I said.'

He whisked them off to prison for three days to think it over.

Then he summoned them back into his presence.

'If you want to save your lives, do what I tell you,' he said. 'I am a man of my word. You are honest men, you say. Well, one of you can stay in prison as hostage; the rest of you can go home with food and then bring your youngest brother back here. That will prove the truth of your tale and save you from the death penalty.'

They all agreed.

'It's our brother's death that's brought us to this,' they said to one another. 'We are guilty men. He pleaded for mercy and we wouldn't listen. That's why we're now in trouble.'

'I told you at the time,' said Reuben. 'I told you that you were treating the boy brutally, but you took no notice. Now you've got to pay for his death.'

They didn't know that Joseph could follow all they were saying. The interpreter standing by him made them think that he spoke only Egyptian. Joseph couldn't face them any longer; he went out of the room and tears streamed down his face. Then he went back. He had Simeon seized and bound in their presence. Then he played a trick on them. He gave secret orders for their sacks to be filled with grain and their money to be put in with it. They were given food for the homeward journey.

The men loaded their donkeys and set off.

When they got home, they told their father all that had happened—how they had been arrested as spies; how they had protested their innocence and told the Viceroy about their family; how he had

Rembrandt: *Joseph's brothers requesting Benjamin from their father*

imprisoned Simeon and told them to bring Benjamin back with them.

Then they opened their sacks—and there were their money-packets in the sacks with the grain! When they saw the money, they and their father were filled with dismay.

'You've robbed me of all my children,' said Jacob. 'Joseph's gone; Simeon's gone; and now you are taking Benjamin from me! And I've got to suffer it all!'

'I'll bring him back safely,' said Reuben. 'You can kill my own two sons if I don't. Let me take charge of him. I'll bring him home.'

'He's staying here,' said Jacob. 'His brother's dead; he is all I've left. If anything should happen to him, I should die with grief.'

The famine grew worse, and the grain the brothers had brought from Egypt had all been eaten.

'Go back again,' their father told them, 'and get some more grain.'

'Now, be sensible,' said Judah. 'You know what the Viceroy said— no brother, no audience with him. If you'll send Benjamin with us, all right—we'll go and buy grain; if you won't let him go, we stay here. The Viceroy warned us quite clearly.'

'You could have spared me all this trouble,' said Jacob. 'Why did you tell him you had another brother?'

'The man asked us all sorts of questions,' his sons told him. 'He asked about the family—"Is your father alive?" "Have you another brother?" All we could do was to answer him honestly. How could we know he would want us to bring Benjamin back with us?'

'Let the lad go with me,' said Judah, 'and we'll get off and escape dying here—with you and the children—from starvation. I will go bail for him; hold me responsible. If I don't bring him back to you, you may blame me for it all my life. If we hadn't been held up like this, we could have been to Egypt and back twice by now.'

Jacob gave in.

'All right,' he said. 'If it must be, it must be. But take a present for the Viceroy. Put some fine fruit in your sacks, and a little balm, a little honey, gum, myrrh, pistachio nuts and almonds. Take twice the money needed—the money-packets in the sacks were perhaps a mistake. And take your brother too. May God Almighty look after you and get the Viceroy to send both Simeon and Benjamin back to me. But if I am bereaved, I am bereaved.'

So the men set off for Egypt.

They were ushered into Joseph's presence—and Joseph caught sight of Benjamin. He immediately gave orders to the Master of Ceremonies.

'Bring the men into the palace,' he said. 'They are to dine with me at noon.'

The officer led the men to the palace. When they saw where they were being taken, they were in a panic.

'It's that money,' they said to one another. 'He just wants an excuse to set his guards on us, make us slaves and take our donkeys.'

Once through the palace gates, they went up to the Master of Ceremonies and tried to explain.

'If you please, sir,' they said, 'when we came here the first time, we came to buy food. We found the money-packets only when we opened our sacks at home; we've brought them back—and more money to buy more food. We don't know how the packets got into our sacks.'

'Don't worry,' said the officer. 'There's nothing to be frightened of. Your God must have put the money there; you settled up with me all right.'

He brought Simeon out to them.

They were taken on into the palace, and given water to wash their feet and fodder to feed their donkeys. They got their present for the Viceroy ready to give him when he came in at noon—they had already been told they were to have dinner with him.

Joseph came back to the palace. The men gave him the present they had brought, bowing to the ground before him. He asked about their welfare and about the family.

'Is your father well, the old man you told me about?' he asked. 'Is he still living?'

'Your servant, our father, is alive and well,' they said.

Joseph looked up and saw Benjamin, his own brother.

'You told me about your youngest brother,' he said. 'Is this your youngest brother? May God be gracious to you, my son.'

Joseph hurried out of the room. He couldn't hold back his tears any longer, he was so deeply moved by meeting his own brother again like this. He was overcome by emotion and had to stay in his room for some time. At last, he washed his face and came out. He now kept his feelings in hand.

'Let dinner be served,' he said.

Dinner followed Egyptian custom: Joseph dined by himself, the Hebrew shepherds by themselves and the members of Joseph's court by themselves—eating with foreigners was taboo.

The brothers sat in order of age; this surprised them. Food was taken to them from Joseph's table; Benjamin's portion was five times that of any of his brothers.

They all drank and had a good time together.

Joseph again gave orders to his Master of Ceremonies.

'Fill the men's sacks with as much food as they can carry,' he said, 'and put my cup—the silver cup—in the youngest brother's sack.' This was done.

At dawn next day, the men were sent off home.

They had not gone far beyond the city when Joseph summoned an officer.

'Up and after the men,' he said. 'When you overtake them, ask them why they have returned evil for good and stolen the silver cup I use for drinking and divining—a wicked thing to do!'

This the officer did.

'How can you say this, sir?' the men protested. 'We would never do anything of the sort. We brought our money back, didn't we? Why should we try to steal gold or silver from the palace? If you find the cup, let the man whose sack you find it in die; the others can be your slaves.'

'Fair enough,' said the officer. 'But only the man himself will be my slave; the rest can go free.'

Soon the sacks were on the ground and being opened. The officer began with the eldest brother and worked down to the youngest. The cup was found in Benjamin's sack.

The men were in a panic. They loaded the donkeys and went back to the city.

Joseph was still in the palace when they got back. They flung themselves on the ground before him.

'What have you been up to?' he asked. 'Didn't you know that a man in my position can easily find things out by divination?'

'What can we say, sir?' said Judah. 'We don't know how to explain it or how to clear ourselves. God has found out our crime. We are your slaves—all of us.'

'No, no,' said Joseph. 'Only the man who stole the cup shall be my slave; the rest of you can go back home to your father.'

Judah went up to Joseph.

'May I have a private word with you, sir?' he asked. 'Don't be angry with me—I know you are the Viceroy. My lord asked us if we had a father or a brother. We told you "We have a father, an old man, and a young brother, born to him in his old age; his brother is dead—he alone is left of his mother's children and he is his father's favourite son."

'We told our father all this. When he asked us to come here again to buy food, we told him plainly that we couldn't come unless the lad came with us. Then your servant my father said "My wife Rachel bore me two sons. One disappeared—surely mauled by a wild beast; I have never seen him since. If this lad leaves me and comes to harm, I shall die of grief—and it will be your fault." What will happen if, when I get home, the lad he loves so much is not with us? It will be the death of him. I guaranteed his safe return. I now ask one thing: let me stay here as your slave instead of the lad; let him go home with his brothers. How can I go home without him? I fear to think what will happen to my father.'

Joseph could hold back his feelings no longer. He ordered all officials out of the audience room. Then he broke down—everybody in the palace could hear his weeping.

'Come near to me,' he said to his brothers.

They gathered round him.

'I am your brother Joseph,' he told them. 'Now don't be angry with yourselves for what you did. There are five more years of famine ahead of us; God sent me here so that our family might survive. You must go back home with a message from me to my father: "God has made me Viceroy of Egypt. Make haste and come down to me. You can live in the land of Goshen, near me—you and the whole clan with your flocks and possessions. I will look after you and see that you don't starve."

'You and my brother Benjamin,' he went on, 'can see that I really am Joseph.'

He put his arms round his brother's neck and they both wept for joy.

Joseph and his father

Joseph gave his brothers all they needed for their journey home; and he also gave them each a splendid coat—he gave Benjamin five coats and a large sum of money. To his father he sent ten donkeys loaded with fine Egyptian food and ten donkeys loaded with bread and grain, and food for his journey to Egypt.

'Joseph is still alive!' they told their father when they got home. 'He is Viceroy of Egypt!'

The old man was stunned by the news; he wouldn't believe a word of it until he saw the cavalcade Joseph had sent. Then he began to realize what had happened.

'It's enough!' he said. 'My son Joseph is still alive; I will go and see him before I die.'

He set off with all his possessions and reached the land of Goshen.

Meanwhile Joseph had ordered his chariot out and went to meet him. He put his arms round his father's neck and wept for joy.

'I can now die happy,' said Jacob. 'I have seen you—you are still alive!'

'I'll report your arrival to Pharaoh,' Joseph said.

Now his brothers were shepherds and had brought their flocks and herds and possessions with them.

'When Pharaoh asks about your occupation,' Joseph went on, 'tell him you are cattle-men. That will secure the border land of Goshen for you—Egyptians have a taboo about shepherds.'

Joseph sought an audience with Pharaoh.

'My father and my brothers have arrived in Goshen,' he reported. He had brought five of his brothers with him to present to Pharaoh.

'What's your occupation?' he asked.

'Your servants are shepherds, your Majesty, as our fathers were,' they answered. 'We have come to settle here as immigrants. There's no pasture left at home—the famine there is terrible. We ask permission to settle here.'

'Let them settle in Goshen,' said Pharaoh. 'If they have any competent men among them, they can be my cattle-men.'

Jacob was now very old, and he knew he had not long to live. He asked Joseph to come and see him.

'I want you to make me a promise,' he said. 'I want you to give me your solemn word that you won't bury me in Egypt. Bury me with my fathers in our ancestral burying ground.'

'I will carry out your wishes,' said Joseph.

'You swear that you will do it?' said Jacob.

'I do,' said Joseph.

Jacob lay back in his bed. Not long afterwards he died; Joseph buried him in the ancestral burying ground in Canaan, and then went back to Egypt.

The last test

Now that their father was dead, Joseph's brothers were frightened; they wondered what he would do now.

'He'll perhaps pay us back for what we did to him,' they said to one another. 'He must hate us.'

So they sent a message to him:

'Your father told us before he died, to tell you this: "Tell Joseph to forgive his brothers for what they did to him." We beg you to forgive us. We are the servants of your father's God.'

Then they sought an audience with him.

Joseph was deeply moved when he met them. They flung themselves down on the ground before him.

'We are your slaves,' they said.

'Don't be afraid,' said Joseph. 'I am not God. You meant to do me harm, but God planned to bring good out of it—to save the lives of many people, as he has done. So don't get frightened. I will look after you and your children.'

He reassured them and spoke kindly to them.

Joseph went on living in Egypt. At last he died. His body was embalmed and laid in a coffin. Years later, his bones were carried to Shechem and buried there.

Two Prophetic Stories

The men who wrote these stories were trying to keep alive the old prophetic faith and to recall their countrymen to their world-mission—to be 'God's Servant' and the servant of their fellow-men. They were protesting against the 'isolationist' and 'apartheid' policies of their contemporaries. They could no longer speak openly on the streets (the small community of city and villages was too tightly knit); they probably put what they had to say down in writing.

The Story of Jonah is centred on Nineveh, the capital city of their hated enemies, the Assyrians. It is the story of how this city repented at the preaching of an Israelite prophet who symbolized the Israelite people. *The Story of Ruth* is a story of a Moabite girl and her loyalty to GOD's Way (see Nehemiah's and Ezra's attitude to such foreign girls, pp. 199, 201). The sting of both stories is in the ending.

Jonah : Enemies are Persons

Once upon a time GOD spoke to Jonah.

'Get up,' he said, 'and go to that great city, Nineveh. Pronounce its doom—its shameful wickedness has been reported to me.'

Jonah set off—but he made for Tartessus in the far west, right away from GOD. He went down to the port of Joppa. There was a large cargo-boat in the harbour. He paid his passage and went on board; he didn't want to have anything to do with GOD and his commands.

Out at sea they ran into a hurricane. The sea was so rough that the ship seemed about to break up. The sailors were in a panic, each shouting out to his own god for help. They threw the cargo overboard to lighten the ship.

Jonah had gone down into the hold, and was lying there fast asleep. The captain went down to see what he was doing.

'What do you mean by sleeping like this?' he shouted. 'Get up and pray to your God. He might take some notice of us and come to our help.'

Meanwhile the sailors were talking together.

'Let's toss up,' they were saying, 'and find out who's to blame for this bad luck.'

They tossed up—it was Jonah!

'Tell us your business,' they said. 'Where do you come from? What's your country? Who are your people?'

'I'm a Hebrew,' he told them. 'I'm running away from GOD—the God of heaven who made the sea and the land.'

'What a thing to do!' they said. 'What shall we do with you to quieten the storm?'

The sea was growing rougher and rougher.

'Throw me overboard,' said Jonah. 'That will calm the sea. I know I am to blame for this hurricane.'

But the men didn't throw him overboard. They rowed as hard as they could to get the ship into harbour. All in vain—the sea grew stormier and stormier still.

Then they prayed to Jonah's God:

'O GOD,' they prayed, 'don't let us die if we throw this man overboard; don't hold it against us. The storm is your doing.'

Then they threw Jonah overboard—and the storm died down.

The sailors were filled with awe in GOD's presence; they worshipped him and vowed to serve him.

GOD sent a great fish. It swallowed Jonah, and there he stayed, inside the fish, for three whole days. He then ordered the fish to put Jonah on shore, and it vomited him out on to the dry land.

GOD spoke to Jonah a second time.

'Get up and go to the great city, Nineveh,' he repreated, 'and pronounce its doom, as I shall tell you.'

This time Jonah got up and went to Nineveh as GOD ordered him.

Now Nineveh was a large city. To walk across it, from city wall to city wall, was a three day's walk. Jonah entered the city and walked for a whole day. He stood and announced its doom.

'In forty days' time,' he shouted, 'this city will become a heap of ruins!'

The citizens of Nineveh at once accepted GOD's word. All of them—from the greatest nobleman to the poorest worker—covered themselves with sackcloth and sat down in grief.

News of all this reached the royal palace. The king got up from his throne and stripped off his royal robes. He, too, put on sackcloth and sat down in grief.

He issued a proclamation and the heralds carried it through the city:

BY ORDER OF THE KING AND HIS MINISTERS!

A FAST IS PROCLAIMED FOR ALL CITIZENS AND ALL ANIMALS. NOTHING SHALL BE EATEN AND NOTHING DRUNK. ALL SHALL PUT ON SACKCLOTH AND PRAY TO GOD WITH THEIR WHOLE HEART. EVERY CITIZEN SHALL TURN FROM HIS EVIL WAYS AND FROM EVERY ACT OF VIOLENCE.

'Who knows?' thought the king. 'GOD may yet change his mind, and stop being angry with us; the city may be saved.'

Indeed, when GOD saw what they had done—how they had given up all their evil ways—he changed his mind. He did not destroy the city.

Jonah was very angry indeed.

'Isn't this just what I said would happen when I was back at home?' he said to GOD. 'That's why I ran away to the west. I know the sort of God you are—"Kind and merciful, slow to anger, quick to love men with all your heart", as the hymn[1] says. I knew you would change your mind. I'd rather be dead than alive!'

'Is anger all you can think of?' asked GOD.

Jonah just walked out of the East Gate of the city and sat down to see what would happen.

GOD made a plant grow up to shade his head—the great heat of the

[1] Ps 103.8

Rembrandt: *Jonah at the walls of Nineveh*

sun was too much for him. That made Jonah happier. But at dawn, next day, a worm attacked the plant and it died. The sun rose, a scorching east wind blew and the heat beat down on Jonah. He nearly fainted.

'I'd rather be dead than alive!' he groaned.

'Is being angry like this right?' asked GOD.

'It is!' said Jonah. 'I could die with anger!'

'But Jonah,' said GOD, 'you are sorry for a plant which grew up in a night and died in a night—a plant you hadn't done anything for and which grew without your help. Shouldn't I be sorry for the great city of Nineveh (even if it is a foreign city) with its hundred and twenty thousand ignorant people—and its animals?'

Ruth: Race doesn't count with God

Naomi and Ruth

Once upon a time, in the days when the Hebrew tribes were settled in the highlands, there was a great drought; the villagers were facing starvation. A family in Bethlehem were forced to emigrate to find food —Elimelech and his wife Naomi and their two sons Mahlon and Chilion. They settled in Moab, and the two sons married Moabite girls, Orpah and Ruth.

Then Elimelech died. The family stayed on in Moab, and for ten years everything went happily. Then both the sons died. Naomi who had now lost both husband and sons, decided to go home to Bethlehem (news had come that there was no shortage of food there) and, with the help of her two daughters-in-law, began to get ready for the journey.

The three women left the village and set off down the road to the Jordan Valley.

'Now you must both go home to your families,' said Naomi to the two girls. 'May GOD be as good to you as you have been to me and my husband. He will help you to marry again and find another good home.'

She kissed them goodbye, and they both burst out crying.

'No, no!' they said. 'We'll go with you to your ancestral home.'

'Now listen to me,' said Naomi, 'you must go home. There's no point in going with me. I've no more sons for you to marry, and I'm too old to marry again and have children. You wouldn't want to stay unmarried all that time, anyhow, just to marry sons of mine. No. I'm very sorry for your sakes that all this trouble has happened to me.'

The girls burst into tears again. Then Orpah kissed Naomi goodbye. Ruth held her in her arms.

'Look!' said Naomi. 'Orpah's gone back to her own people and her own religion. You go back with her.'

'Don't make me leave you!' said Ruth. 'Don't make me go home! I want to go where you go and to live where you live. Your people are my people now, your God is my God. I'll die where you die and be buried where you are buried. Only death itself will separate us from one another!'

When Naomi saw that Ruth was not to be argued with, she said no more. They went on together across the river and climbed the mountain road to Bethlehem.

When they got there, the village buzzed with gossip.

'It can't be Naomi, can it?' the women were saying.

'Don't call me Naomi ("My sweet one") any more,' said Naomi. 'You'd better change my name to Mara ("Bitter"). I've had a dreadful time. When I went away we were all happy together; but I've come home alone. Naomi is no name for me now!'

That is how Naomi and Ruth, the Moabite girl, came home to Bethlehem. It was April, the beginning of the barley harvest.

Ruth and Boaz

There was a rich farmer living in Bethlehem, Boaz, a relative of Elimelech's and a member of the same clan.

'Let me go down to the harvest fields,' said Ruth to Naomi one day. 'Someone will be kind enough to let me follow him and pick any barley that's dropped.'

'Yes, you go,' said Naomi.

Off she went. She followed some reapers in a field and started picking up barley stalks. The field happened to belong to Boaz.

Just then, Boaz himself came into the field from the village.

'GOD bless you all!' he called out to the reapers.

'Who's that girl over there?' he asked a reaper.

'Oh, it's the Moabite girl who came back with Naomi,' he said. 'She asked if she could follow us up the field. She's been busy picking up barley ever since dawn.'

Boaz went over to her.

'Now listen to me, my girl,' he said. 'Stay in this field and don't go wandering off. And keep close to the women—go where they go. I've told the young fellows that they're not to start interfering with you. The water jugs are there—use them when you're thirsty.'

Ruth flung herself on the ground before him.

'You're very kind,' she said. 'I don't know why you should be so kind to a foreigner like me.'

'Oh, I've heard all about you,' said Boaz, 'how you've looked after your mother-in-law since she's been widowed—and how you left your home and country to come and live here among strangers. GOD bless you!'

'You've cheered me up, sir,' said Ruth, 'and made me feel quite at home—even though I'm not one of your workers.'

It was now noon.

'Come and help yourself to some bread,' said Boaz, 'and dip it in the wine.'

Ruth sat down with the other reapers and he passed her some popped corn. She had more to eat than she needed. Then she went back into the field.

'Let her pick up what she wants,' Boaz told his men, 'and no getting fresh with her. You can drop some of the barley for her to pick up. And remember—leave her alone.'

Ruth stayed in the field until dark. She beat the barley stalks and found she had nearly a bushel of barley grain. She carried it back to the village and gave it to Naomi.

'Where did you go?' she asked. 'Where was the field? GOD bless the man who took so much notice of you.'

'Well, the man's name was Boaz,' said Ruth. 'I worked with him.'

'GOD bless him!' said Naomi. 'You know he's a relative of ours, don't you?'

'He told me to keep close to his reapers,' said Ruth, 'and I can stay there till harvest's over.'

'You keep close to the women,' said Naomi. 'You'll get into trouble if you go wandering off into another field.'

So Ruth spent all the days of both the barley and the wheat harvests out in the fields, and went back home each night to Naomi.

'I think you ought to be married,' Naomi said to Ruth one day. 'What do you think of Boaz? Now I'll tell you what to do. He's winnowing the grain tonight down at the threshing floor. Make yourself as pretty as you can and put your best dress on. Go down to the threshing floor. Wait till supper is over before you let him know who you are. Notice where he lies down to sleep. Then go and lie down at his feet and pull his blanket over you. He'll tell you what to do.'

'As you say,' said Ruth.

So she went to the threshing floor and did just what Naomi told her.

At last, supper was over. Boaz was in a merry mood and he lay down beside a heap of grain. Ruth crept quietly up, lifted the blanket at his feet and lay down. Boaz was fast asleep. In the middle of the night, he suddenly awoke, and, turning over, found the girl lying at his feet.

'Who on earth are you?' he asked.

'I'm Ruth,' she said. 'I'm asking you to marry me— it's your duty, you know.'

'GOD has blessed you, my girl!' he said. 'You've proved to me your loyalty to your family—in the field and here tonight at the threshing floor. You haven't been flirting with the boys and trying to find out who's got money and who hasn't. You're a good girl—everybody knows that. I'll do what you ask—it's my duty. But I'm not your nearest relative, you know. There's a man who's a closer relative and it's really his duty to marry you. Stay here tonight, and tomorrow morning I'll have a word with him. If he'll fulfil his legal duty to you, well and good—he can do so. But if he won't, then as GOD lives, I will. Now go to sleep.'

She went to sleep again. But she got up before it was light; she didn't want anybody to recognize her. Boaz thought it best that nobody should know she'd been to the threshing floor that night.

'Hold out the wrap you are wearing,' he said.

He filled it with a bushel of barley grain and helped her to put it on her back. She went back into the village.

'Well, how did it go?' asked Naomi.

Ruth told her.

'And he gave me this bushel of barley,' she added. 'He said I mustn't go home without something for you.'

'Now, take it quietly,' said Naomi. 'We'll see how it all turns out. Boaz won't rest until he has cleared the matter up.'

Happy ending

Boaz went up to the village gate (where the law-court was held) and sat down. After a time, he saw the man whose duty it was, as her nearest relative, to marry Ruth. He called after him as he was walking by:

'Hi, friend! Come and sit down here!'

Boaz got ten of the village elders to form a court. Then he spoke to the man.

'Now,' he said, 'you know all about Naomi. She's come back home and she's going to sell her husband's field. I thought you ought to know. You're her nearest relative. You ought to have the chance of buying it in the presence of these elders as witnesses. If you want to buy it, say so. If you don't, I'd like to know. You have first claim; I come next.'

'Right,' he said, 'I'll buy it.'

'But wait a moment,' said Boaz. 'If you buy the field, you must also marry Ruth the Moabite girl—she's the widow of the heir. The field must go eventually, as you know, to his family.'

'That puts a different light on the matter,' said the man. 'Buying it under those conditions will reduce my estate. I renounce my claim. You can have it.'

The man took off his sandal and gave it to Boaz.

'You buy the field,' he said.

Boaz turned to the assembled court.

'You are witnesses,' he said. 'I have agreed to buy all the property that belonged to the three men—Elimelech, Chilion and Mahlon. And I have agreed to marry Ruth and see that the property eventually goes to her children, so that Elimelech's name shall not die out. I call you all to witness the contract.'

'We are witnesses,' they said. 'May GOD bless you and your bride and give you prosperity.'

Ruth and Boaz were married; and in due time a son was born.

'May GOD be blessed!' all her neighbours said to Naomi. 'He isn't leaving you without somebody to look after you. May your grandson become a famous man! He'll be a joy to you in your old age—isn't he Ruth's child and hasn't she been as good as seven sons to you?'

Naomi picked the baby up and cuddled it.

'We must give the baby a name,' said the neighbours. 'Let's call him Obed.' So Obed was his name.

Obed was King David's grandfather.

Two Prophetic Poems: Living in a Common World

The second poem may be older than Isaiah; the first poem may be a temple hymn that Isaiah and Micah knew and used. The nationalism they protest against can be found in every century, the century of Amos, the century of Nehemiah—and the twentieth century!

In the days that are to be
   the mountain of GOD's temple
shall tower high above
   the highest mountain ranges.

The people of the world
   shall make pilgrimages to it:
'Come, let us climb GOD's mountain
   to the temple of his people's God;
he will teach us the good life
   and help us to live in his Way.
From Jerusalem and its holy mountain
   GOD's true word—true religion—
     spreads over the whole earth!'

GOD shall quell the world's quarrels—
   even among distant empires:
sword and spear shall be forged
   into ploughshare and pruning knife;
there shall be no more war,
   no more training camps,
     no more parade grounds!

When GOD's Day comes
there will be an open road
from the Nile to the Euphrates!
Assyrians will go as pilgrims to Egypt,
Egyptians as pilgrims to Assyria,
worshipping together.

In that day
Israel will be the Third People,
comrade of Egypt and Assyria,
living for the good of the world
which GOD has blessed:
'Happy is Egypt my people,
happy Assyria my workmanship,
happy Israel my heritage!'

◄ Our twentieth-century world: a century of wars

A Scholar's Poem: Real Wisdom

Scholars ('wise men'), as well as prophets and priests, played their part in the life of GOD's people. We give here a scholar's poem which is now found in *The Book of Job*. The scholars were not philosophers (as in Greece) but askers of questions—some sceptical like the author of *Ecclesiastes* (p. 379), many deeply religious like the author of *Job* (p. 359) or the writer of Psalm 73 (p. 406), some historians like the author of *The Court History* (p. 63). Here is a scholar's meditation on GOD's Way which for him was real wisdom.

> Where can Wisdom be tracked down?
>   Where are the springs of Understanding?
>
> Silver is mined, iron dug,
>   gold refined, copper smelted—
> from seams that run into darkness,
>   into the earth's far darkness.
>
> Unknown men hew out tunnels,
>   lost from human sight:
> above—corn shining in the sunlight;
>   below—men raking earth like fire,
>   wresting from rock the sky-blue stone
>   speckled with gold,
>   beyond the flight of carrion-crow,
>   unseen by falcon's eye,
>   unknown to the lion,
>   unvisited by the snake.
>
> Man yet finds his way there—
>   smashing the granite,
>   uprooting the mountains,
>   thrusting tunnels
>   into the gem-starred rock,
>   damming the sources of streams,
>   tapping the hidden wealth of the earth.
>
> But where can Wisdom be tracked down?
>   Where are the springs of Understanding?
>
> No-one knows the way to Wisdom
>   or can find it in the world of men:

the Ocean and the far seas confess—
  'It is not in us'.
Nobody can buy it in the market
  with gold or silver,
or weigh it against Arabian gold
  or African topaz,
    cornelian, chrysolite,
    crystal, coral.

Where, then, can Wisdom be tracked down?
  Where, then, are the springs of Understanding?

Wild beasts and wild birds
  know nothing of it,
disaster and death hear
  only distant rumours.

God alone,
  surveying earth and sky,
knows the way to Wisdom,
  to the place where it is found.

When, in the beginning,
  he curbed wind and water,
    set bounds to rain and thunder,
he discovered it,
  weighed its worth,
    dug down to its depths.

To Man he said:
  Living in GOD's Way
    is Wisdom,
  having nothing to do with evil
    is Understanding.

Job: What can we know about God?

The Book of Job is one of the greatest poems in the literature of the world. It comes from the circles of the 'wise men', the scholars; *A Scholar's Poem* (p. 355) may actually have been written by its author.

The pattern of the book is this:

> The Prologue
> The Poem
>> Job speaks
>> Job and his friends state their case
>> Job speaks again
>> God answers Job
>> Job answers God
> The Epilogue

The Prologue and the Epilogue are in prose and give the beginning and ending of an old folktale about a legendary figure of the distant past: a very rich man, Job, and his family fall on evil days but finally all live happily ever after. The poet uses only the beginning and the ending; we do not know what other adventures the main body of the folktale recounted. The poem begins at the point in the folktale when overwhelming disaster has fallen on Job. The poem itself may have been many years in the making. Perhaps the poet-scholar began it by discussing the folktale with his students and using it as a starting point for a wider enquiry into some important religious questions. The undeserved suffering of an innocent man provokes not only the question 'Why suffering in a world controlled by a good God?' but also the deeper question 'What can we know about God at all?'

It has been suggested that the original work consisted of the Prologue and Epilogue and the poems where Job and God speak to one another,[1] and that, as the poem grew, poems about Job and his friends were added. Later still, other poems were added by the poet or by the poet's students or later editors, to give the book the form it now has.

We give the folktale and the main argument of the poem—the speeches of Job and God.

(Note: 'Satan' here is not a proper name. The Hebrew has 'The Satan', that is 'The Adversary', the officer of the Heavenly Court charged with the supervision of the human race—God's Inspector-General.)

---

[1] See N. H. Snaith, 'The First Book of Job', *The Book of Job*, pp. 34–44.

Prologue

Once upon a time there was a wealthy Edomite sheik called Job, the most outstanding sheik in all the East. He was, moreover, a good man, a genuinely innocent man. His religion was real religion and he would have nothing to do with evil of any kind. He had a large family— seven sons and three daughters—and immense wealth.

One day GOD summoned the Heavenly Court. It met in his presence, and among the members of the court was 'The Satan'—GOD's Inspector-General.

GOD turned to him.

'Where have you been?' he asked.

'On the earth,' he reported. 'I've been wandering north, south, east and west.'

'Did you come across my servant Job?' GOD asked. 'Now he's a good man for you—a genuinely innocent man. His religion is real religion and he won't have anything to do with evil of any kind.'

'Yes, I met him,' said the Satan. 'He's a good man, I admit. But then —he has every reason to be! He has nothing to fear—you stand guard over him and his family and his wealth. Indeed, it is you who have made him as wealthy as he is. But just touch that wealth of his—or his family—and he'll curse you to your face!'

'Very well,' said GOD. 'He's in your hands—you do just that. But leave the man himself alone.'

The Satan left the court.

One day the young people were having a banquet at the eldest son's house. Job himself was at home.

Then—disaster followed disaster.

One after another, messengers came running with news—

'Arab raiders have carried off the oxen and asses from the fields and murdered your herdsmen! I'm the only one to escape!'

'Lightning has killed all your sheep and shepherds! I'm the only one to escape!'

'Wild tribes from the desert—three bands of them—have driven your camels off and killed all your camel-drivers! I'm the only one to escape!'

'A desert hurricane has blown your son's house down. The young people were buried in the rubble—and they're all dead! I'm the only one to escape!'

Job was hard hit. But he knelt down in prayer—

'One after another, messengers came running with news.' Engraving by William Blake

> 'I came naked from the earth,
>   to the earth I shall go naked back.
> GOD gave,
>   GOD takes back—
>   blessed be his name!'

All through these disasters Job never lost his trust in God—or said a word against him.

The Heavenly Court was again in session. The Satan was there to give his report.

'Well,' said GOD. 'Where have you been this time?'

'Wandering on the earth,' he said, 'north, south, east and west.'

'And what about Job now?' GOD asked him. 'He's still the kind of man I said he was—in spite of the disasters you prompted me to send to ruin him. You haven't broken him.'

'Skin for skin, as the proverb puts it,' retorted the Satan. 'You touch the man himself—and see what happens. You'll get his curses then!'

'Very well,' said GOD. 'You are free to do what you want to him—short of actually killing him.'

The Satan left the court and went back to earth. He struck Job with Egyptian boils[1] from head to foot, and Job sat itching in the ash-pit, scratching himself with a piece of broken crockery.

'And you still trust him!' his wife scolded. 'Curse him—and die!'

'That's a wicked thing to say,' said Job. 'You're talking just like a scurrilous street gossip! You know that we must take GOD on his own terms, whether it's good or evil he sends. That's no more than our duty.'

The Poem

Job Speaks[2]

> May the day when I was born
>   vanish from the calendar of men—
> vanish into dawn-less darkness
>   into fog and gloom,
> lost under smothering cloud
>   and sunless skies
>   and the blind blackness of the night;
> with no touch of life
>   or cry of joy;
> cursed by sorcerer and magician
>   whose spells bind the sea monster himself!
> May it never see
>   the stars shining in a lightening sky,
> may it wait in vain for the dawn
>   and the eyelids of the morning!—
> it did not make my mother childless
>   and keep me out of sight of sorrow.
>
> Why didn't I die
>   when I was born?
> Why live to lie on her knees
>   and feed at her breasts?
> Why wasn't I buried

---

[1] 'The traditional dreadful and shameful disease of the wicked', N. H. Snaith, *The Book of Job*, p. 28; cf. Deuteronomy 28.27, 35.

[2] See Jeremiah's poem, p. 265.

'Why didn't I die when I was born?' Engraving by William Blake

like a still-born baby?
I would now have been lying
    with kings and viceroys and princes,
(palace and gilded house
    tumbled to rubble!)
dead in a quiet grave,
    resting and sleeping.
Where the dead are—
    bad men's bullying ways,
    workmen's hard labour,
        are done with;
    prisoners, left alone at last,
        jogged awake by no gaoler's shout.
Everybody is there—
    king and commoner alike,
        and the slave,
        a free man at last!

Why are grief-stricken men
   forced into the light?
Why are the broken and bitter
   burdened with life?
All they can do is to dream of death,
   hunting it down like hidden treasure—
      death that never comes!
Their only joy
   the burial mound and the grave!

Why should a man be doomed
   to grope his way blindfold,
      shut in by God's unceasing No?

All that I have to sustain me
   are my sighs;
all I have to give
   the tumbling torrent of my groans.
All I feared and dreaded
   has happened to me.
I don't know the meaning
   of peace or quiet—
I toss and toss
   in restless torment.

Oh for the old days
   when God was my guardian—
his lamp shining down on me
   lighting my way through the darkness!

When I took my seat in the Council
   in the square by the Town Gate,
young men stepped aside,
   old men stood up,
the talking stopped,
   leaders were silent—
everybody hung on my words,
   waiting for what I had to say.

I was eyes to the blind
   and feet to the lame,
father to the poor,
   defender to the stranger,
a terror to the criminal,
   rescuer of his victims.

I dreamed of my old age—
  'A man of vigour
    to the last—
  like a tree
    with its roots drinking the water,
    its branches bright with dew—
  gripping a new bow,
    arrows enough in my sheath!'

But now—
young people
  laugh at me,
young people whose fathers
  I wouldn't put with my sheep-dogs!
I am sung about in street ballads,
  chattered about in gossip—
loathed and passed by
  and spat at.

I looked forward to good—
  but evil has overtaken me.
I dreamed of light—
  but I walk in darkness!
I am ill and restless,
  miserable day following miserable day.
I have neither hope nor friends;
  if ever I speak in the Council,
    I speak but as a beggar.
I am an outcast—
  the wolf my brother,
    the desert owls my friends!
The sun blackens my blistered body,
  fever burns my bones.
Harp and flute
  are fit only for mourners' dirges.

What fate or reward
  does God Almighty hand out to men—
if not ruin for the wrong-doer,
  calamity for the criminal?
Doesn't he mark, then, what kind of man I am,
  count every step I take?

Neither falsehood nor fraud
   has found a friend in me;
I made a covenant with my eyes
   not to look at a girl.
Let God test my innocence
   in the scales of justice!

If I have wandered from the right way,
   let my eyes rule my heart,
      dirt stick to my hands—
may others eat my harvests,
   my spring crops be rooted up!

If I ever lusted after a woman
   or haunted a neighbour's door—
may my wife grind another's corn
   and sleep in other men's beds!

If I have ever been unjust
   to slave or slave-girl,
what answer can I give
   when God faces me as my judge?
The same God who created me
   created them!

If I have done nothing to help the poor
   or been untouched by a widow's tears;
if I have eaten my food at home
   without sharing it with the orphan;
if I have watched a beggar die
   for want of clothing,
giving him no reason at all to thank me
   for warming him (as I could have done)
   with a fleece from my flock;
if I have charged the innocent falsely,
   knowing the Court would take my side—
God's terror would crush me;
   how could I stand
      in the presence of his greatness?

I have never put my wealth first,
   set simply on making money.
I have never worshipped the splendour of the sun
   or the majesty of the moon—

either in the secrecy of my heart
  or in public worship.
The ruin of my enemy
  never made me happy—
the disasters that destroyed him
  were no joy to me.
Has it not been a family saying:
  'We can't say a word against him;
  no stranger has ever had to sleep in the street.'—
My home has been open
  for every traveller.

I have never hidden my sins,
  keeping my guilt to myself—
for I have never been afraid
  of street gossip or public scorn,
holding my tongue
  and hiding at home.

Oh that someone were listening!
  I am hiding nothing—
    let God answer me!
If he would write his charges out plainly
  I would flaunt them on my shoulder
    or wear them on my head like a crown!
I stake my case
  on the record of my life—
I will enter his presence
  like a prince!

GOD answers Job out of the storm-wind

Who darkens debate
  with ignorant talk?
Pull yourself together like a man
  and answer my questions.

You're a knowledgeable man—
  you must know!
Were you there
  when I made the world—
settling its shape and size
  and measuring it off?

'God answers Job out of the storm wind'. Engraving by William Blake

Tell me—
where were its pillars sunk,
   who laid the corner-stones
when the morning stars burst into song
   and the hosts of heaven shouted aloud?
Where were you when the sea was born
   tumbling in tumult from the earth—
blanketed in cloud
   and swathed in fog?
when I fixed its final shores
   like a bolted door:
'So far and no further—
   here shall your surging stop!'?

Tell me—
Have you ever ordered the dawn,
   commanded the morning
to grip the edges of the world,
   shake the stars from the sky,

cut the sky-line clear like sculpture,
   dip it in dye like a dress?
Have you watched the Dog-star grow dim
   and the points of the Plough go out?

Tell me—
Have you seen the springs of the Sea,
   gone down into the great deep,
discovered the gates of death
   and the guardians of the dark?
Have you ever studied
   the vastness of the earth?
Tell me about it—
   if you really know:
how do you reach the home of light
   or the dwelling of darkness?
Can you put them at their proper stations
   and lead them home again?
How old you must be
   if you were born when they were born!

Tell me—
Have you ever visited the snow-fields
   or the home of the hail?
Where does the hot wind come from
   or the east wind go?
Who cut the channels for the rainstorm
   and a road for the thunder—
storm over no-man's-land,
   thunder over the desert,
clothing desolate wastes with green,
   dry land with grass?
Has the rain a father
   and the dew a sire?
Who gave birth to the ice
   and was mother to the frost?—
the frost that freezes
   the very seas to stone?

Tell me—
Can you bind the Pleiades
   or break Orion's fetters,
tame the Zodiac
   or guide the Bear and her cubs?

Have you taught the sky its duty
  or the earth its routine?
Can you make the clouds hear you
  and command a cloud-burst?
Can you send the lightning on errands
  and does it salute you, 'Sir!'?
Who musters the cloudy battalions
  and tips up the pitchers of the sky?—
making the soil set hard as iron
  and clod cleave to clod?

Do you really think I'm unjust—
  or are you just proving me wrong
    to prove yourself right?
Are you as strong as I am,
  can your voice thunder like mine?
Put on your might and majesty,
  your glory and grandeur—
then humble the proud man with your anger,
  crush criminals in their tracks,
bury them all in the dust they came from,
  silenced in an unknown grave!
And I—even I—will praise you
  for being strong enough to save yourself!

Is my prosecutor sticking to his case?
  Is my critic answering me back?

Job speaks

What can I say?
  I'm too petty,
    I can only keep quiet.
I've had my say—
  I'll not say it again.
I've said too much,
  I'll say no more.

All I said was hearsay,
  but now we stand face to face.
I take back what I said,
  I repent of my empty and foolish talk.

Epilogue

GOD gave Job everything back—indeed he made him twice as wealthy as he had been before.

His kinsmen and friends held a banquet in his honour. They sat down together at table and consoled him for all the misfortunes he had gone through. They each gave him a silver coin and a gold ring.

Job's wealth was now immense. And he had a second family—seven sons and three daughters as before. The girls were the most beautiful girls in the world (he called the youngest 'Bright Eyes'!) and in his will he went beyond the law and treated them like their brothers.

He lived for a long time after this. He had great-great-grandchildren, and was a very old man when he died.

Daniel: Backs to the Wall

In 168 B.C.E. the Jews faced one of their gravest crises. The year before, they had revolted against Antiochus IV (whose capital city was Antioch in Syria) and defied his attempt, with the help of influential Jews in Jerusalem, to force a Greek way of life upon the city and its citizens. Antiochus learned about all this on his way back from defeating the Egyptians and turned aside to deal with the situation. What began as a civil war (between liberal and orthodox Jews) became a major struggle between rebel Jews and the whole military power of the empire. The Syrian soldiers ran riot in the city and many people died at their hands. The temple was desecrated and plundered—a pig was sacrificed on the altar.

The story of what happened afterwards is told in *First Maccabees* in *The Apocrypha*. The Jewish religion was proscribed and a garrison stationed in Jerusalem to enforce obedience. The standard of revolt was raised in the village of Modein. The Jewish rebels fled to the hills. Guerilla warfare against the Syrian army followed and the rebellion spread. Eventually Jerusalem was recaptured and the temple rededicated (163) and full religious freedom secured (163). The rebellion is known as the Maccabaean Rebellion after its most famous leader, Judas Maccabaeus, 'the Hammerer'.

It was in the early days of the rebellion that *The Book of Daniel* appeared, as a tract for the times. It is a strange book containing stories and visions. The stories are of Daniel and his friends who had been taken prisoners to Babylon after the fall of Jerusalem in 586 and who refused to compromise their Jewish faith; Daniel's visions, which follow the stories, are full of strange symbolism, proclaim the fall of the great military empires of Assyria, Babylon, Persia and Greece and predict the defeat of Antiochus IV and the rise of the Jewish people to power and world dominion.

The stories of Daniel and his friends are old popular stories. The author retells them to inspire common people to stand firm in the face of persecution. 'Look at your ancestors,' they say. 'They faced death for their faith but God took care of them. You must fight for your ancestral faith as they did. Take your courage in your hands. God will again give us the victory.' The visions, with their summaries of world history, confirm the message of the stories. Here are three of the stories and the first vision.

A Faith to live for

Long ago, the emperor of Babylon, Nebuchadnezzar, captured Jerusalem and took King Jehoiakim back to Babylonia as a prisoner.[1] He

---

[1] There is some confusion of dates and names here. See p. 182 where it is Jehoiachin who is deported,

ransacked the temple and looted its precious plate for the treasury of his own pagan temple.

He ordered his Lord High Chamberlain to choose some of the young men of the Jewish royal family and nobility for the service of the palace—fine, good-looking, well-educated, bright and clever young men —and to teach them to speak the Babylonian language. He made them a handsome allowance of food and wine. They were to be given three years' training.

Among those chosen were four young men, Daniel, Hananiah, Mishael and Azariah. The Lord High Chamberlain gave them Babylonian names—Belteshazzar, Shadrach, Meshach and Abednego.

Daniel was a sincere worshipper of God and he made up his mind that he would not deny his Jewish convictions by eating forbidden foreign food. He explained this to the Lord High Chamberlain and asked him not to make him do anything against his conscience. The Lord High Chamberlain rather liked Daniel.

'It's the emperor I'm afraid of,' he told him. 'His orders must be obeyed; he settled what food you should be given. If, at the end of your training, you weren't as fit as the others, I'd be executed.'

Daniel tackled the guard in charge of the four of them.

'Give us ten days' test,' he said. 'Vegetables and water are all we want. In ten days' time compare our fitness with the fitness of the others.'

The guard agreed. When the ten days were over, they looked better and fitter than all the young men who had been given the rich food and wine the emperor had ordered. That settled the matter. They could have their vegetables.

The four young men proved brilliant students in all the subjects they had to study; Daniel himself also proved his skill in interpreting dreams and visions.

The three years' training were at last over. The emperor ordered all the young men into his presence; he wanted to talk to them himself. The four young men—Daniel, Hananiah, Mishael and Azariah—stood the test far better than any of the others; and the emperor chose them as his personal attendants. He often consulted them and he found them ten times better than all his official magicians and enchanters.

A Faith to die for

One day the emperor, Nebuchadnezzar, ordered a huge golden statue to be made—ninety feet high and nine feet wide. He had it set up on the Dura Plain, and issued an edict summoning all the important officers of state—from viceroys to provincial officials—to attend its dedication.

The Dedication opened with a proclamation by the Royal Herald:

PEOPLES AND NATIONS:
WHATEVER LANGUAGE YOU SPEAK, YOU ARE COMMANDED, AT THE SOUND OF THE MUSICIANS AND CHOIR, TO FALL DOWN ON YOUR FACES AND WORSHIP THE GOLDEN STATUE THE EMPEROR HAS SET UP. THE PENALTY FOR DISOBEDIENCE WILL BE DEATH IN THE RAGING FIRE OF A FURNACE.

The music burst on the great assembly, and the vast crowd fell on their faces and worshipped.

Certain Babylonian officials sought an audience with the emperor to lay a charge against their Jewish fellow-officials.

'Long live your Majesty!' they said. 'Your Majesty issued an edict about the Service of Dedication: that at the sound of musicians and choir, the assembly were to fall down on their faces and worship the golden statue; the penalty for disobedience would be death in the raging fire of a furnace. We beg to report that three Jewish officials—royal officials, your Majesty—of the province of Babylonia disobeyed your royal edict. They refused to worship your Majesty's God—or the golden statue your Majesty set up.'

The emperor was furiously angry. He ordered Shadrach, Meshach and Abednego to be arrested and brought into his presence.

'Shadrach, Meshach and Abednego,' he said. 'Tell me the truth. Do you refuse to worship my god and to fall down on your faces before the golden statue? I'll give you another chance. If at the sound of musicians and choir you fall down on your faces before my statue, we will say no more. If you refuse to do so, you will be thrown into the raging fire of a furnace. Who is the god who will rescue you then from my power?'

'Your Majesty,' the three men answered, 'this is no time for words. Our God, the God we worship, can rescue us; and he will rescue us—from the furnace's raging fire and from your Majesty's power. But even if he doesn't, we want to make it plain to your Majesty that we will not worship either your god or your golden statue.'

This made the emperor blaze with anger. His face was distorted with rage at the sight of the three men before him.

He gave orders for the heating of the furnace—it was to be made seven times hotter than usual. His guards were to tie up the three men and throw them into the furnace fire.

The men were tied up just as they were—with their clothes and hats on—and thrown into the furnace. The heat was so great that the execution squad themselves died in the flames belching out of the furnace. The three men fell, bound as they were, into it.

The emperor watched through the side hole of the furnace.

Suddenly he stepped back in alarm.

'It was three men we threw into the fire, wasn't it?' he asked his ministers.

'Your Majesty is correct,' they replied.

'But there are four men there,' he said. 'They are all walking unbound in the heart of the fire, quite unhurt. The fourth man looks like a god!'

The emperor went back to the side hole of the furnace.

'Shadrach, Meshach and Abednego, servants of the Most High God!' he called out. 'Come out and come here to me!'

The three men climbed out.

The emperor and his ministers stared at them: the fire hadn't touched them—their hair wasn't even singed, their clothes weren't scorched, there was no smell of burning.

'Blessed is the God of Shadrach, Meshach and Abednego!' the emperor exclaimed. 'He sent his angel to rescue his servants—men who trusted him, defied my Royal Edict and would rather die than worship any other god than their own God. Let a new edict be issued:

WHOEVER SPEAKS AGAINST THE GOD OF SHADRACH, MESHACH AND ABEDNEGO SHALL BE TORN LIMB FROM LIMB AND HIS HOUSE BURNED DOWN.

'There's no other God who can rescue like this!' he added.

The three men were promoted to high office.

A Faith to witness for

This happened at the time of the Persian Emperor Darius.

The emperor divided his empire into one hundred and twenty provinces, each under a viceroy. He appointed three presidents over the viceroys, to receive their reports and to prevent any government corruption. Daniel was one of the presidents—the most distinguished of the three; he was a very able administrator. It was the emperor's intention to make him his President-in-Chief with responsibility for the whole empire.

The other two presidents and the viceroys were jealous of him; they tried to find some incident in his administration that would give them ground for complaint. They could find none; his skill and reliability were outstanding.

'We shall have to go for his religion,' they said. 'We can't find anything else to complain of.'

So they laid their plans.

They sought an audience with the emperor.

'Long live your Majesty!' they said. 'The presidents and viceroys in council have been concerned about the religion of the empire. We beg your Majesty to issue an edict that, for a whole month, nobody shall make any petition to God or man except to your Majesty. The penalty for disobedience shall be death—by being thrown to the lions. We beg your Majesty to issue this edict in written form; it will then be unalterable, as is the customary practice of Persian law.'

The emperor signed the document publishing the edict.

Now Daniel had always been a faithful Jew. He had had windows put in the room in the roof of his Residence facing west towards Jerusalem. It was his habit to go there three times a day, to kneel down and pray to God.

When he heard about the edict, he went straight up to the room on the roof and did what he had done every day—he knelt down by the window and prayed to God.

The Persian officials knew this, and they came to his Residence at the time of prayer and found him on his knees praying to God.

They quickly sought an audience with the emperor.

'Your Majesty!' they said. 'You are aware that you signed the edict prohibiting any prayer to man or God except to your Majesty, for a whole month, on pain of death?'

'I am,' said the emperor, 'and I made it an unalterable law.'

'Daniel the Jew has defied your Majesty,' they said. 'He has ignored the edict. He still prays to his God three times a day.'

The emperor was deeply troubled when he heard this. He was determined to save Daniel somehow; he wracked his brain till sunset in vain. His officials came back to the palace—the whole crowd of them.

'Your Majesty!' they said. 'You are aware that no edict or statute, issued by your Majesty's authority, can be altered in any way?'

There was nothing else for the emperor to do but to order Daniel's arrest and execution.

'Your God, to whom you are faithful, will rescue you!' he said to him.

Daniel was thrown into the lions' pit. A large stone was placed over its entrance, and sealed with the emperor's own seal and the state seal. There was to be no altering of the law for Daniel's sake.

The emperor went back to the palace and spent a worried, sleepless night, refusing all food and entertainment.

At daybreak, he hurried anxiously out to the pit. He had hardly reached it when, with broken voice, he called out Daniel's name.

'Servant of the living God!' he called out. 'Has your God, to whom you have been so faithful, rescued you?'

To his glad surprise, Daniel called back 'Long live your Majesty! God sent his angel and shut the lions' mouths. I'm quite unhurt. I was innocent before God; I never did your Majesty any wrong.'

The emperor quickly ordered Daniel's release. He was taken up out of the pit unhurt. He had put his whole trust in God.

The emperor ordered the arrest of his accusers and sentenced them and their families to the fate they had intended for Daniel—they were thrown into the lions' pit themselves. They had scarcely fallen on the pit's floor when the lions leaped on them and crunched them up.

The emperor then sent a letter throughout the whole Empire:

MAY EVERYBODY ENJOY PEACE! I AM ISSUING A NEW EDICT THAT EVERYBODY THROUGHOUT THE WHOLE OF MY DOMINIONS SHALL WORSHIP IN SINCERITY THE GOD OF DANIEL.

So Daniel went from strength to strength.

A Vision of the Future

Daniel wrote down the dreams and visions which he saw when he was lying on his bed at night. This, in his own words, is the first vision:

In my first vision I was staring at the stormy sea—all the winds of heaven were blowing. Four monstrous Beasts came up out of it, each quite unlike the others: a Lion with an eagle's wings; a Bear half crouching, ferocious and greedy; a Leopard with four heads and four bird's wings growing out of its back; and a powerful, terrifying Beast I could find no name for. This last Beast was stamping round and crunching with its terrible teeth, and unlike the others, had ten Horns—an eleventh little Horn grew up while I stood staring. The little Horn had a man's eyes and spoke with a loud boasting voice. I kept on staring; then—

> Thrones were set up,
>   and the Everlasting God
> with hair like wool
>   and snow-white robes
> took his seat on a throne
>   swirling with flaming fire.

The Court was crowded—
　　there were thousands upon thousands
　　and myriads upon myriads there.
The trial began,
　　the books were opened.

Judgment was passed on the Beasts—the last proud Beast was condemned to death (his carcase to be burned); the other Beasts to be tamed and their lives spared for a short time.

I was still staring at the scene when—

A Man-like Being,
　　escorted by the clouds of heaven,
approached the Everlasting God
　　and was presented to him.
The Man-like Being was crowned king,
　　with all the glory and honour
　　　of a great king—
with authority over the whole world,
　　authority lasting for ever.
His kingdom
　　shall never know defeat.

I, Daniel, was troubled and frightened at the vision. I went up to one of the angelic attendants and asked him what it all meant. He explained it to me.

'The Four Beasts,' he said, 'represent Four Empires[1] rising out of the earth; but it is to God's People[2] that enduring, imperial authority will be given.'

'But what does the last Beast represent?' I asked, 'the terrible Beast with the ten Horns and the little boastful Horn that overshadowed the others?'

'The Fourth Beast (he said)
　　shall be the Fourth Empire[3]
　　　unlike the other empires—
a brutal tyranny
　　trampling down the whole earth.
The Ten Horns
　　are ten emperors;
The Eleventh Horn
　　another very different emperor[4]

---

[1] Babylonia, Media (not known), Persia, Greece.
[2] God's People are represented by the 'Man-like Being' in the first part of the vision.
[3] Greece or Alexander the Great.
[4] Antiochus IV (popularly known as 'the Madman' throughout his empire). See p. 371.

murdering those who stand in his way,
  defying even God himself,
persecuting God's people,
  changing their Festivals and Law,
holding them in his grasp
  for three years and a half.
The Heavenly Court
  shall condemn him to death,
  stripping him of his sovereignty;
all his imperial power and authority
  shall be given to God's people;
much more shall be given to them—
  the splendour and obedience
    of the whole earth.
Their universal rule
  shall last for ever!'

The vision ended. I was greatly troubled and turned pale. But I went on thinking about what I had seen.

Other Voices

'Nothing's worthwhile!'

These three passages come from a book whose main theme is the meaninglessness of all human experience. Life is just one thing after another. There is no
meaning in the disastrous story of God's people. The author was an out-and-out
sceptic who says what he has to say with 'shocking honesty'. The last poem
we give puts his scepticism bluntly, pouring scorn on the convictions of his
fellow-countrymen: 'If you're going to be religious, you'd better be religious
when you're young. You'll learn better when you grow older and find out
what life is really like—just meaningless.' But there is something deeply moving
in the almost savage picture he paints, and what he has to say is not to be
glibly dismissed.

> Empty and meaningless (says the Preacher),
>   everything is meaningless!
> What does a man get by endless toil,
>   sweating under the hot sun?
> Families come, families go,
>   only the earth goes on for ever.
> The sun rises in the east, sets in the west,
>   then back to the east again!
> The wind blows south today,
>   tomorrow it blows north—
> going round and round,
>   turning and returning in its tracks.
> Rivers run down to the sea—
>   the ever-greedy sea—
> flowing, flowing
>   where rivers have to flow.
> The world tires a man out—
>   there's no telling how tired!
> The eye tires of looking,
>   the ear tires of listening.
> What has been will be,
>   what's done must be done again,
>   there's nothing new under the sun!
> Can anybody say of anything—
>   'Look—I've found something new?'—
> it was old
>   centuries ago!
> We can't remember what happened yesterday;

> in the years to be
> nobody will remember
> what happens now!

I began to think about what we mean when we say 'He's wise!' or 'He's mad!' or 'He's stupid!'

I can see one thing—wisdom is like light, stupidity like darkness: the wise man can see where he's going; the fool stumbles in the dark.

I can see another thing: they both come to the same end.

'What happens to the fool,' I said to myself, 'will happen to me. Why have I been bothering about "wisdom"?'

'It's all meaningless,' I told myself.

Nobody remembers either the wise man or the fool—in a hundred years' time they'll both be dead and forgotten.

The wise man dies like the fool.

I hated being alive; all humanity just disgusted me!

Everything is meaningless—like chasing the wind!

> Being young—
>   excited by a dawning world—
>   is all meaningless.
> You'd better remember your Creator
>   when you're young:
> you'll soon be telling yourself—
>   'I'm bored stiff!'
> Everything goes sour
>   or grows old.

> So remember your Creator—
> before
> light, sun, moon, stars grow dark
>   and cloudy skies come back with the rain;
> and the day comes when
>   householders hobble along,
>   strong men are bent double,
>   women no longer grind at the grindstone;
>   daylight through the windows is failing,
>   street doors are shut;
>   a man can't hear the village mill
>   or a bird singing
>   (all songbirds are silent for him!)
>   and climbing a hill is scaring,
>   just walking is frightening—

and all the while
the almond tree is in flower,
the grasshopper too full to hop,
the caper bursting into bloom!

before
the light goes out—
the silver cord snaps,
the golden lamp is smashed!

and winter wastes away—
pitcher and spindle
are broken at the well!

Everything is meaningless (says the Preacher)
everything is meaningless!

The Loveliest Song

One book in the Old Testament stands out from all the others. Tucked away
among histories, hymnbooks and the books of the prophets we suddenly
come upon a book of love poems—a lyric poet celebrating human love. His
poems are probably based on traditional village songs, reminding us that the
grim story we have been reading is not the whole story. Life in the villages
went on as usual—boys and girls fell in love, weddings were celebrated with
dancing and singing. (Some of these songs were still being sung, we are told, at
banquets in the time of Jesus.) The setting of the poems is the countryside;
the characters are a girl and her lover. We give verses that describe their
meeting.

Girl   My sweetheart's voice!
                   He's coming to me—
                      leaping over the hills!
                   He's standing
                      outside our wall,
                         peeping in at the windows,
                         peering through the lattice!

Her Lover   Awake, my sweetheart!
                   My lovely one, come away!
                Winter's gone,
                   skies are clear,
                flowers colour the countryside,
                   birds will soon be singing,
                fig-trees are touched with red,
                   vine-buds full of scent!
                Up, my sweetheart,
                   my lovely one, let's away!
                I want to see your face
                   and hear your voice—
                no hiding away, like a bird
                   in the cranny of the cliffs!

Girl   My love's my very own—
                   and I am his!

                While the air is cool,
                   and the twilight lingers,
                come back to me, my sweetheart,
                   let me gaze at you
                      strong and supple

like a wild goat
  on the Bether hills!
How I dreamed of him!

Night after night
  I lay awake
    watching for him,
    vainly watching.
'I will up and scour
  the squares and streets,'
    said I,
  'seeking my sweetheart.'

I looked and looked—
  he was nowhere to be found!
I called his name—
  no answering voice!
I asked the passing watchmen
  'Haven't you seen my sweetheart?'—
    they vanished into the night.

Then—
  there he was!
I crushed him in my arms,
  I clung to him,
I brought him home
  to my mother's room!

Her Lover   By the spirits of the countryside,
               by the goddesses of the fields,
                 don't wake her,
                 don't touch her—
                   she's asleep.

The Voice of Worship

We come now, finally, to listen again to the hymns the Jewish people sang (see notes on p. 202). Here we can see what their convictions really were, with their depth and their limitations. All hymns bear the marks of their time, but the greatest hymns speak to all times. They need no comment.

A Song of Trust in God

Psalm 91

The People   Happy the man who is kept safe by GOD,
    who lives in his shadow,
who can say to him, 'I trust you,
    my refuge and my fortress!'

He will snatch you from the bird-catcher's trap,
    and his treacherous pit!
He will shelter and protect you
    with his wings.

By night, there is no terror to fear,
    by day, no sunstroke;
in darkness or broad daylight,
    no plague or pestilence.
It may strike thousands of your fellows,
    it shall not strike you.

His faithfulness guards you
    like a shield or a city wall.
You will see for yourself
    what really happens to wicked people.

GOD is your shelter,
    the Most High your refuge;
your home is safe
    from deadly dangers.
His angels will escort you
    wherever you go:
their hands will carry you—
    you'll not stub your foot on a stone;

you will tread and trample
on asp and cobra and dragon,
snake and serpent
without hurt.

The Priest   Since he loves me with his whole heart
(speaking in   I will rescue him;
GOD's name) I will guard him from danger
for he knows who I am.
I will answer his prayer,
I will be with him in trouble.
I will give him the joy of a long life,
he will know what my rescue means!

GOD—Lord of Nature

Psalm 29

People   Give GOD his due, you pagan gods!
and Choir   Acknowledge his glory and strength!
Acknowledge the glory due to him,
worship him in festal dress!

People   GOD's voice sounds over the great waters,
the glorious God thunders!

Choir   GOD over the great waters!

People   GOD's strong voice!
GOD's majestic voice!
GOD's voice shattering the cedars!

Choir   GOD splits the forest cedars—
makes Lebanon Mountain skip like a calf,
Hermon Mountain like a wild ox!

People   GOD's voice shakes the Desert!

Choir   GOD shakes the Kadesh Desert!

A twentieth-century city ▶

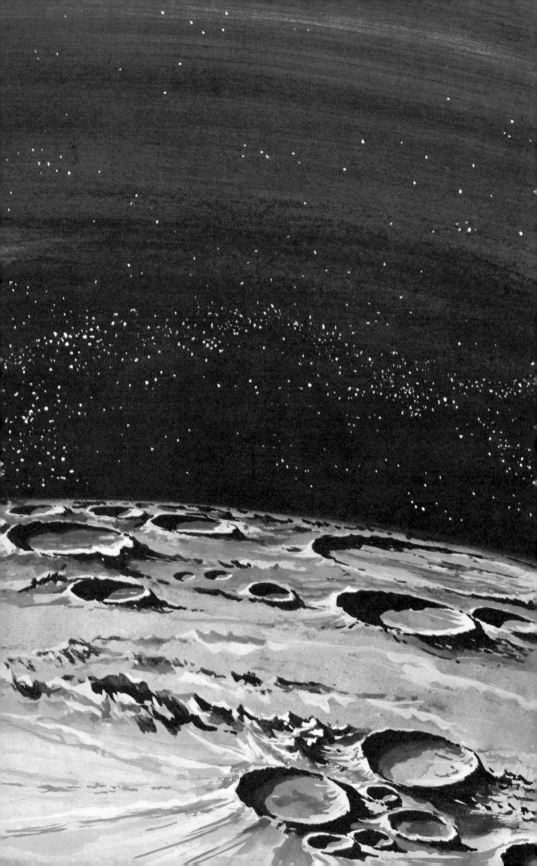

People   GOD's voice sets the oak trees whirling
                    strips the forest bare!
                        In his temple everything cries 'Glory!'

Choir   GOD rules the Great Deep,
                    king enthroned for ever!
             giving his people strength,
                    blessing his people with peace!

Psalm 104

Bless GOD, O my soul!

My GOD, how great you are,
    dressed in splendour and majesty,
    clothed with light;
stretching out the sky like a tent,
    laying its foundations in the Great Deep;
driving the dark storm as your chariot,
    riding on the clouds as your horses—
the winds your heralds,
    the lightnings your ministers!

You built the earth on its pillars,
    set firm for ever,
the ocean covering it like a cloak,
    drowning the mountains!

At your command the waters took flight,
    at the sound of your thunder they fled—
over the hills,
    down the valleys,
        rushing to their appointed place!
You set their final frontiers,
    never again to drown the earth!

You make springs
    flow down the valleys
        between the mountain ranges,
giving drink to the wild beasts,
    quenching the zebra's thirst—
while the wild birds
    are singing in the trees.

◄ Twentieth-century exploration

You water the mountains
  and saturate the earth
    from your storehouse in the sky,
making green grass grow for the cattle,
  fodder for the farm,
food from the soil for man
  and wine to make him happy,
oil for his face
  and bread for his strength.

The great trees are green with leaves,
  the mighty cedars of Lebanon
where the birds nest—
  the stork in the topmost branches;
the high hills are the home of wild goats,
  the rocks the refuge of wild badgers.

The moon marks the seasons,
  the sun knows where to set.
You make it dark and it is night
  when the wild beast goes out prowling,

young lions roar after their prey
   asking you for their food.
Day dawns and off they slink
   to lie down in their lairs.
Man is starting his work
   labouring on till dark.

How many things you have made, O GOD,
   made in your wisdom,
     crowding the earth!

There is the vast and endless sea
   with its innumerable living things;
there go the ships,
   there the sea-monster you made for a plaything!

All of them look eagerly to you
   at their feeding times—
you give and they gather,
   you open your hand, they eat their fill.
You hide your face, they are frightened,
   you take their breath away, they gasp;
you breathe on them, they become themselves again,
   and you renew the whole earth!

I will sing to GOD as long as I live,
   I will sing his praise all my living days!
Bless GOD, O my soul,
   praise GOD!

Psalm 148

Praise GOD
   from the sky
     and from far above the sky,
all his heralds,
   all his host!

Praise him—
   sun and moon,
     you shining stars,
   the high sky
     and waters above it!
Praise GOD's name!

At a word of command he made them,
  established them for ever!
GOD's law
  can never pass away!

Praise GOD—
  from the earth,
    water-spouts and oceans!
  fire, hail, snow, ice,
    storm-wind blowing at his command!
  mountains, hills,
    fruit trees, cedars!
  wild beasts, farm animals,
    snakes, birds on the wing!
  kings, princes,
    governors, judges!
  boys, girls,
    old men, children!
Let them all praise GOD's name!

His name alone is exalted!
  His splendour shines down
    on earth and sky!
Praise GOD!

Songs of the New Year

Psalm 8

O GOD our king
  how majestic you are!
Your glory is in the earth,
  your splendour in the skies!
When I gaze at the sky
  your fingers formed,
the moon and the stars
  you have set there—
'What is man,' I cry,
  'that you should notice him,
mortal man,
    that you should care about him?'

Yet you made him
   a little lower than a god,
crowning him
   with glory and majesty,
making him master
   of all you have made,
   lord of all creation:
of sheep and cattle,
   wild beasts and wild birds,
      fish and the teeming life of the sea.

O GOD, our king,
   how majestic you are
      in all the earth!

Psalm 98

It's a new song
   you must sing to GOD—
      his deeds have been marvellous.

His power and his goodness
   have won him a great victory;
he has shown to the whole world
   the just deliverance of his people—
he has remembered them
   in steadfast love and loyalty.
The whole world has seen
   the victories he has won!

O world! Lift up your voice
   in singing and praise to GOD!
With harp and guitar and trumpet
   raise your voices high
     to GOD our king!

Let the sea's thunder
   match men's voices!
Let the storm floods
   clap their hands,
the mountain ranges
   sing with happiness
     in GOD's presence!

For he comes
   to judge mankind,
to judge men
   with truth and justice!

Psalm 93

GOD is king!

Splendour and strength his armour,
   his belt tightened on!

'You have made the earth
   firm and fixed,
     your firm and ancient throne;
from all eternity
   you are God!

'Yet the vast waters heave, O GOD,
   filling the sky with thunder,
     the boom of battering waves.'

Mightier
   than the waters' thunder,
   than the sea's breakers
      is GOD on high!

Psalm 96

Sing a new song to GOD
   O wide, wide world!—
sing to GOD and bless him,
   announce his victory day by day,
   tell his glory and great deeds
      to everybody everywhere!

The gods men worship are mere idols—
   GOD made the sky!
Majesty and splendour,
   strength and beauty
   attend him in his temple!

You Family of Man,
   ascribe to GOD—
   ascribe to GOD glory and strength,
      the glory which is his due!
Worship in his temple,
   bringing your gift for him,
      doing him homage
         in the splendour of holiness!
O wide, wide world!
   dance to his praise!
Let everybody everywhere know—
   'GOD is king!
      He has made the earth
         firm and fixed!
      He will judge the world
         with justice!'

Let earth and sky be glad,
   let the sea and all its creatures roar,
let the fields and all that grows rejoice,
   let the wild trees shout for joy
      in GOD's presence—
he has come to judge the earth;
   he will judge the world justly,
      the peoples fairly!

Songs of the Temple

Psalm 46

God is our unconquered stronghold,
   helper in our distress!
We are not afraid of earthquakes,
   of mountains tumbling into the sea!
Let the seas surge and thunder!
   Let the waves be white with foam!
     Let the proud mountains tremble!

     GOD is with us!
      Our fathers' God is our high fortress!

A river with its streams gladdens the city
   which God, Most High, has made his home.
God lives in her—
   she will stand firm!
God will help her
   at the first light of day!
Raging storms rock the world:
   God speaks—the earth quakes!

     GOD is with us!
      Our fathers' God is our high fortress!

See what GOD has done—
   he has defeated the whole world!
War everywhere is over—
   bows broken,
   spears snapped,
   shields burned to ashes!—
'Stop! Know that I am God,
   Lord of the nations,
   Lord of the earth!'

     GOD is with us!
      Our fathers' God is our high fortress!

Psalm 81

People
Sing aloud with joy to God our strength—
    our God and our fathers' God!
Let the song ring out to the music
    of the whole orchestra!
At new-moon festival, at full-moon festival
    let the trumpet sound!

Celebrate the Covenant,
    the Covenant made with our fathers,
the Covenant God made with our fathers
    when they escaped from Egypt!

A Temple
Prophet
(*speaking in*
GOD's *name*)
I heard a strange Voice—
    'Speak! I will tell you what to say:
I lifted the burden from your shoulder,
    I carried your baskets of brick!
In distress you called to me—
    I rescued you,
        answering you in mountain thunders,
        testing you at Meribah Kadesh.
I fed and satisfied my people
    with fine wheat and rock honey!

'Listen, my people, and let me teach you—
    if only you would listen, my people!
No pagan god shall claim your country,
    no pagan shrine your worship!
I am GOD—your God!
    I rescued you from Egypt!

'But my people did not listen—
    they would have nothing to do with me!
I left them to their own ways,
    to their stubborn, evil ways.

'If only my people would listen to me,
    if only they would walk in my Way!
I would soon deal with your enemies,
    soon conquer them—
they would come suing for peace,
    scared and cringing!'

Psalm 100

O wide, wide world! Shout to GOD,
worship him with joy,
come with songs into his presence!

Know that he alone is God;
he made us, we are his—
his people, the flock he shepherds.

Enter his temple with gifts,
enter his courts with praise—
thank him and bless him!

GOD is good,
men can trust his steadfast love
as generation follows generation
for ever!

Psalm 121

Worshipper   I will look up at the mountains—
but where can I get help?

Priest   Your help comes from GOD,
maker of heaven and earth!

Worshipper   May my helper never lose grip of me,
never be too sleepy to take care of me.

Priest   GOD, guardian of his people,
is never drowsy or sleepy.
GOD is your guardian,
standing guard at your side.
No harm shall come to you
from the sun in the daytime,
from the moon at night.
GOD will guard your whole life
from every danger—
when you go out, when you come home,
from now on and for ever!

National Lament

Psalm 90

O GOD, you have been our home
    from generation to generation!

Before the birth of the mountains,
    before the creation of the world itself,
from everlasting to everlasting,
    you are God.

You turn men back to dust
    with the command 'Return, O man!'
For you a thousand years
    are like an ended day,
        like sentry-duty at night
    when the guard's relieved
        and turns in to sleep;
    like fresh morning grass
        withered and dead at nightfall!

We die in your anger—
  we have nothing to say in our defence.
You continually remember our wrong-doing,
  continually stare at our secret sins;
our days darken in your anger,
  our years end in a sigh.

We live for seventy years—
  if we are strong, for eighty—
brief years of toil and trouble,
  swiftly passing,
    soon forgotten.
Who knows how to bear your anger
  which our faith in you has brought home to us?
Teach us to grow old
  learning your wisdom.

How long, O GOD, before you relent
  and have pity on your people?
Match the morning with your mercy:
  help us to live with joy,
turn our suffering into happiness,
  make good the agony of the years.

Let your people see your power,
  their descendants know your presence.
Give us your joy, O GOD,
  and make our daily work worthwhile.

Psalm 44

O God, we ourselves have heard—
  our fathers have told us—
all you did in their days
  long ago:
uprooting and planting peoples,
  hewing down and transplanting.
It wasn't our soldiers who conquered the country,
  or our arms that won us the victory;
it was the strength of your hand and arm,
  the light of your face—
    your good favour.

You are my king and my God—
  you who are your people's conquering commander.
By your help we attack our enemies,
  by your help tread down our foes.
It is not my bow I trust,
  my sword will not save me.
It is you who rescue us,
  humiliate our enemies.
In God we will boast all the day,
  to your name for ever give thanks!

Yet it is us you have spurned and shamed—
  you lead our armies no more.
Our enemies have thrown us back
  plundering to their heart's desire—
we are butchered like sheep,
  scattered over the world:
    sold cheap,
    no gain to you,
    insulted and laughed at
    by our neighbours,
    a by-word and laughing-stock
    to everybody.

I can't forget my daily disgrace,
  my face is red with shame
listening to taunting, blaspheming voices,
  watching hostile, avenging faces.

All this is our fate;
  yet we have not forgotten you,
  nor been false to your Covenant,
  nor changed our heart's love,
  nor swerved from your Way—
though it is us you have broken,
  not the dragon,
us you have overwhelmed
  in blackest night!
If we had forgotten your name
  or prayed to pagan gods
    wouldn't you have found it out?
You know the secrets of our heart!

But it's for you
  we are murdered every day,
  butchered like sheep!

Rise up, O God! Why are you sleeping?
  Awake! Don't abandon us for ever!
Why do you hide your face?
  Why take no notice of our distress?
We fall on the dusty ground,
  clinging to the very earth!
Rise up! Come to our help!
  Rescue us in your steadfast love!

National Thanksgiving

Psalm 65 (vv. 5–12)

Answer us with deeds not words,
  with terror and victory,
  O God who rescued us!—
hope of remotest peoples
  and far-away islands!

You build up the mountain ranges
  in your great strength;
you calm the stormy seas
  and the wild waves;
  sea monsters cower
  at your wonders;
you make dawn and sunset
  sing aloud for joy.

You come and water the earth,
  its richness is your gift:
mighty rivers flow full with rain
  making the earth ready for sowing;
in wet furrows, pressed sods,
  softened with steady showers,
  you bless the growing grain.
You crown the year with your bounty—
  wagon tracks drip with blessings.

'You crown the year with your bounty' ▶

The wild moors shout,
   the hills gird themselves
   with happiness and joy!
Sheep clothe the hills like a cloak,
   the valleys are dressed with corn,
   shouting and singing for joy!

A Morning Hymn

Psalm 19 (vv. 1–6)

The sky proclaims God's glory,
   its dome his handicraft:
day to following day,
   night to following night
     tells his story.

No speech, no words,
   no human voice is heard.
Yet their music echoes across the world,
   their speech to remotest peoples!

The sun pitches his tent in the sea,
   happy as a bridegroom,
exulting like a champion runner,
   eager to win the race!

From the eastern horizon
   to the farthest west
he runs his race—
   nothing escapes his heat!

Individual Lament

Psalm 51

Be merciful to me, O God,
  blot out all the wrong I've done—
I trust your steadfast love,
  your lavish kindness.
Wash me clean
  of all my sin!

I know the wrong I've done,
  I can't forget it.
It's you I've sinned against, you only—
  I've done what you condemn.
Your sentence on me is a right sentence,
  I cannot complain of your judgment:
I was conceived and born
  in sin.

You have searched out the truth
  in the depth of my being;
teach me wisdom
  in my secret heart.

Make me really clean,
  whiter than snow.
Fill me with joy and gladness;
  may I, crushed as I am, rejoice.
Don't look at the wrong I've done,
  blot it all out!

Give me a clean heart, O God,
  a new and steadfast spirit.
Don't send me away,
  don't leave me.
Let me know again the joy of being rescued by you,
  hold me up and give me a willing spirit.

Teach me to sing, O God,
  and I will sing your praise!
It isn't sacrifice you want—
  if I brought a whole burnt-offering
    you wouldn't be pleased.
My only sacrifice is a broken heart—
  and this you don't despise!

Individual Thanksgiving

Psalm 139 (vv. 1–18)

You have searched the depth of my being, O GOD,
   you know all about me—
      when I'm resting,
      when I'm working.

You have probed my deepest intentions,
   tracking out the road I take
   and my camping grounds.
You know me through and through,
   understanding better than I what I'm trying to say.
You have laid siege to me
   behind me and before me;
you have put your hand on my shoulder—
   I don't know why.
All this is beyond me,
   out of my reach—
      I can't grasp it.

Where can I go to escape you?
   You are wherever I am.
If I climb the skies
   or explore the underworld,
      you are there!
If I fly with the sun
   from dawn to dark,
your hand's still on my shoulder,
your right hand grips me!
If I say 'I'll lose myself in the darkness,
   vanish in the night!'
darkness is no darkness to you,
   night is bright as day,
      darkness as light!

I thank you for being what you are—
   awe-inspiring, wonderful,
      wonderful in all you do.
You made me the man I am
   in the depth of my being;
you've known what I am really like
   from the moment I was born.
You have watched the marvel of my body,
   the wonder of my birth;

you've seen me grow up
  and marked all I've done—
no day passed by uncounted,
  slipped by unnoticed.

What you think of me matters to me, O God,
    more than anything else—
        how much you know about me!
I cannot fathom your thoughts
    any more than I can count the sand on the shore!
Yet after all my searching
    I am still in your presence!

A Scholar's Hymn

Psalm 73

To the upright and pure in heart
    how good God is!

But it was the way bad men grow rich—
    and boast about it—
that started me slipping
    and losing my foothold:
they don't know what pain means,
    they are bursting with health;
they have none of the troubles and suffering
    of common men and women.
They display their pride in public
    and make violence a habit.
Their eyes shine in their fat faces
    mirroring their empty minds.
They live for sneer and slander,
    for scorn and lies;
yet my people look up to them
    as their 'leaders' and 'heroes' (says God)
in spite of their boasting words—
    'God's an ignoramus;
    he doesn't know or care!'
That's what bad men and rogues are like—
    yet they are the ones who make good,
    it's they who make the money!

And I began to grumble:
    what's the point of 'keeping my heart pure'
    and 'keeping my hands clean',

when all I get is daily trouble
   and daily suffering?
But, if I'd let myself go grumbling on like this,
   I would have betrayed your family, O God.
I tried to make sense of it all,
   but it was beyond my grasp—
until I worshipped in your temple
   and saw what really happens to evil men.
It is they whom you have set
   on slippery and dangerous ground.
They are living in a world of dreams,
   dreams which a waking man knows are only dreams—
dreams suddenly and totally ended
   by death and destruction.

It was my bitter heart
   that made me envious—
I would not understand,
   dunce that I was;
I was living as a mere animal
   in your presence, O God.
Yet how different the truth is:
   I am your friend!
You hold my right hand,
   guide me with your counsel,
     receive me afterward in honour!

In the heavens above I have only you!
   On earth below, having you, I have enough!
Ill and weak though I may be,
   you are mine for ever;
all I desire now, O God,
   is to be near you.
I have made you, O God,
   my fortress!

The Heart of the Matter

Psalm 23

GOD is my shepherd!

I shall lack nothing—
   he lets me lie down on green grass,
leads my by quiet streams,
   makes me a new man.
He guides me along the right tracks,
   because he is what he is;
when I go through the pitch-black gorge,
   nothing frightens me!

You are with me,
   club and staff at the ready—
      making me strong!

You are my host, I am your guest
   while enemies look helplessly on!
You bathe my head with oil,
   fill my cup to the brim!

Your goodness and love shall follow me
   all my days!
GOD's home is my home
   for ever!

Postscript

We have now come to the end of our account of the heart of the Old Testament. We have seen something of the story of Hebrew tribesmen, Israelite highlanders and Jewish exiles, and the convictions by which their best men and women lived—convictions forged in the face of a brutal experience that has overwhelmed more than one small nation.

The core of their faith is to be found in the memory of their escape from Egypt under Moses, told, discussed, pondered, sung, lived by for a thousand years. This faith, growing and deepening as the centuries passed, was held in many ways—with profound insight by their greatest thinkers, with more ambiguity by ordinary people. They had to fight for it against their own doubts and hesitations and fears and littleness. It was threatened, in later centuries most severely, by the sheer desperate need to survive; for theirs was a landscape across which armies and refugees moved.

It was a different thing for a Moses or a David, an Ahab or a Josiah, an Amos or a Jeremiah—kings were not always wrong nor prophets always right—for a Nehemiah or a writer like the writer of *The Book of Jonah*, or for men like the freedom fighters of the Great Rebellion of 168 B.C.E. or young people and women of whom we hear so little. But all would say 'God is with us', 'We must live as God's People', 'God has the last word'.

What these convictions really meant had to be worked out by every individual person—and every generation—in his own way; and, as we have seen, they can offer growing insights or become deadening clichés.

For there is no magic way to human maturity—or learning to live in God's Way as God's People. We can only walk by whatever light we have; and we have to learn to live with unanswered questions. The men without whom there would have been no Old Testament were not dreaming about some utopia—though many people, of course, especially in the later centuries, did do so; they were dealing with the world we live in as it really is and learning how to live in it with honesty and confidence and joy. Their clue was trusting, even in the darkest days, in God's 'steadfast love', and accepting it as their way too. For them, the world is God's world, and he is at work in it all the time.

We do not, therefore, turn to the Old Testament for historical or scientific information (we must get this from present-day historian or scientist) but as a guide to human experience.

Read with insight and understanding, 'it teaches us how to look at the world in a religious light, how to experience the divine power in nature' (and I would add, in history—in the lives of men and women), 'how to increase our ability to meet the full force of creation';[1] in a word, what it means to trust in God and live in his Way in the world as we know it to be today.

Further: it makes quite clear 'the menace which a supernatural religion can offer the world if it is not accompanied, at every inch of the way, with an insistence on the supremacy of charity'[2]—steadfast love.

[1] John Wilson, *Philosophy and Religion*, p. 116.
[2] Herbert Butterfield *The Methodist Recorder*, 24.7.69—see also his *History and Human Relations*, pp. 37ff.

Notes on Some Important Words and Names

Ark. This was a sacred chest or box, made of acacia wood. It was carried by the Israelites on their march across the desert and then kept in the central shrine at Shiloh. Eventually King David brought it to Jerusalem. When King Solomon built the temple there, it was kept in 'The Holiest Shrine' (see p. 153). It symbolized GOD's presence with his people, and was later thought of as his throne. What it meant to the Israelites changed as time went by. In earlier days it was carried into battle (see p. 21). It disappeared at the fall of Jerusalem.

Baal. This word means 'master' or 'lord'. Baal was one of the gods of the Canaanites. The chief god of the Canaanite pantheon—El—was remote; Baal was the young god of vegetation and fertility who each year died, went down into the underworld and rose again: hence autumn and spring. He was also god of storm and rain. His wife (or sister) was Asherah. The word 'asherah' was also used to describe a wooden object used in her worship.

Beersheba. The name means 'Well of Seven'. Because the Hebrew words for 'seven' and 'swear an oath' were similar, it is interpreted in some parts of the Old Testament as 'Well of the Covenant'. It was an important town in the Negeb. Isaac was associated with the shrine there. It was thought of as the southernmost limit of Israelite territory; the Israelites spoke of 'From Dan to Beersheba' as we say 'From John o' Groats to Land's End'.

Bethel. The name means 'House of God'. The site seems to have been occupied about or before 2000 B.C.E. and was an important religious centre from earliest times. It was destroyed by the Israelites; and then, after a break, it was rebuilt. It was associated with Jacob (see p. 327). It reached the height of its fame when it became a religious centre and royal city of the North. Amos preached here (p. 232). It was destroyed again in the Assyrian invasion.

Canaan. This was the old name of the land between the Mediterranean Sea and the Desert. It was used by Semitic peoples of Mesopotamia to describe the coast from Alexandretta in the north to Gaza in the south. It means 'Purple Country' from the name of the famous purple dye ('kinahhu') which was produced by the shellfish native to this coast. The name 'Palestine' comes from the word 'Philistines' who invaded the southern part of the coast in the eleventh century, and became the name used in the West for the southern part of Canaan where the Israelites settled.

Canaanites. The name of the inhabitants of Canaan. They were Amorite in origin and therefore akin to the Israelites, but they had attained a much higher standard of culture than the latter. They were merchants and the Hebrew word for 'Canaanite' means 'merchant' as well.

Carmel. This is the name of two places: 1. a town in the south where

Nabal the farmer lived (p. 46); 2. the well-wooded mountain range on the coast where Elijah met the prophets of Baal (p.226).

Covenant. This word means 'binding' and describes a treaty or agreement between groups or individuals. It is one of the great words of the Old Testament because it was used by the Israelites to describe the great 'Agreement' which GOD made with his people at the Holy Mountain (p. 110). From it come the names which Christians use to describe the Jewish and Christian parts of the Bible: Old Testament and New Testament—'Old Covenant' and 'New Covenant'.

Ephod. This word has two meanings: 1. a garment, especially a garment worn by the High Priest; 2. idols of some sort, sometimes used in connection with divination (p. 51). In the latter sense, the ephod may have some connection with Urim and Thummim, stones which some scholars think may have been kept in the pocket of the garment or idol and shaken to find out answers to questions. Urim and Thummim were possibly two flat stones one side of which meant Yes and the other side No. If both sides fell the same way up, that meant Yes or No as the case might be; if they showed different sides, that meant there was no answer to be given (as in the story of Saul, p. 31).

GOD. See 'Yahweh'.

Hebrews. Although we often refer to the people of the Old Testament as Hebrews, the word only occurs some thirty times, and (except for two references in *Jeremiah* and one in *Jonah*) only in *Genesis, Exodus, Deuteronomy* (once) and 1 *Samuel.* Most frequently it is used by people speaking of them as foreigners and as inferiors. It is possible that the name is connected with one that appears frequently in Mesopotamian and Egyptian documents which refer to them as stateless people in many parts of the ancient world, sometimes as freebooters, as mercenary soldiers or as slaves. If this is so, the Hebrews of the Old Testament would be a particular group associated with the patriarchs Abraham, Isaac and Jacob (Israel). The name Hebrew is replaced by 'Israelite' for the people of the covenant who were led by Joshua into Canaan.

Hebron. This was originally a Canaanite town. It became the tribal centre of the Southern tribes, and here David was crowned king of the South. Its shrine was associated with Abraham. It was the rallying point of Absalom's revolt and its people seem to have resented David's choice of Jerusalem as the capital city of all Israelites, North and South.

Israelites. This was an old tribal name ('Israel' was another name for Jacob). In the Old Testament it is used in two ways: 1. as a general name for the people of the covenant ('GOD's People')—we use it in this version in this sense; 2. as the name for the northern tribes who revolted against Jeroboam and formed a separate kingdom in the north which we call 'The North'.

Jerusalem. This was the name of the fortress which David captured and made his capital city. It was a very old fortified city, inhabited by Jebusites. The city itself was confined to the southern part of the eastern ridge which overlooked the Kidron Valley on the east and the

Tyropaean Valley on the west. David called it after his own name 'Davidstown'. Solomon enlarged it by extending it to the north and building there his palace and the temple. Later on the city spread to the north and the west. The city lacked adequate water supplies—the early city was built on the eastern ridge in order to use the only available spring, the Gihon Spring ('Bubbling Spring') in the Kidron Valley (see p. 61). Later Hezekiah cut a long tunnel to let the spring water flow into Siloam Pool on the west side of the hill. When David's attempt to weld all the people into one nation failed, Jerusalem became simply the capital city of the South. After the fall of Samaria and the Exile it became the spiritual capital of all Jewish people all over the world. See 'Zion'.

Judah.   See 'The South'.

Negeb.   The rocky wastes in the southernmost part of the country.

'The North'.   We use this name for the Northern Kingdom ('Israel'). The deep division between North and South ('Judah') goes back to the earliest times and may be due to the fact that the Northern tribes had been in Egypt, while the Southern tribes had not. This division was strengthened in the days of the tribal league because communication between north and south was made difficult by the existence of Canaanite fortresses like Jerusalem and those of the Esdraelon Valley. The North always thought of itself as the real home of the traditions of Moses—the central shrine of the tribal league was first at Shechem and then at Shiloh, both in the north. They had their own tribal traditions which were gathered together about 750 B.C.E. (referred to by scholars as 'E' because in their stories of the earliest days they used the name 'Elohim' for God and not 'Yahweh').

Passover.   A very old spring festival, associated with the killing and eating of a lamb and daubing its blood on the lintels and doorposts of houses. In early Israelite history, the festival celebrated their deliverance from Egypt. Later it was linked with the Canaanite spring festival of Cakes-made-without-Yeast (see p. 189)—perhaps because, when they settled in the highlands they found themselves celebrating their own Passover Festival at the same time as the Canaanite farmers there were celebrating their spring agricultural festival. The main importance of the festival in the Old Testament is as the celebration of the founding of GOD's people of which the escape from Egypt was the dramatic beginning, and as the supreme illustration of God's undeserved love.

Priests.   Officials who looked after the worship in shrines and temples. After the Exile, Jewish priests were the civil as well as the religious authorities in Jerusalem. They undertook the rewriting of their national history (called 'P') and to them we owe the later account of the story of creation (p. 307).

Prophets.   See p. 221.

The Sea of Reeds.   See p. 106.

'The South'.   The name we use for the Southern Kingdom ('Judah'). Here, as in the North, the Israelite tribes had their own traditions

(referred to by scholars as 'J') which were gathered together about 950 B.C.E.

Urim and Thummim.   See 'Ephod'.

Yahweh.   This is the personal name of God, usually appearing as 'the LORD' in English Bibles. The reason for this is that the later Jew ceased to pronounce the sacred name 'Yahweh' and substituted the Hebrew word for 'Lord' when he met it in his scriptures. In order to remind themselves, Jewish scholars put the vowels for the Hebrew word for 'Lord' with the consonants of the sacred name (YHWH) and this caused Christian readers to pronounce the word as 'Jehovah'. The sacred name also appears as 'Jah' as in 'Hallelujah' ('Praise Yahweh'). The meaning of the name is uncertain, but tradition associated it with a verb which means 'He shows himself to be' or 'He is present and active' (see p. 96).

Other names for God are 'El', translated as 'God' but really a proper name of the chief Canaanite god. It is sometimes combined with 'Elyon' and translated as 'God Most High'. 'Shaddai' ('Almighty'), another name for God, seems to mean 'He of the Mountain'.

In this version, 'GOD' stands for 'Yahweh', 'God' for other names.

Zion.   The name of the old Canaanite fortress of Jerusalem before the Israelites captured it. Later it was used, especially in psalms and prophetic poetry, as the beloved name of their Holy City.

THE GREAT EMPIRES

'GOD'S PEOPLE'

DATE	'GOD'S PEOPLE'	Egypt	Assyria	Babylon	Persia	Greece	Rome
1800	**Tribal Wanderings**						
1500							
1400	**Slaves in Egypt**						
1300	c.1370 Hebrews in Egypt	Rameses II					
	1250 Escape from Egypt (Moses)						
	Covenant at the mountain						
	March to the Jordan						
	The making of the People						
1200	Settling in the Highlands						
1100	Philistines occupy the plain						
	The making of the Nation						
	1020 Saul						
1000	1000 David						
	961 Solomon						
	First Hebrew Historians						
	922 Northern Rebellion						
	THE NORTH / THE SOUTH						
900	873 Jehoshaphat (THE SOUTH)						
	860 Ahab (THE NORTH)						
	Elijah						
	842 Jehu						
800	760 *Amos*		March to the West				
	721 Fall of Samaria						

The Nation is divided		
700	715 Hezekiah / *Isaiah*	701 Invades the South
		663 Invades Egypt
	640 Josiah	
	621 *Deuteronomy* / *Jeremiah*	
600	609 Battle Megiddo	612 Fall of Nineveh
	597 First capture of Jerusalem	605 Battle of Carchemish Invades Palestine
	586 Fall of Jerusalem	
	Deportation to Babylon	539 Fall of Babylon
	c.540 *Prophet of the Exile*	Cyrus
500	538 Some Jews return	
	520-16 Temple rebuilt	
400	444 Nehemiah Governor	
	397 Ezra Commissioner	
Rebirth of the City		
	Alexander in Palestine	323 Ptolomies
		Middle East becomes part of Alexander's Empire
		GREEK CULTURE SPREADS THROUGHOUT THE KNOWN WORLD
		Alexander's Conquests
300	168 Maccabean rebellion	312 Seleucids (Antioch)
200	c.165 *The Book of Daniel*	175 Antiochus Epiphanes
	142 Jews independent	ROMAN EMPIRE IS SPREADING EASTWARD
100	63 Pompey captures Jerusalem	

The Pattern of the Old Testament and the Pattern of 'Winding Quest'

Books of the Old Testament (Order of Hebrew Old Testament)	Dates	Theme	Sources	Winding Quest
TORAH (c 450 B.C.E.)	Period dealt with			
Genesis	1800–1400	Creation; Prehistory The Founding Fathers	⎫ Tribal ⎬ traditions ⎭	V: What Kind of World do we live in? V: What Kind of Persons should we be?
Exodus Numbers	1250–1200	Escape from Egypt and March to Jordan River (Making of the People)		11: Memories of the Past: Escape from Egypt
Two Lawbooks: (Leviticus) Deuteronomy		Law (c 550) Law (found in temple 621)	Various legal codes	p. 184: The New Lawbook in III
PROPHETS (c 250 B.C.E.) *Former Prophets*				
Joshua	1200 ⎫	Settlement in the Highlands	Tribal traditions	II: Memories of the Past: In the Highlands
Judges	1200–1020 ⎬	Monarchy: Saul; David (Making of the Nation)	Written documents and traditional stories	I: Brief Hour of Glory
Samuel	1020–961 ⎭			
Kings	961–561	The Two Kingdoms		III: The Death of Two Cities
Later Prophets	Time of Prophetic Activity			
Isaiah (1–39) (45–55) (55–65)	(742–700) 546–538 (586–400)	Interpretation of the Story	Collections of prophetic poetry	IV: Making Sense of the Story
Jeremiah	626–580			
(Ezekiel)	(593–571)			
The Twelve: Amos	c 760			
'Jonah'	c 350	What about foreigners?	Story	p. 346: Enemies are Persons in V
(other prophetic books)				

Books of the Old Testament WRITINGS (c 90 B.C.E.)	Dates WRITINGS (c 90 B.C.E.)	Theme	Sources	Winding Quest
Psalms	Time of writing 900 onwards	Worship in the Temple	Hymnbooks	III: The Story in Worship, p. 202 V: The Voice of Worship, p. 385 V: Enduring Convictions
Job	450–400	What can we know about God?	Poetry	V: Enduring Convictions
(Proverbs)	(various dates)			
Ruth	450–400	What about foreigners?	Historical novel	V: Enduring Convictions
Song of Songs	c 250	Human love	Love Songs	V: Enduring Convictions
Ecclesiastes	c 250	Meaningless of life	Poems	V: Enduring Convictions
Lamentations	after 587	Dirges on the fall of Jerusalem	Poems	see III, p. 191
(Esther)	(c 150)		Historical novel	
Daniel	c 165	Religious persecution	Stories; visions	V: Enduring Convictions III: Not the End but the Beginning, p. 192. Also pp. 173–4
Ezra Nehemiah } one book Chronicles }	c 300	History of the people from the death of Saul to the time of Ezra	Samuel, Kings diaries and other sources	

Note: Old Testament books enclosed in brackets have not been used in *Winding Quest*.

Where to Find a Passage in the Bible

Where to Find Familiar Names and Stories

Bible References

Suggestions for Background Reading

How to read the Bible	F. C. Grant	Nelson
An Approach to the Old Testament	R. Martin-Achard	Lutterworth
The Old Testament	R. Davidson	Hodder & Stoughton
A Concise History of Israel	Ernst Erlich	Darton, Longman & Todd
What about the Old Testament ?	John Bowden	S.C.M.
The People of the Old Testament	P. R. Ackroyd	Christopher
The Old Testament Tradition	P. R. Ackroyd	The National Society
The Old Testament Prophets	E. W. Heaton	Pelican
The Conscience of the Nation	R. E. Clements	O.U.P.
Documents from Old Testament Times	D. Winton Thomas	Nelson
Geographical Companion to the Bible	Denis Bayly	Lutterworth
Oxford Bible Atlas	ed H. G. May	O.U.P.
Biblical Archeology	G. E. Wright	S.C.M.
One Volume Bible Commentary	W. Neil	Hodder & Stoughton

The Torch Commentaries on individual books   S.C.M.

For browsing, reading and consulting (especially the maps):

The Westminster Atlas to the Bible	G. E. Wright and F. W. Filson	S.C.M.
Atlas of the Bible	L. H. Grollenberg	Nelson
New Atlas of the Bible	Jan H. Negenman	Collins